THE ZOMBIE SURVIVAL GUIDE

The
ZOMBIE
Survival Guide

Complete Protection from the Living Dead

Max Brooks

Illustrations by Max Werner

THREE RIVERS PRESS • NEW YORK

Published by Three Rivers Press, New York, New York.
Member of the Crown Publishing Group, a division of Random House, Inc.

www.randomhouse.com

THREE RIVERS PRESS and the Tugboat design
are registered trademarks of Random House, Inc.

Printed in the United States of America

Design by Debbie Glasserman

Library of Congress Cataloging-in-Publication Data
Brooks, Max.
The zombie survival guide : complete protection from the living dead / Max Brooks.
1. Zombies—Humor. I. Title.
PN6231.Z65 B76   2003
818'.602—dc21   2002155370
ISBN 1-4000-4962-8

25
First Edition

For Mom and Dad.
And for Michelle,
who makes life
worth fighting for.

CONTENTS

INTRODUCTION

The dead walk among us. Zombies, ghouls—no matter what their label—these somnambulists are the greatest threat to humanity, other than humanity itself. To call them predators and us prey would be inaccurate. They are a plague, and the human race their host. The lucky victims are devoured, their bones scraped clean, their flesh consumed. Those not so fortunate join the ranks of their attackers, transformed into putrid, carnivorous monsters. Conventional warfare is useless against these creatures, as is conventional thought. The science of ending life, developed and perfected since the beginning of our existence, cannot protect us from an enemy that has no "life" to end. Does this mean the living dead are invincible? No. Can these creatures be stopped? Yes. Ignorance is the undead's strongest ally, knowledge their deadliest enemy. That is why this book was written: to provide the knowledge necessary for survival against these subhuman beasts.

Survival is the key word to remember—not victory, not conquest, just survival. This book will not teach you to become a professional zombie hunter. Anyone wishing to devote their life to such a profession must seek training elsewhere. This book was not written for the police, military, or any government agency. These organizations, if they choose to recognize and prepare for the threat, will have access to resources far beyond those of private citizens. It is for them that this survival guide was written—private citizens, people with limited time and resources who nonetheless have refused to be victimized.

Naturally, many other skills—wilderness survival, leadership, even basic first aid—will be necessary in any encounter with the living dead. These were not included in this work, as they can be found in conventional texts. Common sense will dictate what else should be studied to complement this manual. Subsequently, all subjects not directly related to the living dead have been omitted.

From this book, you will learn to recognize your enemy, to choose the right weapons, about killing techniques, and about preparation and improvisation when on the defense, on the run, or on the attack. It will also discuss the possibility of a doomsday scenario, in which the living dead have replaced humanity as the planet's dominant species.

Do not discount any section of this book as hypothetical drama. Every ounce of knowledge was accumulated by hard-won research and experience. Historical data, laboratory experiments, field research, and eyewitness accounts (including those of the author) have all served to create this work. Even the doomsday scenario is an extrapolation of true-life events. Many actual occurrences are chronicled in the chapter of recorded outbreaks. Studying them will prove that every lesson in this book is rooted in historical fact.

That said, knowledge is only part of the fight for survival. The rest must come from you. Personal choice, the will to live, must be paramount when the dead begin to rise. Without it, nothing will protect you. On the last page of this book, ask yourself one question: What will you do—end your existence in passive acceptance, or stand up and shout, "I will not be their victim! I will survive!" The choice is yours.

THE ZOMBIE SURVIVAL GUIDE

THE UNDEAD: MYTHS AND REALITIES

He comes from the grave, his body a home of worms and filth. No life in his eyes, no warmth of his skin, no beating of his breast. His soul, as empty and dark as the night sky. He laughs at the blade, spits at the arrow, for they will not harm his flesh. For eternity, he will walk the earth, smelling the sweet blood of the living, feasting upon the bones of the damned. Beware, for he is the living dead.

—OBSCURE HINDU TEXT, CIRCA 1000 B.C.E.

ZOM-BIE: (Zom'be) n. also ZOM-BIES pl. 1. An animated corpse that feeds on living human flesh. 2. A voodoo spell that raises the dead. 3. A Voodoo snake god. 4. One who moves or acts in a daze "like a zombie." [a word of West African origin]

What is a zombie? How are they created? What are their strengths and weaknesses? What are their needs, their desires? Why are they hostile to humanity? Before discussing any survival techniques, you must first learn what you are trying to survive.

We must begin by separating fact from fiction. The walking dead are neither a work of "black magic" nor any other supernatural force.

Their origin stems from a virus known as *Solanum,* a Latin word used by Jan Vanderhaven, who first "discovered" the disease.

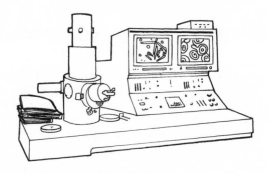

SOLANUM: THE VIRUS

Solanum works by traveling through the bloodstream, from the initial point of entry to the brain. Through means not yet fully understood, the virus uses the cells of the frontal lobe for replication, destroying them in the process. During this period, all bodily functions cease. By stopping the heart, the infected subject is rendered "dead." The brain, however, remains alive but dormant, while the virus mutates its cells into a completely new organ. The most critical trait of this new organ is its independence from oxygen. By removing the need for this all-important resource, the undead brain can utilize, but is in no way dependent upon, the complex support mechanism of the human body. Once mutation is complete, this new organ reanimates the body into a form that bears little resemblance (physiologically speaking) to the original corpse. Some bodily functions remain constant, others operate in a modified capacity, and the remainder shut down completely. This new organism is a zombie, a member of the living dead.

1. SOURCE
Unfortunately, extensive research has yet to find an isolated example of Solanum in nature. Water, air, and soil in all ecosystems, from all

parts of the world, have turned up negative, as have their accompanying flora and fauna. At the time of this writing, the search continues.

2. SYMPTOMS
The timetable below outlines the process of an infected human (give or take several hours, depending on the individual).

Hour 1: Pain and discoloration (brown-purple) of the infected area. Immediate clotting of the wound (provided the infection came from a wound).

Hour 5: Fever (99–103 degrees F), chills, slight dementia, vomiting, acute pain in the joints.

Hour 8: Numbing of extremities and infected area, increased fever (103–106 degrees F), increased dementia, loss of muscular coordination.

Hour 11: Paralysis in the lower body, overall numbness, slowed heart rate.

Hour 16: Coma.

Hour 20: Heart stoppage. Zero brain activity.

Hour 23: Reanimation.

3. TRANSFERENCE
Solanum is 100 percent communicable and 100 percent fatal. Fortunately for the human race, the virus is neither waterborne nor airborne. Humans have never been known to contract the virus from elements in nature. Infection can occur only through direct fluidic contact. A zombie bite, although by far the most recognizable means of transference, is by no means the only one. Humans have been infected by brushing their open wounds against those of a zombie or by being splattered by its remains after an explosion. Ingestion of infected flesh (provided the person has no open mouth sores), however,

results in permanent death rather than infection. Infected flesh has proven to be highly toxic.

No information—historical, experimental, or otherwise—has surfaced regarding the results of sexual relations with an undead specimen, but as previously noted, the nature of Solanum suggests a high danger of infection. Warning against such an act would be useless, as the only people deranged enough to try would be unconcerned for their own safety. Many have argued that, given the congealed nature of undead bodily fluids, the chances of infection from a non-bite contact should be low. However, it must be remembered that even one organism is enough to begin the cycle.

4. Cross-Species Infection
Solanum is fatal to all living creatures, regardless of size, species, or ecosystem. Reanimation, however, takes place only in humans. Studies have shown that Solanum infecting a non-human brain will die within hours of the death of its host, making the carcass safe to handle. Infected animals expire before the virus can replicate throughout their bodies. Infection from insect bites such as from mosquitoes can also be discounted. Experiments have proven that all parasitic insects can sense and will reject an infected host 100 percent of the time.

5. Treatment
Once a human is infected, little can be done to save him or her. Because Solanum is a virus and not a bacteria, antibiotics have no effect. Immunization, the only way to combat a virus, is equally useless, as even

the most minute dosage will lead to a full-blown infection. Genetic research is under way. Goals range from stronger human antibodies to resistant cell structure to a counter-virus designed to identify and destroy Solanum. This and other, more radical treatments are still in the earliest stages, with no foreseeable success in the near future. Battlefield experiences have led to the immediate severing of the infected limb (provided this is the location of the bite), but such treatments are dubious at best, with less than a 10 percent success rate. Chances are, the infected human was doomed from the moment the virus entered his or her system. Should the infected human choose suicide, he should remember that the brain must be eliminated first. Cases have been recorded in which recently infected subjects, deceased by means other than the virus, will nonetheless reanimate. Such cases usually occur when the subject expires after the fifth hour of infection. Regardless, any person killed after being bitten or otherwise infected by the undead should be immediately disposed of. (See "Disposal," page 19.)

6. REANIMATING THE ALREADY DECEASED

It has been suggested that fresh human corpses could reanimate if Solanum were introduced after their demise. This is a fallacy. Zombies ignore necrotic flesh and therefore could not transfer the virus. Experiments conducted during and after World War II (see "Recorded Attacks," pages 216ff) have proven that injecting Solanum into a cadaver would be futile because a stagnant bloodstream could not transport the virus to the brain. Injection directly into a dead brain would be equally useless, as the expired cells could not respond to the virus. Solanum does *not* create life—it alters it.

ZOMBIE ATTRIBUTES

1. PHYSICAL ABILITIES

Too often, the undead have been said to possess superhuman powers: unusual strength, lightning speed, telepathy, etc. Stories range from zombies flying through the air to their scaling vertical surfaces like spiders. While these traits might make for fascinating drama, the individual ghoul is far from a magical, omnipotent demon. Never forget that the body of the undead is, for all practical purposes, human. What changes do occur are in the way this new, reanimated body is used by the now-infected brain. There is no way a zombie could fly unless the human it used to be could fly. The same goes for projecting force fields, teleportation, moving through solid objects, transforming into a wolf, breathing fire, or a variety of other mystical talents attributed to the walking dead. Imagine the human body as a tool kit. The somnambulist brain has those tools, and *only* those tools, at its disposal. It cannot create new ones out of thin air. But it can, as you will see, use these tools in unconventional combinations, or push their durability beyond normal human limits.

A. Sight

The eyes of a zombie are no different than those of a normal human. While still capable (given their rate of decomposition) of transmitting visual signals to the brain, how the brain interprets these signals is another matter. Studies are inconclusive regarding the undead's visual abilities. They can spot prey at distances comparable to a human, but whether they can distinguish a human from one of their own is still up for debate. One theory suggests that the movements made by humans, which are quicker and smoother than those of the undead, is what causes them to stand out to the zombie eye. Experiments have been done in which humans have attempted to confuse approaching ghouls by mimicking their motions and adopting a shambling, awkward limp.

To date, none of these attempts have succeeded. It has been suggested that zombies possess night vision, a fact that explains their skill at nocturnal hunting. This theory has been debunked by the fact that all zombies are expert night feeders, even those without eyes.

B. Sound
There is no question that zombies have excellent hearing. Not only can they detect sound—they can determine its direction. The basic range appears to be the same as that for humans. Experiments with extreme high and low frequencies have yielded negative results. Tests have also shown that zombies are attracted by any sounds, not just those made by living creatures. It has been recorded that ghouls will notice sounds ignored by living humans. The most likely, if unproven, explanation is that zombies depend on all their senses equally. Humans are sight-oriented from birth, depending on other senses only if the primary one is lost. Perhaps this is not a handicap shared by the walking dead. If so, it would explain their ability to hunt, fight, and feed in total darkness.

C. Smell
Unlike with sound, the undead have a more acute sense of smell. In both combat situations and laboratory tests, they have been able to distinguish the smell of living prey above all others. In many cases, and given ideal wind conditions, zombies have been known to smell fresh corpses from a distance of more than a mile. Again, this does not mean

that ghouls have a greater sense of smell than humans, simply that they rely on it more. It is not known exactly what particular secretion signals the presence of prey: sweat, pheromones, blood, etc. In the past, people seeking to move undetected through infested areas have attempted to "mask" their human scent with perfumes, deodorants, or other strong-smelling chemicals. None were successful. Experiments are now under way to synthesize the smells of living creatures as a decoy or even repellent to the walking dead. A successful product is still years away.

D. Taste
Little is known about the altered taste buds of the walking dead. Zombies do have the ability to tell human flesh apart from that of animals, and they prefer the former. Ghouls also have a remarkable ability to reject carrion in favor of freshly killed meat. A human body that has been dead longer than twelve to eighteen hours will be rejected as food. The same goes for cadavers that have been embalmed or otherwise preserved. Whether this has anything to do with "taste" is not yet certain. It may have to do with smell or, perhaps, another instinct that has not been discovered. As to exactly why human flesh is preferable,

science has yet to find an answer to this confounding, frustrating, terrifying question.

E. Touch

Zombies have, literally, no physical sensations. All nerve receptors throughout the body remain dead after reanimation. This is truly their greatest and most terrifying advantage over the living. We, as humans, have the ability to experience physical pain as a signal of bodily damage. Our brain classifies such sensations, matches them to the experience that instigated them, and then files the information away for use as a warning against future harm. It is this gift of physiology and instinct that has allowed us to survive as a species. It is why we value virtues such as courage, which inspires people to perform actions despite warnings of danger. The inability to recognize and avoid pain is what makes the walking dead so formidable. Wounds will not be noticed and, therefore, will not deter an attack. Even if a zombie's body is severely damaged, it will continue to attack until nothing remains.

F. Sixth Sense

Historical research, coupled with laboratory and field observation, have shown that the walking dead have been known to attack even when all their sensory organs have been damaged or completely decomposed. Does this mean that zombies possess a sixth sense? Perhaps. Living humans use less than 5 percent of their brain capacity. It is possible that the virus can stimulate another sensory ability that has been forgotten by evolution. This theory is one of the most hotly debated in the war against the undead. So far, no scientific evidence has been found to support either side.

G. Healing

Despite legends and ancient folklore, undead physiology has been proven to possess no powers of regeneration. Cells that are damaged stay damaged. Any wounds, no matter what their size and nature, will

remain for the duration of that body's reanimation. A variety of medical treatments have been attempted to stimulate the healing process in
captured ghouls. None were successful. This inability to self-repair,
something that we as living beings take for granted, is a severe disadvantage to the undead. For example, every time we physically exert
ourselves, we tear our muscles. With time, these muscles rebuild to a
stronger state than before. A ghoul's muscle mass will remain damaged, reducing its effectiveness every time it is used.

H. Decomposition

The average zombie "life span"—how long it is able to function before
completely rotting away—is estimated at three to five years. As fantastic as this sounds—a human corpse able to ward off the natural
effects of decay—its cause is rooted in basic biology. When a human
body dies, its flesh is immediately set upon by billions of microscopic
organisms. These organisms were always present, in the external environment and within the body itself. In life, the immune system stood
as a barrier between these organisms and their target. In death, that barrier is removed. The organisms begin multiplying exponentially as
they proceed to eat and, thereby, break down the corpse on a cellular
level. The smell and discoloration associated with any decaying meat
are the biological process of these microbes at work. When you order
an "aged" steak, you are ordering a piece of meat that has begun to rot,
its formerly toughened flesh softened by microorganisms breaking
down its sturdy fiber. Within a short time, that steak, like a human
corpse, will dissolve to nothing, leaving behind only material too hard
or innutritious for any microbe, such as bone, teeth, nails, and hair.
This is the normal cycle of life, nature's way of recycling nutrients
back into the food chain. To halt this process, and preserve dead tissue, it is necessary to place it in an environment unsuitable for bacteria, such as in extreme low or high temperatures, in toxic chemicals
such as formaldehyde, or, in this case, to saturate it with Solanum.

Almost all the microbe species involved in normal human decomposition have repeatedly rejected flesh infected by the virus, effec-

tively embalming the zombie. Were this not the case, combating the living dead would be as easy as avoiding them for several weeks or even days until they rotted away to bones. Research has yet to discover the exact cause of this condition. It has been determined that at least some microbe species ignore the repelling effects of Solanum—otherwise, the undead would remain perfectly preserved forever. It has also been determined that natural conditions such as moisture and temperature play an important role as well. Undead that prowl the bayous of Louisiana are unlikely to last as long as those in the cold, dry Gobi desert. Extreme situations, such as deep freezing or immersion in preservative fluid, could, hypothetically, allow an undead specimen to exist indefinitely. These techniques have been known to allow zombies to function for decades, if not centuries. (See "Recorded Attacks," pages 193ff.) Decomposition does not mean that a member of the walking dead will simply drop. Decay may affect various parts of the body at different times. Specimens have been found with brains intact but nearly disintegrated bodies. Others with partially rotted brains may control some bodily functions but be completely paralyzed in others. A popular theory has recently circulated that attempts to explain the story of the ancient Egyptian mummy as one of the first examples of an embalmed zombie. The preservation techniques allowed it to function several thousand years after being entombed. Anyone with a rudimentary knowledge of ancient Egypt would find this story almost laughably untrue: The most important and complicated step in preparing a pharaoh for burial was the removal of the brain!

I. Digestion

Recent evidence has once and for all discounted the theory that human flesh is the fuel for the undead. A zombie's digestive tract is completely dormant. The complex system that processes food, extracts nutrition, and excretes waste does not factor into a zombie's physiology. Autopsies conducted on neutralized undead have shown that their "food" lies in its original, undigested state at all sections of the tract. This partially chewed, slowly rotting matter will continue to accumulate, as the zombie devours more victims, until it is forced through the anus, or literally bursts through the stomach or intestinal lining. While this more dramatic example of non-digestion is rare, hundreds of eyewitness reports have confirmed undead to have distended bellies. One captured and dissected specimen was found to contain 211 pounds of flesh within its system! Even rarer accounts have confirmed that zombies continue to feed long after their digestive tracts have exploded from within.

J. Respiration

The lungs of the undead continue to function in that they draw air into and expel it from the body. This function accounts for a zombie's signature moan. What the lungs and body chemistry fail to accomplish, however, is to extract oxygen and remove carbon dioxide. Given that Solanum obviates the need for both of these functions, the entire human respiratory system is obsolete in the body of a ghoul. This explains how the living dead can "walk underwater" or survive in environments lethal to humans. Their brains, as noted earlier, are oxygen-independent.

K. Circulation

It would be inaccurate to say that zombies have no heart. It would *not* be inaccurate, however, to say that they find no use for it. The circulatory system of the undead is little more than a network of useless tubes filled with congealed blood. The same applies to the lymphatic system as well as all other bodily fluids. Although this mutation would appear to give the undead one more advantage over humanity, it has actually proved to be a godsend. The lack of fluid mass prevents easy transmission of the virus. Were this not true, hand-to-hand combat would be nearly impossible, as the defending human would almost certainly be splattered with blood and/or other fluids.

L. Reproduction

Zombies are sterile creatures. Their sexual organs are necrotic and impotent. Attempts have been made to fertilize zombie eggs with human sperm and vice versa. None has been successful. The undead have also shown no signs of sexual desire, either for their own species or for the living. Until research can prove otherwise, humanity's greatest fear—the dead reproducing the dead—is a comforting impossibility.

M. Strength

Ghouls possess the same brute force as the living. What power can be exerted depends greatly on the individual zombie. What muscle mass a person has in life would be all he possesses in death. Unlike a living body, adrenal glands have not been known to function in the dead, denying zombies the temporary burst of power we humans enjoy. The one solid advantage the living dead do possess is amazing stamina. Imagine working out, or any other act of physical exertion. Chances are that pain and exhaustion will dictate your limits. These factors do not apply to the dead. They will continue an act, with the same dynamic energy, until the muscles supporting it literally disintegrate. While this makes for progressively weaker ghouls, it allows for an all-powerful first attack. Many barricades that would have exhausted three or even four physically fit humans have fallen to a single determined zombie.

N. Speed

The "walking" dead tend to move at a slouch or limp. Even without injuries or advanced decomposition, their lack of coordination makes for an unsteady stride. Speed is mainly determined by leg length. Taller ghouls have longer strides than their shorter counterparts. Zombies appear to be incapable of running. The fastest have been observed to move at a rate of barely one step per 1.5 seconds. Again, as with strength, the dead's advantage over the living is their tirelessness. Humans who believe they have outrun their undead pursuers might do well to remember the story of the tortoise and the hare, adding, of course, that in this instance the hare stands a good chance of being eaten alive.

O. Agility

The average living human possesses a dexterity level 90 percent greater than the strongest ghoul. Some of this comes from the general stiffness of necrotic muscle tissue (hence their awkward stride). The rest is due to their primitive brain functions. Zombies have little hand-eye coordination, one of their greatest weaknesses. No one has ever observed a zombie jumping, either from one spot to another or simply up and down. Balancing on a narrow surface is similarly beyond their ability. Swimming is also a skill reserved for the living. The theory has been put forth that, if an undead corpse were to be bloated enough to rise to the surface, it could present a floating hazard. This is rare, however, as the slow rate of decomposition would not allow by-product gas to accumulate. Zombies who walk or fall into bodies of water will more likely find themselves wandering aimlessly across the bottom until eventually dissolving. They can be successful climbers, but only in certain circumstances. If zombies perceive prey above them, for example, in the second story of a house, they will always attempt to climb to it. Zombies will try to scale any surface no matter how unfeasable or even impossible. In all but the easiest situations, these attempts have met with failure. Even in the case of ladders, when simple hand-over-hand coordination is required, only one in four zombies will succeed.

2. BEHAVIORAL PATTERNS

A. Intelligence

It has been proven, time and again, that our greatest advantage over the undead is our ability to think. The mental capacity of the average zombie ranks somewhere beneath that of an insect. On no occasion have they shown any ability to reason or employ logic. Attempting to accomplish a task, failing, then by trial and error discovering a new solution, is a skill shared by many members of the animal kingdom but lost on the walking dead. Zombies have repeatedly failed laboratory intelligence tests set at the level of rodents. One field case showed a human standing at one end of a collapsed bridge with several dozen zombies on the other side. One by one, the walking dead tumbled over the edge in a futile attempt to reach him. At no time did any of them realize what was happening and change their tactics in any way. Contrary to myth and speculation, zombies have never been observed using tools of any kind. Even picking up a rock to use as a weapon is beyond their grasp. This simple task would prove the basic thought process involved in realizing that the rock is a more efficient weapon than the naked hand. Ironically, the age of artificial intelligence has enabled us to identify more easily with the mind of the zombie than that of our more "primitive" ancestors. With rare exceptions, even the most advanced computers do not have the ability to think on their own. They do what they are programmed to do, nothing more. Imagine a computer programmed to execute one function. This function cannot be paused, modified, or erased. No new data can be stored. No new commands can be installed. This computer will perform that one function, over and over, until its power source eventually shuts down. This is the zombie brain. An instinct-driven, unitask machine that is impervious to tampering and can only be destroyed.

B. Emotions

Feelings of any kind are not known to the walking dead. Every form of psychological warfare, from attempts at enraging the undead to provoking pity have all met with disaster. Joy, sadness, confidence, anxiety, love, hatred, fear—all of these feelings and thousands more that make up the human "heart" are as useless to the living dead as the organ of the same name. Who knows if this is humanity's greatest weakness or strength? The debate continues, and probably will forever.

C. Memories

A modern conceit is that a zombie retains the knowledge of its former life. We hear stories of the dead returning to their places of residence or work, operating familiar machinery, or even showing acts of mercy to loved ones. In truth, not a shred of proof exists to support this wishful thinking. Zombies could not possibly retain memories of their for-

mer lives in either the conscious or subconscious mind, because neither exist! A ghoul will not be distracted by the family pet, living rel-
atives, familiar surroundings, etc. No matter who a person was in his
former life, that person is gone, replaced by a mindless automaton with
no instinct other than for feeding. This begs the question: Why do zombies prefer urban areas to the countryside? First, the undead do not prefer cities, but simply remain where they are reanimated. Second, the
main reason zombies tend to stay in cities instead of fanning out into
the countryside is because an urban zone holds the highest concentration of prey.

D. Physical Needs

Other than hunger (discussed later), the dead have shown none of the
physical wants or needs expressed in mortal life. Zombies have never
been observed to sleep or rest under any circumstances. They have not
reacted to extreme heat or cold. In harsh weather, they have never
sought shelter. Even something as simple as thirst is unknown to the
living dead. Defying all laws of science, Solanum has created what
could be described as a completely self-sufficient organism.

E. Communication

Zombies have no language skills. Although their vocal cords are capable of speech, their brain is not. The only vocal ability appears to be a
deep-throated moan. This moan is released when zombies identify prey.
The sound will remain low and steady until physical contact is made. It
will then shift in tone and volume as the zombie commences its attack.
This eerie sound, so typically associated with the walking dead, serves
as a rallying cry for other zombies and, as has been recently discovered,
is a potent psychological weapon. (See "On the Defense," page 74.)

F. Social Dynamics

Theories have always proliferated that the undead function as a collective force, from an army controlled by Satan to an insect-like
pheromone-driven hive to the most recent notion that they achieve

group consensus by telepathy. The truth is that zombies have no social organization to speak of. There is no hierarchy, no chain of command, no drive toward any type of collectivization. A horde of the undead, regardless of size, regardless of appearance, is simply a mass of individuals. If several hundred ghouls converge on a victim's location, it is because each one is drawn by its own instinct. Zombies appear to be unaware of one another. Individuals have never been observed to react to the sight of one another at any range. This goes back to the question of sense: How does a zombie distinguish between one of its own and a human or other prey at the same range? The answer has yet to be found. Zombies do avoid one another in the same way they avoid inanimate objects. When they bump into one another, they make no attempt to connect or communicate. Zombies feasting on the same corpse will tug repeatedly on the meat in question rather than shove a competitor out of the way. The only suggestion of communal effort is seen in notorious swarm attacks: the moan of a ghoul calling others within earshot. Once they hear the wail, other walking dead will almost always converge on its source. An early study theorized that this was a deliberate act, that a scout used its moan to signal the others to attack. However, we now know that it happens purely by accident. The ghoul that moans at the detection of prey does so as an instinctive reaction, not as an alert.

G. Hunting

Zombies are migratory organisms, with no regard for territory or concept of *home*. They will travel miles and perhaps, given time, cross continents in their search for food. Their hunting pattern is random. Ghouls will feed at night and during the day. They will stumble through an area rather than deliberately searching it. Certain zones or structures will not be singled out as more likely to contain prey. For example, some have been known to search farmhouses and other rural structures while others in the same group have moved by without even a glance. Urban zones take more time to explore, which is why the undead remain longer in these areas, but no building will take precedence over another. Zombies appear to be totally unaware of their surroundings. They do not, for example, move their eyes in a way that would take in the information of a new setting. Shuffling silently, with a thousand-yard stare, they will wander aimlessly, regardless of location, until prey is detected. As discussed earlier, the undead possess an uncanny ability to home in on a victim's precise location. Once contact is made, the previously silent, oblivious automaton transforms into something more closely related to a guided missile. The head turns immediately in the direction of its victim. The jaw drops, lips retract, and, from the depths of its diaphragm, comes the moan. Once contact is made, zombies cannot be distracted by any means. They will continue to pursue their prey, stopping only if they lose contact, make a successful kill, or are destroyed.

H. Motivation

Why do the undead prey upon the living? If it has been proven that human flesh serves no nutritional purpose, why does their instinct drive them to murder? The truth eludes us. Modern science, combined with historical data, has shown that living humans are not the only delights on the undead menu. Rescue teams entering an infested area have consistently reported them stripped of all life. Any creatures, no matter what their size or species, will be consumed by an attacking zombie. Human flesh, however, will always be preferable to other life forms. One experiment presented a captured specimen with two identical cubes of meat: one human, one animal. The zombie repeatedly chose the human. Reasons for this are still unknown. What can be confirmed, beyond any shadow of a doubt, is that instinct brought on by Solanum drives the undead to kill and devour any living creature they discover. There appear to be no exceptions.

I. Killing the Dead

While destroying a zombie may be simple, it is far from easy. As we have seen, zombies require none of the physiological functions that humans need to survive. Destruction or severe damage of the circulatory, digestive, or respiratory system would do nothing to a member of the walking dead, as these functions no longer support the brain. Simply put, there are thousands of ways to kill a human—and only one to kill a zombie. The brain must be obliterated, by any means possible.

J. Disposal

Studies have shown that Solanum can still inhabit the body of a terminated zombie for up to forty-eight hours. Exercise extreme care when disposing of undead corpses. The head in particular possesses the most serious hazard, given its concentration of the virus. Never handle an undead corpse without protective clothing. Treat it as you would any toxic, highly lethal material. Cremation is the safest, most effective way of disposal. Despite rumors that a pile of burning corpses will spread Solanum in a cloud of smoking plague, common sense would dictate that any virus is unable to survive intense heat, to say nothing of an open flame.

K. Domestication?

To reiterate, the zombie brain has proved, so far, to be tamper-proof. Experiments ranging from chemicals to surgery to electromagnetic waves have yielded negative results. Behavioral modification therapy and other such attempts to train the living dead like some kind of pack animal have similarly met with failure. Again, the machine cannot be rewired. It will exist as is, or it will not exist at all.

THE VOODOO ZOMBIE

If zombies are the creation of a virus and not black magic, then how does this explain the so-called "voodoo zombie," a person who has died, been raised from his grave, and is doomed to spend eternity as a slave of the living? Yes, it is true that the word "zombie" originally comes from the Kimbundu word "nzúmbe," a term describing a dead person's soul, and yes, zombies and zombification are integral parts of the Afro-Caribbean religion known as voodoo. However, the origin of their name is the only similarity between the voodoo zombie and the viral zombie. Although it is said that voodoo houngans (priests) can turn humans into zombies by magical means, the practice is rooted in hard, undeniable science. "Zombie powder," the tool used by the houngan for zombification, contains a very powerful neurotoxin (the exact ingredients are a closely guarded secret). The toxin temporarily paralyzes the human nervous system, creating a state of extreme hibernation. With the heart, lungs, and all other bodily functions operating at minimal levels, it would be understandable if an inexperienced coroner declared the paralyzed subject to be dead. Many humans have been buried while in such a state, only to awaken screaming in the pitch darkness of their coffin. So what makes this living human being a zombie? The answer is simple: brain damage. Many who are buried alive quickly use up the air inside their coffins. Those that are recovered (if they are lucky) almost always suffer brain damage from lack of oxygen. These poor souls shamble about with little cognitive skills, or, indeed, free will, and are often mistaken for the living dead. How can you distinguish a voodoo zombie from the genuine article? The telltale signs are obvious.

1. **Voodoo zombies show emotion.** People suffering from zombie powder–induced brain damage are still capable of all normal human feelings. They smile, cry, even growl with anger if hurt or otherwise provoked (something real zombies would never do).

2. **Voodoo zombies exhibit thought.** As has been stated before, when a real zombie encounters you it will immediately home in like a smart bomb. A voodoo zombie will take a moment to try to figure out who or what you are. Maybe it will come toward you, maybe it

will recoil, maybe it will continue its observation as its damaged brain attempts to analyze the information given it. What a voodoo zombie will *not* do is raise its arms, drop its jaw, unleash a hellish moan, and stumble directly toward you.

3. **Voodoo zombies feel pain.** A voodoo zombie that trips and falls will undoubtedly hold its bruised knee and whimper. Likewise, one already suffering from some other wound will nurse it, or, at the very least, be aware of the wound's existence. Voodoo zombies will not ignore deep gashes in their bodies like a real zombie would.

4. **Voodoo zombies recognize fire.** This is not to say that they are afraid of open flames. Some that have suffered severe brain damage may not remember what fire is. They will stop to examine it, perhaps even reach out to touch it, but they will recoil once they realize it causes pain.

5. **Voodoo zombies recognize their surroundings.** Unlike real zombies, who only recognize prey, voodoo zombies will react to sudden changes in light, sound, taste, and smell. Voodoo zombies have been observed watching television or brightly flashing lights, listening to music, cringing at thunder, and even taking notice of one another. This last fact has been critical in several cases of mis-identification. Had the zombies in question not reacted to each other (they looked at each other, made noises, even touched each other's faces), they might have been accidentally exterminated.

6. **Voodoo zombies do NOT have hypersense.** A human who has suffered the debilitating effects of zombie powder is still a sight-dependent human. He cannot operate perfectly in the dark, hear a footstep at 500 yards, or smell a living being on the wind. Voodoo zombies can actually be surprised by someone walking up behind them. This is not recommended, however, as a frightened zombie might react in anger.

7. **Voodoo zombies can communicate.** While this is not always the case, many of these individuals can respond to audiovisual signals. Many understand words; some even comprehend simple sentences. Many voodoo zombies possess the ability to speak, simply, of course, and rarely for extended conversations.

8. **Voodoo zombies can be controlled.** While not always true, many brain damaged humans have lost much of their self-realization, making them very susceptible to suggestion. Simply shouting for a subject to halt or even go away can be enough to get rid of a voodoo zombie. This has created the dangerous situation of confused people believing they could control or train true zombies. Several times headstrong humans have insisted they could simply command their living dead attackers to stop. As cold, rotting hands grabbed their limbs and dirty, worn teeth bit into their flesh, these people discovered, too late, what they were truly dealing with.

These guidelines should give you a good idea of how to tell a voodoo zombie from a true zombie. One final note: Voodoo zombies are almost always encountered in sub-Saharan Africa, the Caribbean, Central and South America, and the southern United States. Although it is not impossible to find someone who has been turned into a zombie by a houngan elsewhere, the chances of such an encounter are slim.

THE HOLLYWOOD ZOMBIE

Since the living dead first stepped onto the silver screen, their greatest enemy has not been hunters, but critics. Scholars, scientists, even concerned citizens have all argued that these movies depict the living dead in a fantastic, unrealistic fashion. Visually stunning weapons, physically impossible action sequences, larger-than-life human characters, and, above all, magical, invincible, even comical ghouls have all added their colors to the controversial rainbow that is "the Zombie Movie." Further criticism argues that this "style over substance" approach to somnambulist cinema teaches human viewers lessons that may get them killed in a real encounter. These serious charges demand an equally serious defense. While some zombie movies are based on actual events*, their goal, indeed the goal of almost every movie in every genre, has always been, first and foremost, to entertain. Unless we are discussing pure documentaries (and even some of those are "sweetened"), moviemakers must take some artistic license to make their work more palatable to the audience. Even movies that are based on actual events will sacrifice pure reality for good storytelling. Certain characters will be an amalgam of real-life individuals. Others may be purely fictional in order to explain certain facts, facilitate the plotline, or simply add flavor to the scene. One might argue that the role of the artist is to challenge, educate, and enlighten her audience. That may be true, but try imparting knowledge to an audience who has either left or fallen asleep within the first ten minutes of the picture. Accept this basic rule of moviemaking and you will understand why Hollywood zombie films stray, in some cases wildly, from the reality on which they are based. In short, use these photo-plays as their makers intended: as a source of temporary, lighthearted entertainment and not a visual aid to your survival.

OUTBREAKS

Although each zombie attack is different, given the number, terrain, reaction of the general populace, etc., its level of intensity can be measured in four distinct classes.

---

*At the behest of the filmmakers and/or their estates, the titles of those movies based on true-life stories have been omitted.

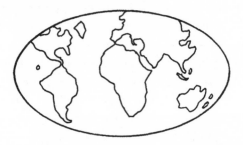

CLASS 1

This is a low-level outbreak, usually in a Third World country or First World rural area. The number of zombies in this class of outbreak ranges between one and twenty. Total human casualties (including those infected) range from one to fifty. The total duration, from the first case to the last (known), will range between twenty-four hours and fourteen days. The infested area will be small, no larger than a twenty-mile radius. In many cases, natural boundaries will determine its limits. Response will be light, either exclusively civilian or with some additional help from local law enforcement. Media coverage will be light, if present at all. If the media is present, look for common stories like homicides or "accidents." This is the most common type of outbreak and also the easiest to go unnoticed.

CLASS 2

Urban or densely populated rural areas are included in this level of outbreak. Total zombies will range between twenty and one hundred. Total human casualties may reach as high as several hundred. The duration of a Class 2 attack may last no longer than a Class 1 outbreak. In some cases, the larger number of zombies will spark a more immediate response. A rural, sparsely populated outbreak may extend to a hundred-mile radius, while an urban outbreak may encompass only several blocks. Suppression will almost certainly be organized. Bands of civilians will be replaced by local, state, even federal law enforcement. Look for an additional, if low-level, military response, the National Guard in the United States or its equivalent abroad. Most often, so as to ease panic, these units will take a more noncombatant role, providing medical assistance, crowd control, and logistical support. Class 2 outbreaks almost always attract the press. Unless the attack occurs in a truly isolated area of the world, or one where the media is strictly controlled, the story will be reported. This does not mean, however, that it will be reported accurately.

CLASS 3

A true crisis. Class 3 outbreaks, more than any other, demonstrate the clear threat posed by the living dead. Zombies will number in the thousands, encompassing an area of several hundred miles. The duration of the attack and a possible lengthy mop-up process could last as long as several months. There will be no chance for a press blackout or cover-up. Even without media attention, the sheer magnitude of the attack will leave too many eyewitnesses. This is a full-blown battle, with law enforcement replaced by units of the regular military. A state of emergency will be declared for the infested zone, as well as the neighboring areas. Expect martial law, restricted travel, rationed supplies, federalized services, and strictly monitored communication. All these measures, however, will take time to implement. The initial phase will be one of chaos as those in power come to grips with the crisis. Riots, looting, and widespread panic will add to their difficulties, further delaying an effective response. While this is happening, those living within the infested area will be at the mercy of the undead. Isolated, abandoned, and surrounded by ghouls, they will have only themselves to depend on.

CLASS 4

(See "Living in an Undead World," pages 154–81.)

DETECTION

Every undead outbreak, regardless of its class, has a beginning. Now that the enemy has been defined, the next step is early warning.

Knowing what a zombie is will not help if you are unable to recognize an outbreak before it's too late. This does not entail building a "zombie command post" in your basement, sticking pins in a map, and huddling around the shortwave radio. All it requires is looking for signs that would slip by the untrained mind. These signs include:

1. Homicides in which the victims were executed by head shots or decapitation. It has happened many times: People recognize an outbreak for what it is and try to take matters into their own hands. Almost always, these people are declared murderers by the local authorities and prosecuted as such.

2. Missing persons, particularly in wilderness or uninhabited areas. Pay careful attention if one or more of the search members end up missing. If the story is televised or photographed, watch to see what level of armament the search parties carry. Any more than one rifle per group could mean that this is more than just a simple rescue operation.

3. Cases of "violent insanity" in which the subject attacked friends or family without the use of weapons. Find out if the attacker bit or tried to bite his victims. If so, are any of the victims still in the hospital? Try to discover if any of these victims mysteriously died within days of their bite.

4. Riots or other civil disturbances that began without provocation or other logical cause. Common sense will dictate that violence on any group level does not simply occur without a catalyst such as racial tension, political actions, or legal decisions. Even so-called "mass hysteria" can always be traced to a root source. If none can be found, the answer may lie elsewhere.

5. Disease-based deaths in which either the cause is undetermined or seems highly suspect. Deaths from infectious disease are rare in the

industrialized world, compared to a century ago. For this reason, new outbreaks always make the news. Look for those cases in which the exact nature of the disease is unexplained. Also, be on the alert for suspicious explanations such as West Nile virus or "mad cow" disease. Either could be examples of a cover-up.

6. *Any* of the above in which media coverage was forbidden. A total press blackout is rare in the United States. The occurrence of one should be regarded as an immediate red flag. Of course, there may be many reasons other than an attack of the living dead. Then again, any event causing a government as media-conscious as our own to clamp down merits close attention. The truth, no matter what it is, cannot be good.

Once an event has tripped your sensors, keep track of it. Note the location, and its distance from you. Watch for similar incidents around or near the original site. If, within a few days or weeks, these incidents do occur, study them carefully. Note the response of law enforcement and other government agencies. If they react more forcefully with each occurrence, chances are that an outbreak is unfolding.

WEAPONS AND COMBAT TECHNIQUES

At least fifteen or twenty of them; men, women, children. We opened up at seventy, maybe eighty meters. I could see chunks of flesh blasting off their bodies. Our rounds were hitting their mark! They kept coming, they just kept coming! I sighted one and let go a full burst from my BXP. I know I snapped his spine, because the man dropped like a leaf. Legs still twitching, he kept crawling after me! At twenty meters, we opened up with the Vektor. Nothing! I watched bits of organ and bone blown out their backs. I watched limbs literally sawed off at the joints. The SS77 is the best MG ever made, 840 meters per second, 800 rounds per minute, and it wasn't doing a goddamn thing! What grenades we had only downed one of them. One! His mangled body lay motionless with a still-snapping head! [Name Withheld] let go with his RPG. The damn rocket went right through its soft target and took out a rock behind it! Finally, at five meters, we used the last bit of fuel in the flamethrower! The sons of bitches lit up like torches but just wouldn't stop! One of them grabbed [Name Withheld], setting him on fire as it bit through his neck. I saw the rest of those things surround him as we took off for the jungle, a mob of burning bodies squatting down to tear another screaming human torch apart. Goddamn the devil's mother, what the hell were we supposed to do!?!

—SERBIAN MERCENARY DURING THE ZAIRIAN CIVIL WAR, 1994

Choosing the right weapons (*never* carry just one) can make the difference between a pile of dead zombies and becoming one yourself. When confronted with the undead, it is easy to believe in the super-commando strategy: Load up with the heaviest, most powerful weapons possible and go out to "kick ass." This is not only foolish—it is suicidal. Zombies are not camp guards in some POW escape movie, crumbling en masse with the first theatrical volley. Arming yourself for a zombie encounter requires careful consideration, a cool head, and a practical analysis of all factors involved.

GENERAL RULES:

1. **OBEY THE LAW!:** Regulations governing weapons such as firearms and explosives depend on your location. Follow them to the letter. Punishment may range from a sizable fine to incarceration. In any case, the resulting criminal record is something you *cannot afford!* When the dead rise, law enforcement must look upon you as a model citizen, someone to be trusted and left alone, not a felon of questionable background who should be interrogated at the first sign of trouble. Fortunately, as this chapter will show, simpler, legal weapons will serve you much better than paramilitary death machines.

2. **TRAIN CONSTANTLY:** No matter what weapon you choose, from a simple machete to a semiautomatic rifle, it must become an extension of your body. Practice as often as possible. If classes are available, by all means sign up. Learning from qualified instructors will save immense time and energy. If the device can be disassembled, do so, both in sunlight and total darkness until you know every pin, every spring, every curve and edge of that all-important machine. With practice will come both experience and confidence, two traits you must develop in order to successfully do battle with the living dead. History has proven that a well-trained individual, with nothing but a rock, has a better chance of survival than a novice with the latest technological marvel.

3. **CARE FOR YOUR TOOLS:** Weapons, no matter how simple they may be, must be cared for as if they were living things. Anyone with firearm experience knows that inspection and cleaning are part of everyday use. This also applies to close-combat weapons. Blades need polish and rust protection. Grips need checking and maintenance. Never abuse your tools or expose them to unnecessary damage. If possible, have them tested regularly by experienced professionals. These experts may detect early-stage defects imperceptible to the amateur user.

4. **BEWARE DISPLAY ITEMS:** Many companies offer a variety of replica weapons, such as swords, bows, etc., that are meant merely for decoration. Always research your chosen item thoroughly and ensure that it is intended for actual use in the real world. Do not rely solely on the company's word. "Battle ready" may mean the item could withstand a few blows on a theatrical stage, or at some historical fair, but it will snap in half during a life-or-death confrontation. If resources permit, purchase a duplicate item and train with it to the breaking point. Only then should you trust in its abilities.

5. **DEVELOP THE FIRST WEAPON:** The human body, if cared for and trained properly, is the greatest weapon on earth. Americans are notorious for their bad diet, lack of exercise, and relentless fetish for labor-saving technology. As recognizable as the term "couch potato" is, a more accurate term would be "cattle": fat, lazy, listless, and ready to be eaten. Weapon No. 1, the biological tool that is our body, can and must be transformed from prey to predator. Obey a strict diet and physical-fitness regimen. Concentrate on cardiovascular instead of strength-building exercise. Monitor any chronic health conditions you may have, no matter how small. Even if your worst ailment is allergies, treat them regularly! When a situation does arise, you must know *exactly* what your body is capable of! Study and master at least one martial art. Make sure its emphasis is on escaping holds rather than delivering blows. Knowing how to

slip from a zombie's clutches is the single most important skill you can possess when you find yourself in close combat.

CLOSE COMBAT

Hand-to-hand combat should almost always be avoided. Given a zombie's lack of speed, it is much easier to run (or walk quickly) than stand and fight. However, it may be necessary to destroy a zombie at close quarters. When this happens, split-second timing is critical. A wrong move, a moment's hesitation, and you may feel cold hands gripping your arm, or sharp, broken teeth biting into your flesh. For this reason above all, choosing a close-combat weapon is more important than any other in this section.

1. BLUDGEONS

When using a blunt weapon, the goal is to crush the brain (remember, the only way to kill a zombie is by destroying its brain). This is not as easy as it sounds. The human skull is one of the hardest, most durable surfaces in nature. So, of course, is the zombie's. Extreme force is needed to fracture, let alone shatter it. However, this must be done, and done with a single, well-placed blow. Missing your target or failing to breach the bone will leave you with no second chance.

Sticks, ax handles, and other wooden clubs are good for knocking a zombie out of the way or beating off an individual attack. What they lack is the weight and strength necessary

for a lethal strike. A section of lead pipe will work for a single encounter but is too heavy for those on the move. A sledgehammer has the same drawback and also requires practice for its user to hit a moving target. Aluminum bats are light enough to work for one, maybe two fights, but are known to bend after prolonged use. The standard, one-handed carpenter's hammer has striking power but severely limited reach. Its short handle allows a zombie to grab your arm and pull it in. The police baton, made of acetate plastic (in most cases), is strong enough for any battle but lacks the lethal power for a one-blow kill. (Note: This was intended in its design.)

The best bludgeon is a steel crowbar. Its relatively lightweight and durable construction makes it ideal for prolonged close combat. Its curved, semi-sharpened edge also allows for a stabbing motion through the eye socket, directly into the brain case. More than one survivor has reported killing zombies in this manner. Another benefit of the crowbar is that it may be necessary to pry open a door, shift a heavy object, or perform other tasks for which it was originally designed. None of these functions can be accomplished with any of the previously mentioned items. Even lighter and more durable than the steel crowbar is the titanium model,

now trickling into Western markets from Eastern Europe and the former Soviet Union.

2. EDGED WEAPONS

Blades, in any form, have advantages and disadvantages over bludgeons. Those that have enough strength to split the skull rarely stand up after many repetitions. For this reason, slicing, particularly decapitation, serves almost the same function as a head blow. (Note: The severed head of a zombie is still able to bite and must be regarded as a threat.) The advantage of slicing over bludgeoning is that it can make killing a zombie unnecessary. 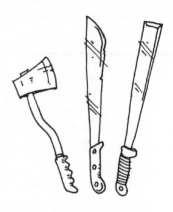 In some cases, simply chopping off a limb or severing the spine is enough to disable an undead assailant. (Note: Severing a limb also brings the possibility of contact with the virus through the exposed area.)

The civilian ax can easily crush a zombie's skull, smashing through bone and brain in one swing. Decapitation is equally easy, which is why the ax has been the favored tool of executioners for centuries. Connecting with a moving head, however, might be difficult. Furthermore, if the swing ends in a total miss, you might be taken off balance.

The smaller, one-handed hatchet is a good weapon of last resort. If you find yourself cornered, and larger weapons are useless, a hatchet blow will more than take care of an attacker.

The sword is the ideal edged weapon, but not every kind will suffice. Foils, rapiers, and similar fencing weapons are not suited for slicing. Their only possible use would be a direct stab through the eye socket followed by a quick swirling action through the brain. This motion, however, has been accomplished only once, by a trained swordsman, and is therefore not recommended.

Single-handed long swords allow you a free hand for other tasks such as opening a door or defending your body with a shield. Their only drawback is the lack of swinging power. One arm may not have the strength to slice through the thick cartilage between bones. Another drawback is its user's notorious lack of accuracy. Scoring a flesh wound anywhere on the body of a living opponent is one thing. Making an exact, clean chop through the neck is something else altogether.

Double-handed swords could be considered the best in their class, providing the strength and accuracy for perfect decapitation. Of this type, the Japanese Samurai Katana ranks first. Its weight (three to five pounds) is perfect for long-term conflicts, and its blade can sever the toughest organic fiber.

In tight quarters, shorter blades hold the advantage. The Roman Gladius is one choice, although combat-ready replicas are hard to find. The Japanese Ninjite boasts a two-handed grip and, in genuine models, renowned tempered steel. Both factors make it a superior weapon. The common machete, because of its size, weight, and availability, is probably your best choice. If possible, find the military type usually sold at Army surplus stores. Its steel tends to be of a higher quality, and its blackened blade helps concealment at night.

3. Miscellaneous Hand Weapons

Spears, pikes, and tridents serve to skewer a zombie, keeping it out of reach but not necessarily scoring a kill. The chance of an eye-socket stab is possible, but remote. The medieval European halberd (an ax-spear hybrid) may serve as a chopping weapon but, again, requires great amounts of skill and practice to accomplish a decapitating blow. Other than using them as bludgeons, or keeping your attacker at a distance, these weapons serve little purpose.

Morning stars or "flails," a spiked ball chained to a rod, do basically the same damage as a crowbar, albeit in a more dramatic way. The owner swings the rod in a wide, circular motion, providing enough momentum to bring the ball crashing through the skull of his or her opponent. Using this weapon takes considerable skill, and it is therefore not recommended.

The medieval European mace serves the same function as the standard household hammer but without benefit of the latter's practical uses. A mace cannot pry open a door or window, drive a chisel, or hammer a nail. Attempting such an act could result in accidental injury. Therefore, carry this medieval weapon only when no alternative is available.

Knives are always useful, serving a variety of functions in a range of situations. Unlike a hatchet, they can kill a zombie only when the blade is stabbed through the temple, eye socket, or base of the skull. On the flip side, knives almost always weigh less than hatchets and, therefore, are better if you are on the move. When choosing a knife, make sure the blade is no more than six inches long and always smooth. Avoid serrated knives and saw-blade combinations found in survival knives, as they tend to become lodged in their victims. Imagine yourself stabbing one zombie through the temple and turning to engage the other three ghouls but not being able to retrieve your blade.

The trench spike is, without a doubt, the best compact anti-zombie weapon on earth. It is a combination of a seven-inch steel spike for a blade and brass knuckles for a handle. It was developed during the vicious hand-to-hand combat of World War I, where soldiers killed each other in trenches no wider than a few feet. Specifically, it was designed to stab downward, through an enemy's steel helmet. You can imagine how effective this weapon would be against a zombie. The user could stab easily through a zombie's skull, withdraw cleanly and quickly, then turn to either brain another zombie or, at the very least, knock one over with a brass-knuckle punch to the face. Original models are extremely rare, with barely a few remaining in museums and the homes of private collectors. However, if accurate, detailed schematics can be found, have one or perhaps two combat-ready, stress-tested replicas made. They will be an investment you will never regret.

The Shaolin Spade

This weapon bears special mention in the anti-ghoul arsenal. It may appear unconventional: a six-foot hardwood staff with a flat, bell-shaped blade on one end and an outward-facing crescent blade on the other. Its roots date back to a bronze-bladed agricultural tool used during the Chinese Shang Dynasty (1766–1122 B.C.E.). When Buddhism migrated to China, the spade was adopted by Shaolin monks as both tool and weapon. On several occasions, it has proven to be surprisingly effective against the living dead. Thrusting forward with either blade will produce instant decapitation, while its length provides complete safety for the user. This length does make it impractical for indoor combat, and it should therefore be avoided in those situations. In open spaces, however, nothing combines the safety of a spear with the killing power of a katana sword like the Shaolin spade.

A variety of other hand weapons exist around the world, and space does not permit the author to discuss each one individually. If you discover an implement or tool that you think might make a good weapon, ask yourself these questions:

1. Can it crush a skull in one blow?
2. If not, can it decapitate in said blow?
3. Is it easy to handle?
4. Is it light?
5. Is it durable?

Questions 3, 4, and 5 will have to depend on your present situation. Questions 1 and 2 are essential!

4. POWER TOOLS

Popular fiction has shown us the awesome, brutal power of the chain-saw. Its lightning-quick, rotating teeth can easily slice through flesh and bone, making the strength and skill required for manual weapons

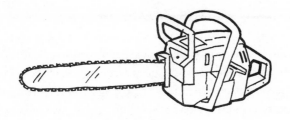

unnecessary. Its roar might also give the owner a much-needed psychological boost—empowerment in a situation where abject terror is a given. How many horror movies have you seen in which this industrial killing machine has spelled doom for anyone and anything it touched? In reality, however, chainsaws and similar powered devices rank extremely low on the list of practical zombie-killing weapons. For starters, their fuel supply is finite. Once drained, they provide as much protection as a hand-held stereo. Carrying extra fuel or power cells

leads to the second inherent problem: weight. The average chainsaw weighs ten pounds, compared to a two-pound machete. Why increase the chances of exhaustion? Safety must also be considered. One slip, and the spinning teeth might be slicing through your skull just as easily as your enemy's. Like any machine, another problem is noise. A chainsaw's distinctive roar, even if running for just a few seconds, will be enough to broadcast to every zombie within earshot, "Dinner is served!"

SLINGS AND ARROWS

It is a commonly held notion that using non-firearm ballistics such as bows and slingshots are a waste of energy and resources. In most cases, this is true. However, if used properly, such a weapon will enable you to score a kill at long range with little or no sound. What if you're attempting to escape an infested area, you turn a corner, and a single ghoul blocks your path? It's too far away for a hand weapon. Before you get close, its moans will betray your position. The crack of a firearm will sound an even louder alarm. What do you do? In cases like these, certain silent weapons may be your only option.

1. THE SLING

Made famous from the biblical story of David and Goliath, this weapon has been part of our heritage since prehistoric times. The user places a smooth, round stone in the wider center of a thin leather strip, grabs both ends, swings it repeatedly in a rapid circle, then releases one end of the strip, loosing the stone at his target. Theoretically, it is possible to dispatch a zombie with a silent headshot at just under thirty paces. However, even with months of training, the chances of scoring such a hit are one in ten at best. With no experience, the wielder would be better off just throwing stones.

2. THE SLINGSHOT

A descendant of the leather strap, the modern slingshot has at least ten times the accuracy of its ancestor, the sling. What it lacks is punch. Small projectiles fired from a modern slingshot simply do not have the force, even at minimum range, to penetrate a zombie's skull. Using this weapon might serve only to alert a ghoul to your presence.

3. THE BLOWGUN
Given that poison has no effect on the undead, discount this weapon entirely.

4. SHURIKEN
These small, multipoint devices were used in feudal Japan to pierce a human skull. In appearance they resemble a steel, two-dimensional replica of a shining star, hence their nickname, "throwing stars." In expert hands, they could easily bring down a zombie. However, as with many weapons discussed, the throwing star requires great expertise. Unless you are one of the few masters of this art (only a handful can still claim this title), refrain from such an exotic method.

5. THROWING KNIVES
As with shuriken, these short-range weapons require weeks of practice to hit something as large as a human body and months to hit something as small as a human head. Only a dedicated expert could even hope for a reliable zombie kill. The time and energy spent training could be much more productive if applied to a conventional weapon. Remember, you have a variety of skills to learn, and not all the time in the world to learn them. Don't waste those valuable hours attempting to master a third-rate weapon.

6. THE LONG OR COMPOUND BOW
To be blunt, hitting a zombie through the head with an arrow is an extremely difficult feat. Even with compound bows and modern sights, only experienced archers have a chance of making a direct shot. The only practical use for this weapon is the delivery of incendiary arrows. For starting fires silently, at long distance,

nothing works better than a flaming arrow. This manner of attack can, and has, been used to set undead individuals on fire. The targeted zombie will not know enough to pull the arrow from its body and might, given the right circumstances, burn other ghouls before succumbing to the flames. (See "Fire," pages 51–54, for appropriate use.)

7. THE CROSSBOW

The power and accuracy of a modern crossbow can send a "bolt" (crossbow arrow) clean through a zombie's skull at over a quarter mile. Small wonder it has been dubbed "the perfect silent killer." Marksmanship is important, but no more so than with a rifle. Reloading requires time and strength, but this should be unnecessary. The crossbow is a sniper's weapon, not a crowd-stopper. Use only against one zombie. Any more, and you might find yourself grabbed and mauled before you have time to load another bolt. As for bolts, either triangular or bullet-shape will suffice. For increased accuracy, a telescopic sight should be added. Unfortunately, the size and weight of any good crossbow will make it the primary weapon. Therefore, choose one only when the situation permits, such as traveling in a group, defending your home, or when no silenced firearms are available.

8. THE HAND BOW

Smaller, one-handed crossbows can serve as a complement to your primary weapon. Carrying one means that a compact, silent weapon will always be on hand if needed. In comparison to the larger crossbow, hand bows have inferior accuracy, power, and range. Using one means getting closer to the target. This increases not only the danger but the risk of detection, which, in turn, negates the need for a silent weapon. Use the hand bow carefully, and sparingly.

FIREARMS

Of all the weapons discussed in this book, nothing is more important than your primary firearm. Keep it cleaned, keep it oiled, keep it loaded, keep it close. With a cool head, steady hand, and plenty of ammunition, one human is more than a match for an army of zombies.

Choosing a firearm must be an exact science, with every variable considered. What is your primary goal: defense, attack, or flight? What outbreak class are you facing? How many people, if any, are in your group? What environment is your battleground? Different firearms serve different functions. Almost none serve all. Selecting the perfect tools means dispelling conventional doctrines of warfare that have worked so well against our fellow humans. Sadly, we know all too well how to kill each other. Killing zombies—that's another story.

1. THE HEAVY MACHINE GUN

Since World War I, this invention has revolutionized human conflict. Its mechanism allows a storm of lead to be discharged in seconds. These tactics may be invaluable on the human battlefield but are a feckless waste against the living dead. Remember, you are going for a head shot: one bullet, precisely placed. As the machine gun is designed for saturation fire, it may take hundreds, even thousands of rounds for one, randomly lethal shot. Even aiming the machine gun as a rifle (a tactic used by U.S. special forces) is a losing proposition. Why hit a zombie with a well-aimed five-round burst when one well-aimed rifle shot produces the same result? In the 1970s, one school of thought favored the "scythe theory": If a machine gun is placed at the head level of an undead crowd, it could mow them down with one long burst. This argument has been debunked—ghouls, like the humans they used to be, are not all the same height. Even if some are destroyed, at least half will survive to close on your position. But what about the massive body damage caused by these weapons? Won't a machine gun have enough punch to rip a body in half, and doesn't that negate the need for a head shot? Yes and no. The standard 5.56-millimeter round used by the U.S. Army SAW (Squad Automatic Weapon) does have the ability to snap a human spine, sever limbs, or yes, tear a zombie's form in two. This, however, does not mean a head shot is unnecessary. For one, the chance of dismembering a zombie is slight and therefore requires large amounts of ammunition. For another, unless the brain is destroyed, the zombie itself is still alive—crippled, yes, perhaps even immobile, but still alive. Why give yourself the unnecessary need of having to finish off a mass of writhing and potentially dangerous body parts?

2. The Submachine Gun

The problem presented by this weapon is similar to that of the heavy machine gun: ammo expended versus living dead dispatched. However, when fighting in tight quarters, the submachine gun finds its niche. The short barrel makes it easier to handle than a rifle, but the folding stock gives it much more support than a pistol. Always be sure to keep it on the single-shot setting. As we discussed, full auto is simply a waste of ammo. Also, be sure to aim it from the shoulder. Shooting from the hip will produce nothing more than a loud noise and a clean miss. One disadvantage is poor accuracy at long range. Because the submachine gun was designed as a close-combat weapon, you will have to get much closer to a zombie than if you were carrying a rifle or assault weapon. This would normally not be a problem except that submachine guns, like all auto and semiautomatic weapons, have the possibility of jamming while in use. At short range, you may be putting yourself at unnecessary risk. This is the only reason to discount a submachine gun as your primary weapon.

3. The Assault Rifle

This weapon was invented originally to bridge the gap between the rifle and submachine gun, offering both range and rapid fire. Wouldn't these traits make it ideal against the undead? Not really. Although range and accuracy are needed, rapid fire, as we've seen, is not. Even though an assault rifle can be set for semiautomatic, just like a submachine gun, the temptation to go full auto still exists, as it does with a submachine gun. When fighting for your life, it may simply be too easy to flip the switch to "rock 'n' roll," no matter how wasteful and useless this might be. If you do choose an assault rifle as your primary weapon, keep in mind the basic questions that apply to all firearms: What is its range? What is its accuracy? Is the appropriate ammunition readily available? How easy is it to clean and maintain?

To answer some of these questions, it is best to examine two extreme examples. The U.S. Army M16A1 is considered by many to be the worst assault rifle ever invented. Its overcomplicated mecha-

nism is both difficult to clean and prone to jamming. Adjusting the sight, something that must be done every time a target shifts its range, requires the use of a nail, ballpoint pen, or similar device. What if you didn't have one, or lost it as several dozen zombies shambled steadily toward you? The delicate plastic stock of the M16A1 obviates bayonet use, and by attempting to use it as such you would risk shattering the hollow, spring-loaded stock. This is a critical flaw. If you were confronted by multiple ghouls and your A1 jammed, you would be unable to use it as a last-ditch hand-to-hand weapon. In the 1960s, the M16 (originally the AR-15) was designed for Air Force base security. For political reasons typical of the military-industrial complex (you buy my weapon, you get my vote and my campaign contribution), it was adopted as the principal infantry weapon for the U.S. Army. So poor was its early battle record that during the Vietnam War, communist guerrillas refused to take them from dead Americans. The newer M16A2, although somewhat of an improvement, is still regarded as a second-class weapon. If given the choice, emulate the Vietcong and ignore the M16 entirely.

On the opposite end of the spectrum, the Soviet AK-47 is considered the best assault rifle ever made. Although heavier than the M16 (10.58 pounds versus 7 pounds) and possessing a considerably harder kick, this weapon is famous for its rugged efficiency and sturdy construction. Its wide, spacious firing mechanism prevents jamming from dirt or sand. In hand-to-hand combat, you could either stab a zombie through the eye socket with the weapon's bayonet or use the solid, steel-backed wooden stock to smash through a zombie's skull. If imi-

tation is the sincerest form of flattery, then several nations have chosen to flatter the AK with either direct copies (Chinese Type 56) or
modified designs (Israeli Galil). Again, although the assault rifle is not
ideal for defense against the living dead, a member of the AK-47 family will be your best bet.

4. THE BOLT-/LEVER-ACTION RIFLE

A product of the mid-nineteenth century, these weapons are often
regarded as obsolete. Why use a hunting rifle when you can own a submachine gun? Such arrogance is simply unfounded, its roots based in
techno-chauvinism and the absence of practical experience. A well-
made, expertly used bolt- or lever-action rifle offers a defense against
the living dead that is as good if not better than the latest military hard-
ware. A rifle's single-shot capability forces the user to make each
round count, increasing the chance of a hit. This feature also eliminates
even the possibility of "rock 'n' rolling," and therefore preserving
ammunition whether the user intends to or not. A third reason is the
relative easiness to clean and operate a rifle, something that must not
be overlooked. Hunting rifles are designed for a civilian market.
Manufacturers know that if they are too complex, sales will plummet.
A fourth and final reason is ready availability of ammunition. As there
are more civilian gun shops than military armories in the United States
(a pattern not shared by the rest of the world), you will find it easier to
obtain ammunition for a hunting rifle than an assault weapon or submachine gun. This will prove critical in any of the scenarios covered
in the latter part of this manual.

When choosing a bolt- or lever-action rifle, try to find an older, military version if possible. This does not mean that civilian models are
inferior weapons—quite the opposite—but almost all military bolt-
action rifles were designed for use in hand-to-hand combat. Make sure
you take the time to study the use of a rifle for this purpose. Simply
swinging it like a club would destroy any weapon, military and civilian alike. Manuals are available that explain how to use a rifle as a
bludgeon. Even old war films can demonstrate how deadly these

weapons are without firing a shot. Examples of bolt-action military rifles are the U.S. Springfield, the British Lee Enfield, and the German Mauser Kar 98k. Many of these still exist, some in good working order. Before choosing, however, make sure the appropriate ammunition is in ready supply. Having an impressive, bolt-action military rifle will do no good if the only rounds available fit civilian models.

5. The Semiautomatic Rifle
Since its debut, this weapon has shown itself to be a superior zombie killer. Given the possibility of wasting ammunition (a round is expended every time the trigger is pulled), a fair amount of discipline is required. However, this option can be a blessing when engaging multiple targets. In one recorded instance, a trapped woman dispatched fifteen attacking zombies in twelve seconds! (See "1947 A.D., Jarvie, British Columbia," pages 223–24.) This story illustrates the potential of a semiautomatic rifle. For close combat or for people on the run, the semiautomatic carbine serves the same function as the larger model. Although possessing half the range, the carbine tends to be lighter and easier to carry, and uses smaller ammunition. Either type will serve you well, depending on the situation. When choosing a semiautomatic weapon, the World War II M1 Garand or M1 Carbine are, in many ways, superior to contemporary weapons. This may be surprising, but these older military weapons were designed to survive the greatest conflict in history. Not only did they meet this task admirably, but the Garand remained the U.S. Army's main rifle through the Korean conflict, while the Carbine saw action up until the first years of Vietnam. Another advantage of the M1 Garand is its secondary role as a hand-to-hand weapon (in WWII, bayonet use was still considered a vital part of combat). Although no longer in production, many Garands still remain on the market with ammunition widely available. The M1 Carbine is, amazingly, still in production. Its light weight and short muzzle perfectly suit this weapon to indoor combat or long journeys on foot. Other, more modern choices include the Ruger Mini-30, Ruger Mini-14, and the Chinese Type 56 (a copy of the Soviet SKS

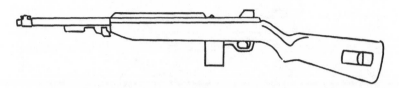

carbine, not to be confused with the assault rifle of the same name). If discipline can be maintained, you will not find a better weapon than the semiautomatic rifle.

6. THE SHOTGUN

At close range against human attackers, this weapon reigns supreme. Against the living dead, this is not entirely true. A good twelve-gauge shotgun can literally blow a zombie's head off. However, the longer the range, the greater the pellet dispersal pattern, and the lesser chance of skull penetration. A solid slug would have the same effect as a rifle, even at greater range (provided the barrel is long enough), but in that case, why not just use a rifle? What shotguns *do* possess is stopping power. The scattering shot acts as a solid wall, whereas a rifle bullet might pass clean through or miss the target altogether. If you are cornered, or on the run, and need time to escape, a good shotgun blast can send several zombies sprawling. The downside of a shotgun is that the large, twelve-gauge shells are bulky and therefore burdensome when traveling and leave less room for other equipment. This must be considered if a long journey is required.

7. THE PISTOL

Americans have a special relationship with handguns. They seem to appear in every movie, every TV show, every pop novel, every comic book. Our heroes have always carried them, from the Old West lawman to the gritty urban cop. Gangsters rap about them; liberals and conservatives fight over them. Parents shelter children from them and manufacturers make untold fortunes from them. Possibly more than the automobile, the handgun is synonymous with America. But how

useful is this cultural icon against a swarm of newly risen flesh-eaters? In truth, not very. Unlike our fictional heroes, the average person may have difficulty hitting anything, let alone something as small and mobile as a zombie's head. Throw in the obvious emotional strain of undead combat, and the possibility of a successful shot ranks one step above negotiating with your attacker. Studies have shown that of all wasted ballistic wounds—e.g., those that struck a zombie in a non-lethal way—73 percent came from some type of handgun. A laser sight increases the odds of accurate aim but does nothing to steady a shaky wrist. Where handguns do come in handy is in extreme circumstances. If you are grabbed by a zombie, a pistol can be a life-saver. Pressing its muzzle against the undead temple and squeezing the trigger takes no skill and ensures a positive kill. The fact that handguns are small, light, and easy to carry make them attractive as a secondary weapon for any scenario. If your primary weapon is a carbine, this adds the possibility of shared ammo and lighter load. For these reasons, a pistol should always be carried when confronting ghouls, but as a backup only. Never forget that many dismembered, half-eaten corpses have been discovered with these wonder weapons still clutched in their cold, dead hands.

8. .22-CALIBER RIMFIRE WEAPONS

These weapons (rifle or pistol) fire a round no wider than a few millimeters and no longer than an inch. In normal circumstances it is usually relegated to practice, competition, or the hunting of small game.

In an attack by the undead, however, the diminutive .22 rimfire stands proudly alongside its heavier cousins. The small size of its rounds allows you to carry three times as much ammunition. This also makes the weapon itself lighter, a godsend on long treks through ghoul-infested territory. The ammunition is also easy to manufacture and plentiful throughout the country. No shop that sells any kind of ammunition would fail to stock .22 rimfire. Two disadvantages present themselves, however, when the use of a .22 is considered. The small round has zero stopping power. People (including former President Reagan) have been shot with .22s and not even realized it until later. A ghoul taking a round to the chest would not even be slowed, let alone stopped, by this puny projectile. Another problem is the lack of skull penetration at longer ranges. With a .22, you might have to get a little too close for comfort, a fact that could increase stress and degrade the odds of a kill. By the same token, the lack of power in a round fired by a .22 has been called a blessing in disguise. Without the force to punch through the back of a zombie's skull, .22 bullets have been known to ricochet inside the brain case, doing as much damage as any .45. So when it comes time to arm yourself against a looming zombie menace, do not discount the small, almost toylike nature of this nimble, efficient firearm.

9. Accessories

Silencers, if attainable, can be a vital attachment to your firearm. Their ability to muffle noise obviates the need for a bow, sling, or other non-ballistic weapon (essential if on the move).

A telescopic sight can increase aim immeasurably, especially for long-range sniper attacks. Laser sights, on the surface, may be your

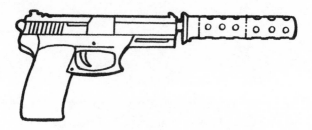

best bet. After all, how hard is it to place a red dot on a ghoul's forehead? The disadvantage is limited battery life. The same goes for night-vision scopes. Although they allow for accurate, long-range hits on zombies after dark, they become nothing more than useless black tubes when the power runs out. Conventional glass and metal sights are the preferable accessory. They may not be fancy, and they may lack the cachet of electronics, but these basic instruments will never let you down.

RANGE VERSUS ACCURACY

Studies have shown that, given the trauma of battle, the closer a human is to a zombie, the wilder his shooting will be. When practicing with your firearm(s), establish a maximum range for repeated accuracy. Practice against moving targets in ideal (stress-free) conditions. Once that range is fixed, divide it by half. This will be your effective kill zone during an actual attack. Make sure the undead do not move closer than this zone, as your accuracy will erode. If engaging a group, make sure to hit those that enter the zone *first* before dispatching the others. Do not discount this advice no matter what your previous experience has been. Street-hardened police officers, decorated combat veterans, even "cold-blooded" murderers have ended up as well-chewed meat because they believed in their "nerves" and not their training.

EXPLOSIVES

Question: What could be better than hurling a hand grenade at a mass of approaching zombies? Answer: almost anything. Anti-personnel explosives kill mainly by shrapnel, metal shards tearing through vital organs. As this will not affect zombies, and the chance of shrapnel penetrating the skull is slim, grenades, bombs, and other explosive tools are inefficient weapons.

These devices should not be completely discounted, though. For blasting through doors, creating instant barricades, or even scattering zombie mobs, nothing works better than a jar of gunpowder.

FIRE

The living dead have no fear of fire. Waving an open flame in a ghoul's face will do nothing to slow or impede its advance. Zombies who have caught fire will neither notice nor react to the engulfing flames in any way. *Too many humans have met with tragedy for failing to understand that fire is no deterrent to zombies!*

As a weapon, however, fire is still humanity's greatest ally. Complete incineration is the best way to destroy a zombie once and for all. Burning eliminates not only the body but all traces of Solanum. However, don't think a flamethrower and several Molotov cocktails

are the solution to all your problems. In actual combat, fire can be as deadly a threat as it is a protector.

Flesh—human, undead, or otherwise—takes a long time to burn. In the minutes or hours before a blazing zombie succumbs, it will become a walking—or to be perfectly accurate, a *shambling*—torch. Several cases have been recorded in which burning ghouls have done more damage, even caused more deaths, than they would have with only their fingernails and teeth.

Fire itself has no loyalty. Consider the flammable nature of your surroundings, the chance of smoke inhalation, the possibility that a blaze will act as a beacon for other zombies. All these factors must be considered before such a powerful and unpredictable weapon is unleashed.

For this reason, fire is mainly considered an attack or flight weapon, and rarely used for static defense.

1. MOLOTOV COCKTAILS

This term applies to any jar of flammable liquid with a primitive fuse. It is a cheap, effective way to kill multiple zombies at once. If the situation permits—e.g., fleeing an advancing horde, clearing a fireproof structure, or destroying a flammable structure with multiple zombies trapped in it—by all means, bombard the ghouls in question until nothing is left but ash.

2. Dousing

The act of dousing consists of simply filling a bucket with flammable liquid (gasoline, kerosene, etc.), throwing it at a zombie or zombies, lighting a match, and running. If there is room for escape and no danger of residual fire damage, the only drawback to this method is the close proximity required to fully drench the enemy.

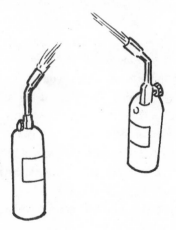

3. The Blowtorch

The common torch, which consists of a propane tank attached to a nozzle, has neither the heating power nor the fuel supply to burn through a zombie skull. But it can be a convenient firestarter if the undead in question have already been soaked in a flammable liquid.

4. THE FLAMETHROWER

This device, perhaps more than any other, strikes people as the ultimate zombie eliminator. A jet of flame, two hundred feet long, composed of jellied gasoline, can turn an undead crowd into a wailing funeral pyre. So why not acquire one? Why not forsake all other weapons for this man-made fire-breathing dragon? The answers are as realistic as they are numerous. The flamethrower was developed purely as a military weapon and is no longer in service with the U.S.

Army and Marine Corps. It would be difficult to find any model, let alone one that works properly. Acquiring the fuel is even more difficult than the thrower. But assuming you can find both, you must consider its practical use. Why carry *seventy pounds* of equipment on your back when only a handful of ghouls are loose? A flamethrower's weight makes it a liability if you are on the move. Unless you are in a fixed position or have access to motorized transport, sheer exhaustion will become as dangerous a threat as the walking dead. Common sense would suggest that a flamethrower's place on the battlefield is against overwhelming numbers, swarms of undead numbering in the hundreds if not thousands. If such a horde were, heaven forbid, to exist, chances are they would be facing a much larger, well-equipped government force rather than one private citizen and his trusty (and let's not forget illegal) flamethrower.

OTHER WEAPONS

Imagination and improvisation are two invaluable assets during clashes with the living dead. By all means, feel free to regard all the materials around you as a cache of potential weapons. But always keep in mind a zombie's physiology, and what your homemade device is likely to accomplish.

1. Acid

Apart from fire, sulfuric acid is the best way to completely destroy a zombie. Implementing it is another matter. If somehow you have the means to acquire or produce large amounts of sulfuric acid, treat it with the same respect you would an incendiary weapon. Not only is this substance as much a danger to yourself as it is to the undead, the time it takes to dissolve zombie flesh and bone is considerable. Acid should be used as a post-encounter disposal tool rather than a combat weapon.

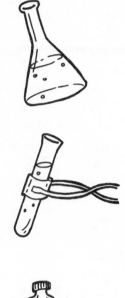

2. Poison

As there are hundreds of thousands of lethal compounds in this world, it is impossible to discuss them all. Instead, we will review some basic rules that govern the physical and physiological makeup of the undead. Zombies are immune to all types of tranquilizers and irritants such as Mace and tear gas. Any compound designed to halt bodily functions would be equally impotent, as the undead no longer require these functions. Zombies do not suffer from heart attacks, nerve paralysis, suffocation, or any other fatal effects caused by poison.

3. Biological Warfare

Wouldn't it be poetic to destroy beings infected by a virus with another virus? Unfortunately, this is not an option. Viruses attack only living cells. They have no effect on the dead. The same is true for all types of bacteria.  Several laboratory attempts have been made to culture and spread *necrotizing fasciitis* (a flesh-eating bacterial disease) among captured zombies. None have proved successful. Experiments are now under way to grow a new strand of bacterium that feeds only on dead flesh. Most experts are skeptical of its success. Tests are ongoing to determine which of the many microorganisms normally involved in decomposition continue to consume flesh in spite of its infected nature. If these microbes can be isolated, reproduced, and delivered in a manner not harmful to its user, they could be humanity's first weapon of mass destruction in the battle against the living dead.

4. ZOOLOGICAL WARFARE

Hundreds of creatures, great and small, feed on carrion. Employing some of these animals to devour the dead before they devour the living might seem the ideal solution. Unfortunately, all species, from hyenas to fire ants, instinctively avoid zombies. The highly toxic nature of Solanum appears to be encoded in the survival patterns of the animal kingdom. This mysterious warning signal that Solanum emits, be it an odor or some kind of "vibe" long forgotten by humans, is impossible to mask by any known substance. (See "1911 A.D., Vitre, Louisiana," pages 215–16.)

5. ELECTROCUTION

As the zombie's muscular system is basically that of a human, electricity does have the ability to temporarily stun or paralyze its body. Lethal results have been seen only in extreme cases such as power lines used to completely char a zombie's brain. This is not a "wonder weapon"—the current that runs through power lines is enough to burn almost any organic matter, living or undead, to a crisp. It requires twice the voltage to stun a zombie that it does to stun a human, so common taser guns are ineffective. Electricity has been used to create a temporary barrier with water-filled, electrified ditches to keep ghouls paralyzed long enough for a secondary fatal method to be employed. Several such incidents have been recorded over the years.

6. RADIATION

Experiments are now being conducted to test the effects of microwaves and other electromagnetic signals on the brains of the undead, on the theory that such a device could generate massive, instant, lethal tumors in a zombie's gray matter. Research is still in its early stages, and results have so far been inconclusive. The only known instance when zombies came into contact with gamma radiation occurred during the notorious Khotan Incident. (See "1987 A.D., Khotan, China," pages 234–35.) In this event, the ghouls were not only unaffected by rads that would have killed humans, but they threatened to spread their contamination throughout the province. For the first time, the world glimpsed a new and even deadlier threat: the radioactive zombie. As much as this sounds like the product of bad 1950s science fiction, it is, or was, a very real and historically significant fact. According to records, the radioactive ghouls possessed no enhanced abilities or magical powers. The threat they posed lay in their ability to spread deadly radiation to everything and everyone they touched. Even people who drank from a water supply the ghouls had touched died soon afterward from radiation sickness. Fortunately, the outbreak was crushed by the overwhelming power of the Chinese army. Not only did this solution put an end to this new danger—it prevented the disaster of the Khotan reactor going critical.

7. GENETIC WARFARE

Some recent proposals recommend a variety of genetic weapons in the war against the undead. The first step would be to map the genetic sequence of Solanum. Next, an agent would be developed to rewrite that sequence, ordering the virus to suspend its attack on human tissue, turn on itself, or simply self-destruct. Instead of retraining the zombie, we would retrain the virus that controls the zombie. If successful, any of these agents would be a revolutionary breakthrough in combating the undead. Through genetic engineering we could find an actual cure. Celebration of this breakthrough, however, will have to wait. The science of genetic therapy is still in its infancy. Even with media attention and massive financial resources, both of which are nonexistent, an agent to combat the virus will have to remain a theory.

8. NANOTHERAPY

Nanotechnology, the study of microscopic machinery, is only in its adolescence. At present, experimental computer chips are being made that are no bigger than a molecule! One day robots that small will be able to perform tasks within the human body. These nanobots, or whatever the accepted term will be, will one day destroy cancer cells, repair damaged tissue, even attack and destroy hostile viruses. Theoretically, there is no reason why they could not be injected by the billions into a recently infected human to identify the Solanum virus and eradicate it from the system. When will this technology be perfected? When will it find its way into the medical profession? When will it be adapted for combating Solanum? Only time will tell.

ARMOR

Speed and agility should be your first defense against the walking dead. Armor will not only decrease both these advantages that you have over zombies, but it will also sap your energy during prolonged conflict. Add the risk of dehydration, and the prospect seems even less

attractive. One final, less obvious disadvantage to armor is not physical but psychological: People wearing protective garb tend to feel more
confident and therefore take greater risks than those in simple clothing. This artificial bravery has resulted in too many senseless deaths.
Simply put, the best protection from a zombie bite is distance. If for
some reason you insist on some type of protective gear, the following summary will provide all the information necessary for prudent
decision-making.

1. PLATE MAIL

This could be defined as the classic "suit of armor." The term itself
conjures up images of seemingly invincible knights dressed from head
to toe in shining steel. With so much protection, wouldn't one be able
to wander among the undead ranks, taunting them at will with no danger of repercussion? In truth, standard medieval armor is far from

invulnerable. The leather or metal joints that hold its many pieces together can be torn apart by an individual's persistent hands, to say nothing of a mob. Even intact, steel suits are heavy, cumbersome, suffocating, dehydrating, and extremely noisy. If possible, study and wear a real suit of armor and practice fighting in it against even one (mock) attacker. You will find the experience uncomfortable at best, excruciating at worst. Now imagine five, ten, fifty attackers, all converging on your position, grabbing at the plates, pulling them in all directions. Without the speed to outrun them or the agility to avoid them, even the necessary vision to find and strike them, you will almost certainly end up as little more than canned food.

2. CHAIN MAIL

If worn from head to toe, this simpler form of armor actually does provide some protection from zombie bites. Teeth will be unable to penetrate its links, thereby saving you from infection. Its flexibility allows for greater movement and speed; its lack of a faceplate allows for greater visibility. Its very nature (unlike solid plates) allows the skin to breathe and thereby cuts down on dehydration and overheating. Drawbacks, however, are still plentiful. Unless you have been training with this armor for years, your combat effectiveness is bound to be impaired. Its weight can still increase exhaustion. Its general discomfort can lead to unwanted distraction, something that must be avoided in battle. Although chain mail may keep you safe from infection, the pressure of a zombie bite may still be enough to crack bones, tear muscles, or rip flesh within the armor. As with plate mail, the clanking of so many chain links will signal to any nearby zombies that prey has arrived. Unless you want your presence announced, discount this idea entirely. On a practical note, if you choose chain mail, make sure it is battle-quality! Much of the medieval or ancient armor produced today is for decoration or stage performance. For this reason, less expensive alloys are used in their production. When purchasing your chain mail, always ensure, through inspection and careful testing, that it can withstand a zombie's bite.

3. THE SHARK SUIT
Although designed for protection against shark bites, this mesh bodysuit can stand up to the toughest undead jaws. Made of either high-tensile steel or titanium, it provides twice the protection of chain mail with half the weight. Noise, however, is still a factor, as well as physical discomfort and decreased speed and agility. Shark suits might come in handy if hunting the dead underwater. (See "Underwater Battles," pages 144–54.)

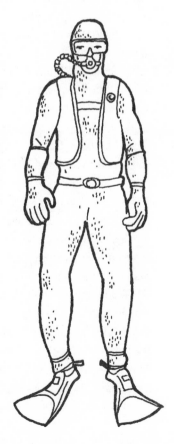

4. HELMETS
This type of armor would be invaluable to ghouls, if only they knew enough to wear them. To humans, they serve no purpose other than obstructing vision. Unless your battle is taking place in a "hard hat area," avoid this cumbersome waste of space.

5. BULLETPROOF VESTS

Because almost all combat-related zombie bites occur on the limbs, this and other torso armor are a total waste of time. One might consider a bulletproof vest *only* in a chaotic situation in which there is a chance of being shot by your own people. Even in this situation, the misguided sniper would probably be going for a head shot.

6. KEVLAR COVERS

In recent years, law enforcement have begun to equip officers with this light, ultra-strong material. While thicker, harder plates are used in vests to stop bullets, a thinner, more flexible version is employed to stop blades and the occasional guard dog. This new version, if covering the lower legs and forearms, can help to reduce the risk of zombie bites in close-quarter situations. If you do acquire Kevlar covers, make sure to wear them only during battle, and do *not* draw any false bravery from them! Many humans in the past have believed that Kevlar or similar kinds of body armor gave them carte blanche to take unnecessary risks. No armor in the world can protect a human from that kind of stupidity. As stated before, your goal is to survive, *only survive,* and never be a hero. Bravado in combat is the surest way to endanger yourself and those around you!

7. TIGHT CLOTHES AND SHORT HAIR

Cold, hard figures have shown that when battling the living dead, nothing has saved more victims than basic, tight clothing and closely cropped hair. The simple fact is that ghouls attack by reaching out to grab their victims, pulling them in, then biting. Logic dictates that the less material a person offers up for grabs, the better his or her chances will be. Baggy clothing, complete with pockets, straps, or anything that might hang freely, will be a convenient handle for grasping zombie claws. Anyone who has worked in factories or with some kind of heavy machinery will tell you the importance of never letting anything hang loose. Tight clothing, obviously within comfort limits, will help

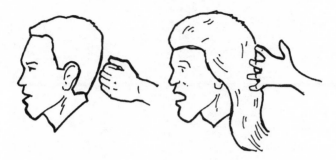

to eliminate this danger. Hair can be a similar hazard. Many times, victims have been seized and even dragged by their hair to a gruesome end. Tying one's hair back before a conflict may work temporarily. However, a short haircut, one inch or shorter, is ideal for hand-to-hand combat.

ON THE DEFENSE

The story of Yahya Bey, a Turkish immigrant to the United Kingdom, describes an attack on his home village of Oltu. According to Bey, a swarm of zombies descended from the surrounding hills in the dead of night. Those who were not devoured fled either to their homes, the town mosque, or the local police station. Several were crushed in the panic to enter this last location while an accidental fire killed everyone inside. Many people, lacking the time and materials to barricade all their doors and windows, were overrun by the undead. Many, suffering from bites, sought shelter in the home of the town doctor. As he attempted to treat his patients, they expired, then reanimated. Bey, a six-year-old boy, managed to climb onto the roof of his house, remained there for most of the night, then took off at first light, jumping from roof to roof until he reached open ground. Although no one in the nearby villages believed his story, a search party was sent to look for human marauders. This group found Oltu in shambles, all buildings burned, smashed, or otherwise destroyed. Half-eaten corpses littered the deserted streets. Dragging footprints, enough to suggest a sizable group, followed a track of fewer, faster tracks into the mountains. Neither group was ever discovered.

•••

What is the perfect protection from the undead? Truthfully, there isn't one. Defense isn't as simple as physical safety. Supposing you manage to find, build, or modify a structure to keep the external threats at bay— then what? Zombies will not just go away, and there's no telling how long it will take for rescue. How will you survive? Hunger, thirst, disease, and many other factors have claimed as many lives as the walking dead. Siege warfare, the type our ancestors faced when their castles or villages were surrounded by enemies, is what you will be facing when the dead walk again. Physical safety is only one part of the equation. To be fully prepared, you must have a working knowledge of stationary survival. In an interdependent world, this art has long since been forgotten. Look around your home. How many items have been manufactured within ten, fifty, even a hundred miles of it? Our way of life, particularly as members of the richest industrialized nation on earth, requires a delicate network of transportation and communication to exist. Remove that network, and we are reduced to a standard of living reminiscent of medieval Europe. Those who comprehend this and plan for such an existence stand a much greater chance of survival. This section shows both how to create a stronghold and how to live within its boundaries.

THE PRIVATE RESIDENCE (DEFENDING YOUR HOME)

For Class 1 conflicts, most people's homes will provide adequate shelter. There is no need to flee the city or town as soon as you hear that the dead are walking. In fact, this is highly discouraged. In the first hours of a zombie attack, most of the population will try desperately to escape. Roads will become a mass of stationary vehicles and panicked people, a situation that is rife with the potential for violence. Until the living destroy the dead, or the dead overrun the living, trying to flee would only add more bodies to the anarchy. So load your weapons, prepare for a fight, but stay put, stay safe, stay alert. And what better place to do so than in the comfort of your own home?

1. PREPARATION PART I: THE HOME

Before the dead rise, before the chaos and carnage begin, certain homeowners will find that they are safer than their neighbors. Although no house was ever constructed for the purpose of zombie defense, several designs have proved remarkably secure. If your house itself is not structurally ready for a zombie attack, various measures can be employed to fortify it.

A. Exceptions

Stilted homes, as seen on beaches and along rivers and other high watermark areas, were built mainly to avoid being overrun by floods. Their height already makes conventional attacks impossible. Doors and windows could even remain open and unboarded. The only entrance and one or two outside staircases could either be barricaded or destroyed once the alarm is sounded. Secure on this raised platform, survival time would be determined only by the amount of provisions a homeowner had stockpiled.

There is another highly protective dwelling that was built to combat a force just as prevalent, and just as deadly, as an undead army:

Tornado-proof "safe houses," now being constructed in the American heartland, are designed to resist mild to moderate twisters. Their layout consists of concrete walls, steel-reinforced doors, and steel shutters neatly concealed behind everyday curtains. On their own, these domiciles could withstand both a Class 1 and Class 2 outbreak.

B. Modifications to Houses

Securing a house against the undead is similar to securing it from the living. One difference is the common burglar alarm. Many of us sleep securely at night only because our alarms are "armed" and working. But what do these devices really do, other than send a signal to a private security or police force? What if these forces don't come? What if they are occupied with other battles? What if they are ordered to protect areas deemed "more important"? What if they have ceased to exist, disappeared into the stomachs of ghouls? In any of these cases, direct means of defense are called for.

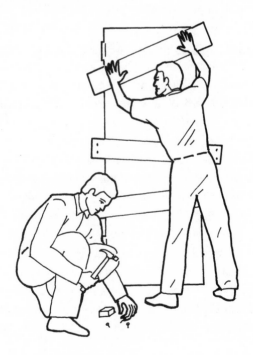

Security bars on doors and windows will stop a group of zombies for a limited amount of time. Experience has shown that as few as three walking dead can tear them down in less than twenty-four hours.

Tempered safety glass prevents entry by smashing but can be forced right out of its pane. This can easily be fixed by installing concrete or steel frames. However, the money it would take to replace each window in an average house could and should be spent instead on purchasing or building one of the two house types discussed above: stilted or tornado-proof domiciles.

A good ten-foot chain-link fence can hold dozens of zombies for weeks, even months, provided their numbers remain at Class 1. A ten-foot cinder-block wall, reinforced with steel rods and filled with concrete, is the safest barrier in both Class 1 and Class 2 outbreaks. Zoning laws may prohibit a wall this high, but don't dismiss it. (Check with your local zoning board.) Although zombies have been known (on rare occasions) to hoist themselves over obstacles as high as six feet, this has never occurred en masse. Several people, well-armed and with good communication, can maintain a six-foot wall, not easily but safely, for as long as the stamina of this group holds out.

A gate should be steel or wrought-iron, solid if possible. It should slide to one side, not swing in or out. Reinforcement is as simple as parking your car up against it. Electric motors make opening easier but will leave you trapped in a power outage or breakdown.

As stated earlier, a ten-foot concrete wall will only provide adequate protection in a Class 1 or Class 2 outbreak. In a Class 3 outbreak, enough zombies can, and will, climb on top of each other until they form an undead ramp right over your wall.

C. Apartments

Apartments and apartment buildings vary in size and layout and, therefore, in defensibility. However, from the squat two-story buildings of Los Angeles to the concrete and glass towers of New York, certain basic rules apply.

First-floor apartments present the highest risk simply because of their accessibility. Tenants living above the ground floor are almost always safer than those in any type of house. Destroying the staircase effectively isolates the rest of the building. With the elevator turned off and the fire escape too high for a zombie to reach (strict limits are imposed by law), any apartment house can become an instant haven from the walking dead.

Another advantage of the apartment complex is its large population. Whereas a private homeowner may be forced to hold the residence by himself, an apartment building can be defended by all of its tenants. This also increases the chances of having multiple skilled experts such as carpenters, electricians, paramedics, and Army reservists (not always the case, but still a possibility). Of course, with additional people comes the challenge of additional social conflicts. This potential problem, however, should never be a deterrent when choosing between a house and an apartment. Given the choice, always pick the latter.

IMPORTANT NOTE: DISCOUNT HOME-DEFENSE MANUALS!
Although almost every other section in this book encourages the use of conventional texts (on weapons use, military tactics, survival skills, and so on), those written to protect a domicile are not recommended. Home-defense books are designed to counter a human adversary with human skills and human intelligence. Many of the tactics and strategies featured in these books, such as employing elaborate alarm systems, booby traps, and painful, but nonlethal devices such as Mace canisters or nail heads in the carpet, would be useless against an undead intruder.

---

2. Preparation Part II: Supplies

Once the private residence is secure, stockpiling for a siege must be undertaken. There is no telling how long it will take for help to arrive. There is no telling if help ever will. Always be prepared for a long siege. Never assume a quick rescue.

A. Weapons

Whereas in the field you must travel light to maintain mobility, in your home you have the luxury of storing and maintaining a plethora of weapons. This does not mean filling your home with any capricious instrument of destruction. Each home arsenal should include:

- Rifle, 500 rounds
- Shotgun, twelve-gauge, 250 shells
- Pistol, .45 caliber, 250 rounds
- Silencer (rifle)
- Silencer (pistol)
- Heavy crossbow (in lieu of silencers), 150 bolts
- Telescopic sight (rifle)
- Night-vision scope (rifle)
- Laser sight (rifle)
- Laser sight (pistol)
- Katana sword
- Wakizashi or other short-bladed sword
- Two knives with smooth, six- to eight-inch blades
- Hand hatchet

(NOTE: This list applies to a single individual. Numbers should be adjusted depending on the number of people in the group.)

B. Equipment

Now that all weapons have been chosen, consider what equipment is necessary for your maintenance and perhaps even survival. In the short run, standard disaster-survival kits will suffice. Any longer, and the material below will be necessary. Common household items such as clothing, toilet paper, etc., are assumed to be kept on hand in reasonable quantities.

- Water, three quarts per day, for cooking and washing
- Hand-pumped water filter
- Four replacement filters
- Cistern for collecting rainwater
- Iodine and/or purification tablets
- Canned food, three cans per day (preferable to dried goods in that they contain some water)
- Two portable electric stoves
- Advanced medical kit (must include field-surgery implements and antibiotics)
- Bicycle-powered electric generator
- Gasoline generator (to be used only in emergencies)
- Twenty gallons of gasoline
- Rechargeable, battery-powered shortwave radio
- Two battery-powered flashlights
- Two rechargeable, battery-powered electric lamps
- Two rechargeable, battery-powered and/or solar-powered radios
- Appropriate reinforcement materials, including lumber, bricks, mortar, etc.
- Extensive tool kit, including sledgehammer, ax, handsaw, etc.
- Lime and/or bleaching powder in sufficient supply to maintain latrine
- One high-powered telescope (80X–100X), with spare lenses and cleaning equipment
- Fifteen emergency flares
- Thirty-five chemical light sticks

- Five fire extinguishers
- Two sets of earplugs
- Spare parts for all aforementioned machinery and user's manuals
- Extensive library of manuals, including a general disaster manual

(NOTE: As with weapons, personal items such as food, water, and medicine must be multiplied for the number of people in your group.)

3. Surviving an Attack

The siege has commenced. Zombies swarm around your home, incessantly attacking but unable to enter. At this point, your worries are far from over. Waiting out a siege does not mean sitting idle. Many tasks will have to be accomplished and repeated for survival in a confined space.

A. Designate one corner of your backyard to serve as a latrine. Most survival manuals will explain the finer points of construction and disposal.

B. If soil and rain permits, dig a vegetable garden. This ready source of food should be consumed first, saving the canned food for an emergency. Keep it as far away from the latrines as possible, to

avoid infection not by waste but by the residual effects that lime or bleach will have on the soil.

C. For electricity, always resort to the manual (bicycle-powered) generator. Not only is the gasoline model loud and potentially dangerous—its fuel is finite. Use it only in extreme circumstances, such as a night attack, when manual power is unfeasible or impossible to generate.

D. Patrol the wall constantly. If you're in a group, run patrols on a twenty-four-hour basis. Always be vigilant for an unlikely but possible infiltration. If you are alone, limit your patrols to daylight hours. At night, make sure all doors are secure (windows should already be barred). Sleep with a flashlight and weapon nearby. Sleep lightly.

E. Maintain a low profile. If you have a basement, do your cooking there, along with power generation and any equipment maintenance. When you monitor the radio, something that should be done every day, use headphones. Keep blackout curtains on all windows, especially at night.

F. Dispose of all bodies. Be it zombie or human, a corpse is still a corpse. The bacteria in rotting flesh can be a serious health hazard. All bodies within your perimeter should be burned or buried. All bodies outside of your wall should be burned. To do this, simply stand on a ladder on your side of the wall, pour gasoline on the freshly slain ghoul, light a match and let it fall. Although this may attract more undead to your dwelling, it is a necessary risk to remove an already-present hazard.

G. Exercise daily. Use of the stationary bicycle, along with basic calisthenics and dynamic tension, will keep your body fit and strong enough for any combat situation. Again, make sure your regimen is quiet. If a basement is not available, use a room in the center of the house. Basic soundproofing such as mattresses and blankets against the walls will help to muffle any sounds.

H. Remain entertained. Despite the need for vigilance, recreation is a must. Make sure a large cache of books, games, and other forms of amusement are available (electronic games are too noisy and energy-inefficient to be considered). In a long and seemingly interminable siege, boredom can lead to paranoia, delusion, and hopelessness. It is as important to keep your mind in good shape as it is your body.

I. Keep your earplugs handy, and use them often. The constant, collective moan of the undead, a sound that will persist at all hours for as long as the siege continues, can be a deadly form of psychological warfare. People with well-protected, well-supplied homes have been known to either kill one another or go insane simply from the incessant moan.

J. Make sure your escape route is planned and your gear ready to go. In the uncertainty of battle, it may be necessary to abandon your home. Perhaps the wall has been breached, perhaps a fire has

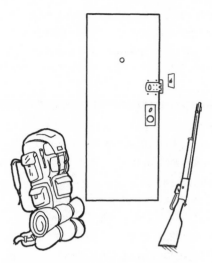

started, perhaps rescue has arrived but is not close enough. For whatever reason, it's time to go. Keep your survival pack and weapon in a readily accessible area, packed, loaded, and ready for action.

4. IMMEDIATE DEFENSE

The dead have risen. You smell the smoke, hear the sirens. Screams and shots fill the air. You have been unable or unwilling to properly

prepare your home—what now? Although the situation looks grim, it by no means signals your demise. If you take the right actions at the right time, you can save yourself and your family from joining the ranks of the undead.

A. Strategies for Two-Story Homes

1. Lock all your doors and windows. Although a pane of glass may not stop a zombie, the sound of its shattering will be the best warning you can get.

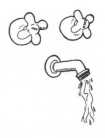

2. Run upstairs and turn on the bathtub. Although this sounds foolish, there is no way of knowing when the water will be cut. After a few days, thirst will become your greatest enemy.
3. Find the best weapons possible. (See previous chapter.) They should be light and, if possible, attachable to your body so you will have the full use of your hands. Those will be busy for the next hour.
4. Begin stockpiling the second story. Use the list on pages 71–72 as your guide. Most households have at least 50 percent of the items listed. Do a quick inventory to see what you have. Don't take everything, just the bare essentials: one or two weapons, some food (you already have a bathtub full of water), a flashlight, and a battery-powered radio. And since most families keep their medical chests upstairs, you won't need anything more. Remember: Time could be short, so don't spend it all gathering supplies when the most important job is still ahead.
5. Demolish the staircase! As zombies are unable to climb, this method guarantees your safety. Many have argued that an easier solution would be to board up all the windows and doors. This method is self-defeating because it would take only a few zombies to break through any homemade barricade. No doubt destroying your staircase will take time and energy, but it must be done. Your life depends on it. Do *not,* under any circumstances, try to burn your stairs away with the hope of controlling the fire. Several people

have attempted to save time in this way; their efforts have ended in either death by fire or the total destruction of their home.

6. If you have a ladder, use it to continue to stock your upstairs refuge. If not, catalog what you do have, fill all sinks and other receptacles with water, and prepare for a long wait.

7. Stay out of sight. If you listen to the radio, do it at a minimum volume. When the skies darken, do not turn on the lights. Do not go near the windows. Try to make it seem as if the house has been abandoned. This may not stop a random zombie intrusion, but it will help to discourage a mass congregation from descending upon your home.

8. Do not use the phone. As in all disasters, the lines will probably be tied up. One more call only contributes to clogging the system. Keep the ringer on the lowest setting. If a call does come through, by all means answer it, but do so quietly.

9. Plan an alternate escape. You may be safe from zombies but not from fire. If a gas line bursts, or some fool down the street goes crazy with a Molotov, you may have to abandon your home. Find a bag or other means of carrying essentials (see "On the Run," pages 94–123), and keep it at the ready.

B. Strategies for Single-Story Homes

If you do not live in a two-story house, the attic will be a less comfortable but equally secure substitute. Most can be secured by simply

raising the retractable staircase or removing the temporary ladder. Zombies lack the cognitive ability to build a ladder of their own. If you stay quiet, they will not even know that an attic exists.

Never use a basement as a shelter. Popular horror flicks have shown that, in a crunch, this subterranean chamber can protect the living from the dead. This is a dangerous fallacy. Burning, suffocating, or simply starving to death in basements have claimed hundreds of lives over the years.

If you find yourself in a one-story home with no attic, grab whatever supplies you can, take hold of a weapon, and climb onto the roof. If the ladder is kicked away, and there is no direct access (a window or trapdoor), the undead will not be able to reach you. Keep still and keep silent to avoid attracting the undead. Zombies in the area will break into the house below you, search it for prey, then wander off. Remain on the roof for as long as you can, until supplies are exhausted or a rescue patrol arrives. It may not be comfortable, but it is your best chance for survival. Eventually, it will become inevitable to abandon this refuge. (See "On the Run," pages 94–123, for details.)

PUBLIC SPACES

As with private homes, safety can be found in public or nonresidential buildings. In some cases, their size and layout may afford more protection than the most secure domiciles. In other cases, the exact opposite is true. Because arming and equipping these structures should be done in the same manner as in private homes, albeit on a grander scale, this section focuses on the best and worst public sanctuaries.

1. OFFICE BUILDINGS
Many of the same rules regarding apartment houses can be applied to office buildings. Once the first floor has been abandoned, the staircases destroyed, and the elevators shut down, an office building can be a tower of safety.

2. SCHOOLS

As there is no generic layout, deciding whether a public school is a good place to hole up can be tricky. Keep in mind the general rules of defense (see "General Rules," pages 86–87). Unfortunately for our society but fortunately for a zombie siege, inner-city schools have taken on a fortress-like atmosphere. Not only are the buildings themselves built to withstand a riot, but chain-link fences surrounding them make these halls of education look more like military compounds. Food and medical supplies should be readily available from the cafeteria, the nurse's station, or the physical-education office. Often, a school is your best bet—perhaps not for education but certainly for protection from an undead attack.

3. HOSPITALS

What would seem to be the safest, most logical place to flee to during an outbreak is actually one of the worst. Yes, hospitals may be stocked with food, medical supplies, and an expert staff. Yes, the structures themselves could be secured, as with any office or apartment building. Yes, they may have security, even a regular police presence. In any other disaster, a hospital should be first on your list of havens. Not so when the dead rise. Even with growing awareness about zombies, Solanum infections are still misdiagnosed. Humans with bites or newly murdered corpses are always brought to hospitals. The majority of first-wave zombies (in some cases 90 percent) consist of medical staff or those involved with the treatment of cadavers. Chronological maps of zombie outbreaks show them literally radiating from these buildings.

4. POLICE STATIONS

Unlike with hospitals, the reason for avoiding police stations has less to do with zombies than with humans. In all probability, the people living in your city or town will flock to the local police station, creating a nexus of chaos, bodies, and eventual blood. Imagine a packed, writhing crowd of frightened people, too many to control, all trying to force their way into the building they think best represents safety. One does not need to be bitten by zombies when beatings, stabbings, accidental shootings, and even tramplings are just as likely. So when the dead rise, locate your local police station—and head the other way.

5. RETAIL STORES

For Class 1 uprisings, many types of retail stores will provide adequate shelter. Those with roll-down gates, solid or otherwise, can stop up to ten zombies for several days. If the siege lasts any longer or if more zombies arrive, the situation may change dramatically. Enough rotting fists, enough heaving forms smashing against the gate will eventually break it down. Always have an alternate escape route planned, so that if the barricade is breached, you can quickly move on. If you can't formulate a solid Plan B, do not consider this place a refuge. Stores without gates should not be considered. Their display windows will do nothing more than advertise you to the zombies.

6. SUPERMARKETS

Although they have enough food to sustain your group for years, supermarkets are also dangerous. Their huge glass doors, even when locked and gated, provide little protection. Reinforcement of these entrances would be difficult. Basically, the exterior of a supermarket is a giant display window, meant to show the fresh, delicious food within. With humans on the inside and zombies on the outside, that is exactly what it will do.

Not all food stores are deathtraps, however. The smaller, family-owned markets and bodegas of the inner city can serve quite well as temporary havens. To protect against theft and, more recently, riot, all have strong steel gates, some even solid roll-down shutters. As with stores, these small markets can provide adequate protection for short-term, low-intensity attacks. If you find yourself in one, remember to eat perishables first and be ready to dispose of the rest if (when) the electricity is cut.

7. SHOPPING MALLS
A practically indefensible structure. Large shopping centers are always targets for both humans and zombies. It is always the case with social disturbance: At the first sign of trouble, these concentrations of wealth swarm with private security, police, even overzealous shop owners. If the crisis occurs suddenly, a large number of shoppers may become trapped within the mall, creating problems of overcrowding, trampling, and suffocation, as well as attracting the dead. In an outbreak of any class, heading for a shopping mall would mean heading for a center of chaos.

8. CHURCHES
Forgive the expression, but places of worship are a mixed blessing. The main advantage of most churches, synagogues, mosques, and other houses of worship is that they are built to withstand forced entry. Most have heavy wood or metal doors. Windows tend to be high off the ground. A majority possess wrought-iron fences that, despite their aesthetic intent, can serve as added protection. When compared to many secular structures of equal size, your typical place of worship is sur-

prisingly secure. However, the protection they offer during an outbreak will never be enough against the horde of zombies that are sure to come. The inevitable onslaught has, of course, nothing to do with the supernatural. Satan's soldiers are not out to invade God's house. Ultimate evil is not doing battle with ultimate good. The walking dead attack churches for one good reason: It's where the food is. Despite their education, technical savvy, and professed disinterest in the spiritual world, urban Americans run, screaming to their gods, at the first sight of zombies. These places of worship, crammed with people loudly praying for their souls, have always served as beacons for the undead. Aerial photographs have shown zombies migrating, slowly, steadily, and with increasing numbers, toward their future slaughterhouse: the nearest church.

9. WAREHOUSES

Given their lack of windows, easily secured entrances, and generally spacious layouts, warehouses can be an ideal refuge for an extended period of time. Many warehouses have a security office, usually

equipped with bathroom facilities and therefore an immediate source of water. If the merchandise that is stored there is both heavy and kept in large, durable crates, consider yourself lucky. These boxes can be used to reinforce doorways, create private rooms, or even, as many of us did when we were children, be used to build a secondary line of defense or "fort" within the main area. There is the possibility, however unlikely, that whatever goods are stored could be helpful to your survival. For all these reasons, rank warehouses among your most attractive hideouts. One caveat concerning location: 50 percent of the time, these buildings are close to shipyards, factories, or other industrial sites. If this is the case, be cautious, observant, and always ready to flee. Also, beware of refrigerated warehouses storing perishable goods. Once electricity is lost, their quick decomposition can become a severe health hazard.

10. Piers and Docks

With some modifications, adequate supplies, and the right location, any dock or pier can be made practically unreachable. Because zombies can neither swim nor climb, their only access would be from land. Destroying that one access point would leave you on an artificial island.

11. Shipyards

Despite the fact that they frequently are the storage site for industrial waste and hazardous materials, shipyards do present undeniable possibilities for refuge. Like warehouses, their containers can be transformed into barriers or, in some cases, even weapons. (See "Mar. 1994 A.D., San Pedro, California," pages 240–41.) The ships themselves become ready havens once the gangway has been secured. But before boarding, make sure you check these waterborne fortresses for infected crew, particularly in smaller, recreational marinas. In the first stages of an outbreak, citizens will no doubt flock to the shoreline, hoping to use (or steal) any available cabin cruiser. Because many marinas are built in relatively shallow water, they are not deep enough

to keep zombies completely submerged. More than once, an unwary, amateur sailor has climbed aboard his boat to find several ravenous, waterlogged zombies waiting for him.

12. BANKS

What could be safer than a stronghold already built to house the most valuable commodity on Earth? Wouldn't a bank be a logical place to prepare a defense? Wouldn't its security measures be more than enough to repel a horde of walking dead? Not in the least. Even the most cursory examination of banks reveals that a majority of their so-called "security" features require the deployment of police and/or outside security. With the police and all other special forces otherwise engaged during an outbreak, silent alarms, surveillance cameras, and waist-high locked gates will be useless when the dead smash through the plate-glass windows, hungry for human flesh. Of course, there is safety in the vault. These titanic constructions would stop even zombies armed with rocket launchers. (No, zombies do not know how to operate rocket launchers.) However, once inside the vault, what next? Given that there is no food, no water, and precious little oxygen, seeking refuge in a vault does little more than give you enough time to place a gun to your head, make peace with your god, and pull the trigger.

13. CEMETERIES

Ironically, and despite many popular myths, cemeteries are not the most dangerous place to be when the dead rise. In fact, they can be a place of temporary rest. As previously stated, infected bodies are more likely to end up in hospitals or morgues, reanimating long before they can be taken to cemeteries for conventional burials. And if by some miracle, a corpse did come to life inside its coffin, would it really "rise from the grave"? To answer this question, one must ask another: how? How would a body with normal human strength claw its way out of a coffin, possibly made of steel, possibly encased in a hermetically sealed box, six feet underground? If one looks at the preservation methods involved in standard American burials, the fact is obvious that any person, undead or otherwise, could not possibly scrape, scratch, and crawl his or her way to the surface. But what if the casket is not made of steel? Even a plain pine box would be prison enough to entomb the most tenacious zombie. What if the wooden casket has rotted? In that case, the body has been lying buried so long that its brain

has rotted away as well. Remember: Bodies that reanimate have to be fresh, reasonably intact, and infected with the virus. Does this describe a long-dead corpse? Although it's seen as an iconic vision of the living dead, like vampires drinking blood or werewolves howling at the full moon, the fact remains that zombies have not and never will rise from the grave.

14. CAPITOLS AND CITY HALLS

Apply the same principles regarding police stations, hospitals, and houses of worship to state, municipal, and federal government buildings. Most will be the focus of concentrated human activity, making them centers of chaos and zombie congregation. Avoid all government buildings if possible.

GENERAL RULES:

Buildings in poorer, inner-city neighborhoods tend to be more secure than others. Their reliance on high fences, razor wire, barred windows, and other anti-crime features make them readily defensible. Buildings in middle- or high-income areas tend to emphasize aesthetics. What rich city council wants an eyesore in its neighborhood? Instead of ugly, even tacky, safety features, these affluent people rely more heavily on law enforcement and private security (forces of proven unreliability). For these reasons, and if the situation permits, head away from the suburbs and toward the inner city.

Avoid "accidents waiting to happen." Many industrial structures of the sort commonly found in inner-city or "downtown" areas house explosive or flammable materials. They also may contain complicated machinery such as power generators and environmental regulators, mechanisms that require constant supervision. Put those two together, and disaster is guaranteed. The Khotan nuclear power plant is only one extreme example. More numerous if less dramatic incidents usually occur with all Class 2 and 3 outbreaks. Do not seek refuge in or near

industrial sites, fuel-storage facilities, airports, or any other place identified as high-risk.

When choosing a refuge, consider these questions carefully:

1. Is there a wall, fence, or other physical perimeter?
2. How many potential entrances/exits are there?
3. Can the people in your party simultaneously defend each fence
   and exit?
4. Is there a secondary defensive position, multiple floors, or an attic?
5. Can the building be secured?
6. Is there a potential escape route?
7. What is the supply situation?
8. Is there a water line?
9. If needed, are weapons or tools available?
10. Are materials available to reinforce the entrances?
11. What about means of communication: phone, radio, Internet, etc.?
12. Given all these factors, how long could you or your group survive
    an extended siege?

Make sure to consider all these questions when choosing where to
make your stand. Resist the urge to dash into the nearest building.
*Remember, no matter how desperate the situation seems, time spent
thinking clearly is never time wasted.*

THE FORTRESS

In Class 3 outbreaks, private homes and even public structures prove
insufficient to support human life. Eventually, the people inside will
have either suffered the eventual degradation of their defenses, or simply run out of supplies. What is needed in a severe outbreak is a nearly
impregnable structure with all the facilities of a self-sustaining bio-
sphere. What is needed is a fortress. This does not mean you must
search one out immediately. The first days, even weeks, of a Class 3

infestation will be marked by utter bedlam, an orgy of panicked violence that will make travel risky. When things have "quieted down," humans in the area will have been organized, evacuated, or completely devoured. Only then should you begin your search for a fortress.

1. MILITARY COMPLEXES

Army, Marine, or even Air Force bases should be your top priority when searching for a fortress. Many are located in sparsely populated and therefore less infested areas. Almost all have elaborate security fences around their perimeters. Some have secondary, even tertiary defensive positions. Most are equipped with fully stocked, fully functional fallout shelters, some with the capabilities of a small city. Because they have multiple means of communication, they will undoubtedly be the last of all global facilities to lose contact with one another. What is most important, however, is not the physical fortifications but the men and women within them. As has been noted, well-trained, well-armed, well-disciplined people are always the best defense. Even with some desertions, a small cadre of soldiers would be enough to hold the perimeter indefinitely. To enter a military base in times of crisis, you would find a self-contained world of trained specialists, most probably with their dependents (families) on base, all ready to defend their new home. The best example of this was Fort Louis Philippe in French North Africa (see pages 211–13), where in 1893 a unit of French Foreign Legionnaires successfully survived a zombie siege for an amazing three years! One expected problem of military bases is that their obvious advantages make them prone to overcrowding during an outbreak, which creates the additional dangers of acute supply consumption and security degradation.

2. PRISONS

Although designed from the ground up to keep the living in, correctional institutions can also be more than efficient in keeping the dead out. Behind their formidable walls, each cell block, corridor, and room is a fortress unto itself.

Problems, of course, do arise when considering prisons as a refuge.

Ironically modern penitentiaries are less defensible than older models because of the way they were designed. High concrete walls are a classic trademark of the pre-1965 prison. Their design is a product of the industrial age, when sheer size was valued as a means of intimidation and respect. Although this psychological aspect may be lost on the dead, anyone seeking refuge could not ask for a better, time-honored barrier than the ones that kept our ancestors safe from society's criminal element. In an age of bottom lines and frugal budgeting, available technology has replaced heavy and expensive construction. Surveillance cameras and motion sensors leave only a double fence of razor wire as the physical deterrents to escape. A dozen zombies would be stopped in their tracks. Hundreds could maybe cause some damage. Several thousand, however, crawling over each other in a writhing, growing mound, would eventually rise high enough to topple the first fence, then the second, then come swarming into the compound. Against this onslaught, who wouldn't trade all the high-tech machinery in the world for twenty feet of old-fashioned concrete?

And what about the inmates? Considering that within a prison's walls are the most dangerous members of our society, wouldn't it be wiser to confront the undead? Most of the time, the answer is yes. Anyone with common sense knows it's safer to take on ten zombies than one hardened criminal. However, in the event of a large-scale, long-term infestation, prisoners will no doubt be released. Some may decide to stay and fight for their safety (see "1960 A.D., Byelgoransk, Soviet Union," pages 226–27), or risk the dangers of the outside for freedom, even a chance to raid the surrounding countryside. Be careful when approaching a prison. Make sure the inmates have not taken over. Use caution if internal leadership consists of a prisoner-guard coalition. In other words, unless the penitentiary is abandoned or populated by civilians and guards, always be on your toes.

Once inside the gates, several major steps must be taken to transform this correctional facility into a self-contained village. The following is a Checklist for Survival should you find the penitentiary abandoned.

A. Locate and catalog all supplies within the walls: weapons, food, tools, blankets, medicine, and other useful items. Prisons will not be high on a looter's list. You may find almost everything you need.

B. Establish a renewable source of water. Exploratory wells and a variety of rain catchers can be used when the lines go dry. Before this happens, make sure that all large containers are filled and covered. Water will not only be important for drinking and cleanliness—it will be vital for agriculture.

C. Plant vegetable and, if possible, grain gardens such as wheat or rye. A long-term emergency could last entire seasons, long enough to harvest and consume several crops. You probably won't find seeds on the premises, so count on raiding the surrounding areas. This is dangerous but necessary, as agriculture will be the only long-term means of sustenance.

D. Harness a source of power. When the grid goes, you may have enough fuel to run the emergency generators for days, even weeks. Muscle-operated dynamos can be easily modified from the existing generators. Operating these machines will also eliminate the need for an exercise regimen. Your generator may not provide the amount of electricity you had while connected to the grid, but it should provide more than enough for a small to medium-sized group.

E. Plan for a breach. What if the gates should suddenly topple? What if a crack should widen somewhere in the wall? What if for some unforeseen reason, the undead come flooding through the compound? No matter how strong your perimeter may seem, always have a backup defense. Plan which cellblock will be your fallback point. Reinforce, arm, and maintain it constantly. This should also be your primary living area, capable of housing your group until the compound can be retaken or an escape can be executed.

F. Remain entertained! As with the private home defense, keeping a positive mental attitude is essential. Find the natural entertainer in your group and encourage him or her to develop a routine of shows. Encourage talent nights and competitions among the others. Music, dance, storytelling, comedy—whatever people can do, no matter how bad it may be. This may seem silly, even ridiculous: Who's going to plan a talent show when hundreds of zombies are scraping at the gates? Someone who knows the importance of morale in any time of crises. Someone who knows the psychological damage a siege can cause. Someone who knows that a group of rattled, angry, frustrated people are just as dangerous as the hundreds of zombies scraping at the gates.

G. Learn! Almost every prison in the United States has its own library. Use your free time (and there will be plenty of it) to read every useful text. Subjects like medicine, mechanics, construction, horticulture, and psychoanalysis—there are so many skills waiting to be learned. Make each member of your group an expert in something. Organize classes to teach one another. You never know when an expert may be lost and another designated to replace him. Knowledge from the prison library will help with every task on this list.

3. OFFSHORE OIL RIGS

When choosing a fortress purely for its safety, nothing on earth holds a candle to these artificial islands. Completely isolated from shore, with living and work spaces towering far above the waterline, even a bloated, floating zombie could never climb aboard. This makes security almost a non-issue, allowing you and your group to concentrate fully on the task of survival.

Offshore platforms also excel in self-containment, especially in the short term. As with ships, they carry their own living and medical facilities. Many are equipped to supply all their crew's needs for up to six months. All have their own distilleries, so fresh water will never be a

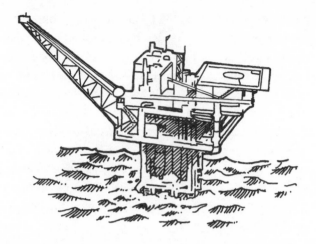

problem. Since all are equipped to mine either oil or natural gas, power will be unlimited.

Food is also plentiful, as the ocean provides a nutritious (and, some would argue, superior) diet of fish, kelp, and if possible, seaborne mammals. Unless the rig is extremely close to land, there is no danger of industrial pollution. People can, and do, live entirely, indefinitely from the riches of the sea.

This complete isolation, as attractive as it sounds, also presents its own brand of difficulties.

Anyone living near the beach will tell you what a killer salt air can be. Corrosion will be your number one enemy, eventually winning out against all preventative measures. Essential machines can be repaired. Cruder distilleries of steel pots and copper tubing work just as well as high-tech desalinizers. Wind- or tidal-powered dynamos could provide more than half the power of the fossil-fuel generators. Sensitive electronic gear, however, such as computers, radios, and medical machinery, will be the first to go and the hardest to replace. Eventually, the entire complex will deteriorate, from a cutting-edge industrial wonder to a crude and rusty albeit still serviceable hulk.

Unlike prisons and military bases, offshore oil rigs will be the first places abandoned. Within the first few days of an outbreak, workers will no doubt demand to get to their families, leaving the rig without a trained staff. If none of your group knows how to operate the machinery, learning might be difficult. Unlike prisons, there may not be a library with how-to books on every shelf. This may require a little creative improvisation, making do with what you can operate instead of, or until you can master, all the technology that can be found on most sophisticated rigs.

Industrial accidents—explosions of stored oil and gas—are bad enough on land. In the middle of the ocean, they have materialized into some of the worst disasters in history. Even with all the firefighting and rescue facilities of a living, functional world, entire crews have been killed when their rigs went up in flames. What would happen if a fire occurred and there was no one to cry to for help? This does not mean that oil rigs are sea-based bombs waiting to go off; it does not mean they should be avoided by all but the most foolhardy. What is recommended, however, is to shut down the drill. This may rob you of new petroleum but will work wonders for your life expectancy. Use already-stored fuel for the generator. As stated above, it will not give you the same amperage as the primary generator, but with the drill off and all industrial facilities closed, what will you need it for?

The ocean can be a source of life, but also a merciless killer. Storms, striking with a ferocity rarely seen on land, can smash even the sturdiest platforms. News tapes of North Sea rigs literally turning over, disintegrating to rubble, then sinking beneath the waves are enough to make anyone think twice about leaving shore. This is, unfortunately, a problem that cannot be remedied by humanity. Nothing in this or any other book can save you from nature when she decides to remove this hunk of steel from her ocean.

ON THE RUN

The 1965 "Lawson Film," as it is now commonly called, is an 8mm home movie of five people attempting to escape the infestation of Lawson, Montana. Its shaky, soundless footage shows the group racing to a school bus, starting the engine, and attempting to drive out of town. After only two blocks, they accidentally rammed several wrecked cars, backed up into a building, and cracked the rear axle. Two members of the group smashed the windshield and tried to make it out on foot. The camera operator filmed one of them being grabbed and mauled by six zombies. The other ran for her life, disappearing around a corner. Moments later, seven zombies surrounded the bus. Fortunately, they were unable to turn the vehicle over or smash the glass of the side door. As the film ran out after only a few minutes, little is known of what happened to the survivors. The bus was eventually found with its door caved in. Dried blood covered the inside.

During the course of an outbreak, you may find it necessary to flee the area. Your fortress may be overrun. You may run out of supplies. You may become critically injured or ill, in need of professional medical attention. Fire, chemicals, or even radiation may be rapidly approaching. Crossing an infested area is generally the most dangerous thing you can do. You will never be safe, never be secure. Always exposed, in hostile territory, you will know what it means to be prey.

GENERAL RULES:

1. **ONE GOAL:** Too often, people who have been holed up in forti-fied dwellings are seduced by the distractions of their initial free-dom. Most of these people never make it to safety. Do not become one of these unnecessary statistics. Your mission is to escape— nothing more, nothing less. Do not look for abandoned valuables. Do not hunt the occasional zombie. Do not investigate any strange noises or lights in the distance. Just get out. Every side trip, every pause in the journey, increases the odds of being found and devoured. If by some chance you come across humans that need assistance, by all means stop to help. (Sometimes logic must give way to humanity.) Otherwise, keep going!

2. **ESTABLISH A DESTINATION:** Where exactly are you headed? Too often, people have abandoned their fortifications to wander aimlessly and hopelessly across an area swarming with ghouls. Without a fixed destination in mind, the chances of sur-viving the journey are slim. Use your radio to discover the nearest haven. If possible, try to communicate with the outside world to confirm that this destination is indeed safe. Always have a backup destination, in case the first is overrun. Unless other humans are waiting, and unless constant communication is maintained, you may arrive to find a gathering of zombies waiting hungrily at the finish line.

3. **GATHER INTELLIGENCE AND PLAN YOUR JOURNEY:** How many zombies (approximately) stand between you and your destination? Where are the natural boundaries? Have there been hazardous accidents such as fires or chemical spills? What are the

safest routes to take? What are the most dangerous? Which have been blocked since the outbreak began? Will weather be a problem? Are there any assets along the way? Are you sure they're still there? Can you think of any information you'd like to have before setting out? Obviously, once you are holed up in your fortress, gathering intelligence will be difficult. It may be impossible to know how many zombies are out there, if a bridge is down, or if all the boats at the marina are gone. So know your terrain. At least that factor will not change with an outbreak. Consider where you will be at the end of each day. Make sure, at least from the map, that it's relatively defensible, with good concealment and several escape routes. Specific gear will also have to be considered, depending on the chosen path. Will rope be required for climbing? What about extra water if there's no natural source?

Once all these factors are calculated, consider the unknown variables and formulate backup plans around them. What will you do if a fire or chemical spill blocks your path? Where will you go if the zombie threat turns out to be greater than anticipated? What if a team member is injured? Consider all the possibilities, and do your best to plan for them. If someone says to you, "Hey, let's just get going and deal with whatever's out there," hand him a pistol with one bullet and tell him that it's an easier way of committing suicide.

4. **GET IN SHAPE:** If the previous instructions have been followed to the letter, your body should already be conditioned for a long journey. If this is not the case, begin a strict cardiovascular regimen. If there is no time, make sure the path you have chosen is within your physical abilities.

5. **AVOID LARGE GROUPS:** When on the defense, the advantage lies in numbers. But when traveling through zombie territory, the opposite holds true. Large groups increase the chances of detection. Even with strict discipline, accidents happen. Larger groups also impede mobility, because the slowest members have to struggle to keep pace with the fastest, and vice versa. Of course, traveling solo has its problems as well. Security, reconnaissance, and, naturally, sleep would all be hampered if someone tried to "go it alone." For ideal performance, keep your team at three members. Four to ten is still manageable. Anything above that is asking for trouble. Three members allow mutual protection in hand-to-hand fighting, dispersion of guard duty at night, and the ability of two members to carry an injured third for short periods of time.

6. **TRAIN YOUR GROUP:** Take stock of your team's individual skills, and use them accordingly. Who can carry the most gear? Who's the fastest runner? Who's the quietest in hand-to-hand combat? Designate individual jobs in both combat and everyday survival. When your team hits the road, everyone should know what's expected of him or her. Working together should also be top priority. Practice mock survival techniques as well as combat drills. For example, time how long it will take to pack up all your gear and move out in a sudden zombie attack. Obviously, time may be critical in your departure. In an ideal situation, your group should move as one, act as one, kill as one.

7. **REMAIN MOBILE:** Once discovered, zombies will converge on you from every direction. Mobility, not firepower, is your best

defense. Be prepared to run at a moment's notice. Never pack more than you can run with. Never unpack all your gear at once. Never remove your shoes unless immediate security is assured! Pace yourself. Undertake high-speed dashes only when necessary, as they squander large amounts of precious energy. Take frequent, short breaks. Do not allow yourself to become too comfortable. Remember to stretch during each break. Never take unnecessary risks. Jumping, climbing, and anything that could cause injury should be avoided if possible. In ghoul-infested territory, the last thing you need is a sprained ankle.

8. **REMAIN INVISIBLE:** Other than speed, your next closest ally will be stealth. Like a mouse trying to crawl through a nest of snakes, you must do everything possible to avoid detection. Turn off any hand-held radios or electronic equipment. If you wear a digital watch, make sure the alarm is deactivated. Tie down all your gear, making sure nothing clanks when you walk. If possible, keep your canteen full (to avoid a "sloshing" sound). If in a group, refrain from talking. Whisper or use visual signals to communicate. Stick to areas with good cover. Travel through open areas only when necessary. At night, refrain from using fires, flashlights, or any other sources of light. This will restrict your mobility to daylight hours and your diet to cold rations, but these sacrifices must be made. Studies have shown that zombies with intact eyes can spot a glowing cigarette ember from over half a mile away. (It is not known whether this causes them to investigate, but why take the chance?)

Fight only when you have to. Delays brought on by battle will serve only to draw more zombies. People have been known to finish off one zombie only to find themselves surrounded by dozens more. If combat proves inevitable, use firearms only in the most desperate of circumstances. Firing a shot is no different than sending up a flare. Its report may attract zombies for miles around. Unless you have a reliable and very speedy means of escape, or unless your firearm is silenced, use a secondary hand weapon. If not, have an escape route planned and ready to use once your shots are fired.

9. **LOOK AND LISTEN:** In addition to staying hidden, you must try to spot potential threats. Watch for any movement. Don't ignore shadows or distant humanoid forms. During breaks and while on the march, pause to listen to your surroundings. Do you hear footsteps or scraping sounds? Are the undead moaning, or is it just the wind? Of course, it is easy to become paranoid, to believe zombies are around every corner. Is that bad? In this instance, no. It's one thing to believe everyone's out to get you, quite another when it's actually true.

10. **SLEEP!:** You or your group are all alone, trying to be silent, trying to be alert. Zombies could be anywhere, hiding, hunting. Dozens could appear at any moment, and help is miles away. So how in heaven's name are you supposed to get any sleep!?! It sounds crazy, it sounds impossible, but it is essential if you're going to make it through this ordeal alive. Without rest, muscles deteriorate, senses dull, and each passing hour reduces your ability to operate. Many a foolhardy human, believing he could load his body with caffeine and "power through" his trek, has realized too late the consequences of such stupidity. One advantage of having to travel by day is that, like it or not, you're not going anywhere for at least several hours. Instead of cursing the darkness, use it. Traveling in small groups, as opposed to solo, allows for more secure sleep because individual members can take shifts standing watch. Of course, even with someone watching over you, dropping off will not be easy. Resist the temptation of sleeping pills. Their effects could leave you unable to function if zombies attack during the night. Other than meditation or other mental exercises, there is no quick fix for getting to sleep in the middle of an infestation.

11. **REFRAIN FROM OVERT SIGNALS:** The first sight of a plane might cause you to try to attract the pilot's attention, firing your weapon, sending up a flare, lighting a signal fire, or by some other dramatic means. This could get the pilot's attention, who could radio for a helicopter or ground rescue team to head for your position. This act will also attract nearby zombies. Unless the helicopter is only minutes away, the zombies will undoubtedly reach you first. Unless the aircraft you see has the potential to land right then and there, do not attempt to signal it with anything other than a radio or mirror. If these are not available, keep going.

12. **AVOID URBAN AREAS:** No matter what your chances for survival are during an infestation, they will undoubtedly drop by 50 if not 75 percent when traversing an urban area. The simple fact is that a place inhabited by more living will have more dead. The more buildings present, the more places to be ambushed. These buildings also decrease your field of vision. Hard cement surfaces, unlike soft ground, do nothing to muffle footsteps. Add to that the chances of simply knocking something over, tripping over debris, or crunching over broken glass, and you have a recipe for a very noisy trip.

Also, as has been and will be stressed again in this chapter, the possibility of being trapped, cornered, or otherwise surrounded in an urban area is infinitely greater than it is in any wilderness setting. Forget for a moment that your problem even comes from the living dead. What about friendly fire, other humans hiding in buildings, or armed bands of hunters that mistake you for a zombie? What about fire, either accidental or intentionally started by hunters? What about chemical spills, poisonous smoke, or other hazardous by-products of urban warfare? What about disease? Remember that bodies of both dead humans and dispatched zombies might be left unattended for weeks. The deadly microorganisms they carry that are spread by the wind will be as potent a health hazard as any other found on city streets. Unless you have some legitimate reason (a rescue attempt or impassable obstacles on either side, not a quick chance to loot), stay away from cities at all costs!

EQUIPMENT

Traveling light is essential to your journey. Before packing anything, ask yourself, "Do I *really* need this?" Once you've compiled your gear, go down the list and ask that question again. Once you've done that, do it again. Of course, traveling light does not mean just holstering a .45, grabbing some beef jerky and a water bottle, and heading down the road. Equipment will be vital, more so than in any other scenario where you are holed up in a place—a prison, a school, your own home—where supplies are in abundance. The equipment you take with you may be all you have. You will carry your hospital, storeroom, and armory on your back. The following is a list of standard equipment you will need for a successful journey. Specific gear such as alpine skis, sunblock, or mosquito netting should be added according to your environment.

- Backpack
- Dependable hiking boots (already broken in)
- Two pairs of socks
- Wide-mouthed, quart-sized water bottle
- Water-purification tablets*
- Wind- and waterproof matches
- Bandanna
- Map**
- Compass**
- Small flashlight (AAA battery) with coated lens
- Poncho
- Small signaling mirror
- Bedroll *or* sleeping bag (both will be too cumbersome)

- Sunglasses (polarized lenses)
- Palm-sized first-aid kit*
- Swiss Army knife or multi-tool
- Hand-held radio with earpiece**
- Knife
- Binoculars**

- Primary firearm (preferably, a semi-automatic carbine)
- Fifty rounds (if in a group, thirty per person)
- Cleaning kit**
- Secondary firearm (preferably a .22 rimfire pistol)*
- Twenty-five rounds*
- Hand weapon (preferably, a machete)
- Signal flares**

*not necessary in groups
**need be carried by only one person if in a group

In addition, all groups should carry:

- Silent ballistic weapon (preferably a silenced firearm or crossbow)
- Extra ammunition for fifteen kills (if weapon differs from standard firearm)
- Telescopic sight
- Medium-sized medical kit
- Two-way radio with headphones
- Crowbar (in lieu of hand weapon)
- Water-purification pump

Once you have chosen your gear, make sure everything works. Try it all, over and over again. Wear your backpack for an entire day. If the weight is too much in the comfort of your fortress, imagine how it will feel after a daylong hike. Some of these problems can be solved by choosing objects that combine various tools (some portable radios come equipped with flashlights, survival knives carry compasses, etc.).

Apply this space-saving philosophy when choosing weapons as well. A silencer for an existing weapon requires less space than a whole new weapon, such as a crossbow and extra bolts. Wearing your pack for a day will also give you an idea where the chafe points are, where the harness needs adjusting, and how best to secure the gear.

VEHICLES

Why walk when you could ride? Americans have always been obsessed with the idea of labor-saving machinery. In all walks of life, industry struggles in an endless race to invent and perfect machines that make the chores of everyday life faster, easier, and more efficient. And what could be a greater deity of American techno-religion than the automobile? No matter what our age, gender, race, economic status, or geographic location, we are taught that this omnipotent machine, in all of its wondrous forms, is the answer to our prayers. Why wouldn't this be true during a zombie outbreak? Wouldn't it make sense to just race across hostile ground? Travel time would be reduced from days to mere hours. Equipment storage would no longer be a problem. And what danger would zombies present when you could simply run them over? These are powerful advantages, to be sure, but with them come a host of equally powerful problems.

Consider fuel consumption. Gas stations may be few and far between. Chances are those you do find will have been drained long ago. Determining the exact mileage of your vehicle, packing it with extra fuel, even planning the exact route may get you only so far.

How will you know which path will lead to safety? Post-infestation studies, particularly in North America, have shown that most roads quickly become blocked by abandoned vehicles. Additional obstacles may include destroyed bridges, piles of debris, and barricades abandoned by last-ditch defenders. Off-roading presents an equal if not greater challenge. (See "Terrain Types," pages 109–17) Driving through the countryside, searching for an open path to freedom, is the best way to run out of gas. More than one vehicle has been found alone in the wilderness, tank dry, blood-smeared cabin empty.

Imagine a breakdown. Most Westerners transporting their vehicles to Third World countries usually pack a full set of replacement parts. The reasoning behind this is simple: The automobile is one of the most complicated machines on earth. On bad roads, without the convenient auto garage, this machine can quickly become a pile of useless junk.

And then there is noise. Roaring through an infestation may seem attractive when things are going well. But any powered engine, no matter how good the muffler, generates more noise than the loudest human footstep. If you find yourself in a vehicle that for whatever reason cannot go another foot, grab your gear and run! Until this moment, you have been announcing your presence to every ghoul in the area. Now, with your mechanized mobility gone, good luck in avoiding them.

Despite these warnings, the lure of motorized transport can seem irresistible. The following is a short list of typical vehicles and their advantages and disadvantages.

1. THE SEDAN

What is otherwise known as your basic "car" has thousands of variations. This makes it difficult to generalize about their advantages and disadvantages. When choosing, look for gas mileage, equipment storage space, and durability. If sedans have one major drawback, it is their lack of all-terrain capability. As stated before, most roads will be blocked, jammed, or destroyed. If you own a sedan, imagine how it would perform crossing a field. Now add snow, mud, rocks, tree stumps, ditches, streambeds, and a variety of rusting, forgotten junk. Chances are that your sedan would not get very far. Too often, the land around an infested area has been littered with broken-down and/or stuck sedans.

2. THE SUV

With a booming economy coupled with an abundance of cheap gasoline, the 1990s saw an explosion of these types of vehicles—road monsters harkening back to the automotive golden age of the 1950s, when bigger was always better. At first glance, they appear to be the ideal means of escape. With the off-road capability of a military vehicle and the comfort and reliability of a sedan, what could be better for fleeing the undead? The answer is: a lot. Despite their appearance, not all SUVs are equipped for all-terrain driving. Many were produced for a consumer who never even contemplated taking his SUV beyond his own neighborhood. But what about safety? Shouldn't the sheer mass of such large vehicles offer more protection? The answer is, again, no. Repeated consumer studies have shown that many SUVs possess safety standards well below that of many mid-sized sedans. That said, some of these vehicles are truly what they appear to be: rugged, dependable workhorses that can handle unforgiving conditions. Research your options carefully so you can tell these genuine models from the gas-guzzling, aesthetically engineered, irresponsibly marketed vanity pieces.

3. THE TRUCK

This class refers to any mid-sized cargo vehicles, from vans to delivery trucks to recreational vehicles. With poor gas mileage, limited off-road capability (depending on the model), and massive, ungainly bulk, these vehicles could be considered the worst choice in transportation. In many cases, trucks have become stuck in both urban and wilderness settings, transforming their occupants into canned food.

4. THE BUS

As with the previous class, these large road monsters can present as much a danger to their drivers as to the living dead. Forget speed, forget maneuverability, forget fuel efficiency, off-road  capability, stealth, or any other feature you will need to escape an infested area. A bus has none of these. Ironically, if a bus has any "advantage," it is as a means not of escape but of defense. Twice, hunting groups have driven police buses into infested areas and used their vehicles as mobile fortresses. Unless you plan to use a bus in this way, steer clear of them.

5. THE ARMORED CAR

These civilian tanks are rare, to say the least. Unless you work for a private security company or have a vast personal fortune, it is unlikely you will have access to one. Despite their poor mileage and lack of all-terrain capability, armored cars present a number of advantages for people on the run.
Their massive armor gives the driver virtual invulnerability. Even in a breakdown, those inside could survive as long as their provisions held out. A zombie horde of any size and strength would be incapable of penetrating the reinforced steel.

6. THE MOTORCYCLE

Definitely the best choice for fleeing an infested area. The motorcycle—specifically the dirt bike—can reach places inaccessible to four-wheeled vehicles. Their speed and maneuverability allows them to be

ridden right through a crowd of
zombies. Their light weight
allows them to be pushed for
miles. Of course, there are drawbacks. Motorcycles have small
gas tanks, and offer no protection
whatsoever. The statistics show,
however, that these are small dis-

advantages. When compared to other motorists attempting to escape a
zombie outbreak, dirt-bike riders have a 23-to-1 survival rate. Sadly,
31 percent of motorcycle fatalities come from ordinary accidents.
Reckless and/or arrogant riders could find themselves killed just as
easily by a crash as by the jaws of walking dead.

7. ADDITIONAL MOTOR-VEHICLE EQUIPMENT

- Tire-patching gear
- Pump
- Extra fuel (as much as can be carried and stored outside of the
  cabin)
- Extra parts (within size limits)
- C.B. radio
- Instruction manual
- Repair kit (jumper cables, jack, etc.)

8. ALTERNATE ROAD TRANSPORTATION

A. *The Horse*

No one can dispute the obvious advantage of an escape on horseback.
Fueling from a gas station becomes irrelevant. Extra supplies are
reduced to feed, blanket, and some additional medicine. Terrain
options increase, as four hooves don't need a road. Before the luxury
of automobiles, people traveled quite efficiently on these fast, sturdy
animals. Before saddling up and hitting the trail, however, keep in
mind these simple warnings. As anyone who's even ridden a pony as

a child will agree, horseback riding requires skill. Forget how easy it looks in Westerns. The skills needed to ride and care for horses are difficult to master. Unless you already know how, don't think you can learn on the go. Another drawback, specific to dealing with zombies, is that horses are notoriously spooked by the undead. Even the scent of a zombie, carried by the wind and maybe miles from the source, will be enough to send most horses into hysterics. This could be an advantageous early-warning system to an extremely experienced rider, one who knows how to control his animal. For most, however, the end result could be a catapult toss to the ground, injuries and all. The horse, at that moment, would not only leave its hapless rider stranded, but its frantic neighing would also serve to alert nearby zombies.

B. The Bicycle

In a class by itself, this vehicle offers the best of both worlds. The common bicycle is fast, quiet, muscle-powered, and easy to maintain. Add to this the additional advantage that it is the only vehicle you can pick up and carry if the terrain gets too rough. People using bicycles to escape from infested areas have almost always fared better than those on foot. For optimum performance, use a mountain bike, as opposed to the racing or recreational model. Don't let your speed and mobility go to your head, however. Wear standard safety gear, and choose caution over speed. The last thing you want is to end up in a ditch, legs broken, bike trashed, with the shuffling of undead feet growing louder with each step.

TERRAIN TYPES

Much of our species' evolution has been a struggle to master our environment. Some would say we've gone too far. This may or may not be true. What cannot be argued, especially in the case of industrialized, First World countries, is that it is possible to assert complete control

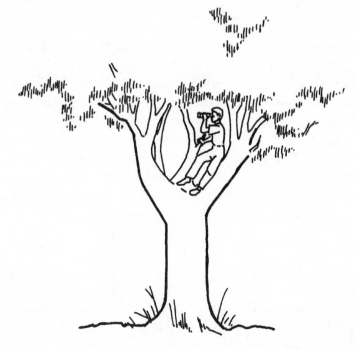

over the forces of nature. In the comforts of your own home, you control the elements. You decide when it should be hot or cold, wet or dry. You decide to erase the day by pulling the shades, or purge the night by simply turning on a lamp. Even the smells and, in some cases, the sounds of the outside world can be expunged by the walls and closed windows of the artificial bubble you call home. In that bubble, the environment takes orders from you; out in the world, on the run from a mob of ferocious zombies, the exact opposite is true. You will be at nature's mercy, unable to change even the slightest aspect of the environment that you previously took for granted. Here, adaptation will be the key to survival, and the first step to that adaptation is to know your terrain. Every environment you encounter will have its own set of rules. These rules must be studied and respected at all times. This respect will determine whether that terrain becomes your ally or enemy.

1. FOREST (TEMPERATE/TROPICAL)

The density of many high trees enhances concealment. Animal noises, or lack thereof, can provide warning of approaching danger. Soft earth will serve to muffle your footsteps. Occasional sources of natural food (nuts, berries, fish, game, etc.) will supplement and extend your packed rations. Sleeping in the branches of a large tree may permit you a safe night's rest. One irritating disadvantage comes from the canopy above. If you hear a helicopter overhead, you will not be able to signal it quickly. Even if the crew does spot you, they'd need a large clearing to land. This may be frustrating as you hear but are unable to see possible salvation flying right above your head.

2. PLAINS

Wide open spaces allow zombies to spot you at great distances. If possible, avoid them. If not, keep a sharp lookout for the undead. Make sure you see them before they see you. Drop to the ground immediately. Wait for them to pass. If motion is necessary, crawl. Stay down until you've cleared the danger zone.

3. FIELDS

For concealment, nothing works better than tall crops. The question is: Will this work to your advantage or to a lurking ghoul's? Noise will be a critical factor. Traipsing through dry crops will create enough din to attract zombies from far and wide. Even at their wettest, travel through fields slowly, listen carefully, and be ready for close combat at any time.

4. HILLS

Traveling through rolling terrain will limit your visibility. If possible, avoid high ground. Stick to valleys. Keep an eye on the surrounding hilltops in case the unexpected zombie should spot you. High ground can be useful for getting your bearings, confirming your route, and confirming zombie locations within the area. Approach high ground with extreme caution. Travel low, on your stomach, with eyes primed for a slouching figure and ears alert for that distinctive moan.

5. SWAMP

If possible, avoid wetlands altogether. The noise of splashing through water prevents any chance of stealth. Poisonous and predatory wildlife are as much a threat as the undead. Soft mud will impede your advance, especially with a heavy pack. Always stick to firm, dry ground. If necessary, wade through only the shallowest water. Watch

for ripples or any subsurface motion. A zombie might have sunk through the soft mud and be trapped just below the waterline. Look for tracks and animal carcasses. As in forests, listen to the wildlife. Their physical presence will also act as an early-warning mechanism. Hundreds of different animal and bird species live in this ecosystem. Only the threat of large predators would be enough to silence them. If you find yourself in the middle of a swamp and suddenly hear absolutely nothing, you will know the undead are close.

6. TUNDRA

This subarctic environment is the most human-friendly on earth. Long winter nights are safe for travel, as the extremely low temperatures

freeze zombies in their tracks. The long summer days put sight-dependent humans on equal parity with their omnisensed, undead pursuers. This allows for more time spent on the go. Ironically, this subarctic twilight has also proven to aid in deeper, more relaxed sleep. Escapees bedding down for the "night" have consistently reported the ability to truly rest without the fear of a putrid mob rushing at them from out of the darkness.

7. DESERT

Apart from urban areas, hot, arid zones can be the most dangerous environments on earth. Even without the threat of zombies, dehydration and/or heatstroke can kill a healthy human in several hours. The best way to avoid these lethal conditions is, obviously, to travel by night. Unfortunately, this will be impossible, as night movement is highly discouraged during an outbreak. Traveling should take place for three hours after dawn and three hours before dusk. The brightest, hottest part of the day should be spent immobile and shaded. Use hours of total darkness for rest. This will slow your journey but greatly

reduce the risks of attack. More than in any other terrain, make sure you either have enough water for the trek or know exactly where to obtain it. If possible, avoid deserts altogether. Never forget that this environment can kill you just as easily as any walking dead.

8. URBAN

As stated before, areas of high population density should be avoided at all costs when on the run. Within their boundaries will be a maelstrom of unspeakable chaos. Imagine a large number of people—say, half a million—left to their own devices in a city without running water, electricity, phones, food delivery, medical attention, garbage collection, fire control, or law enforcement? Now add thousands of carnivorous humanoid creatures prowling the bloodstained streets. Imagine half a million human beings—frightened, frantic, frustrated, fighting for their lives. No conventional battlefield, no riot, no "normal" breakdown in social order can possibly prepare you for the nightmare that is a city besieged by the living dead. If you must ignore all common sense and travel through an urban area, the following rules will improve (if by no means guarantee) your chances of survival:

A. Know the Area!

This rule begs repeating, because nowhere is it more vital than in urban areas. How large is the city you are entering? How wide are its roads? Where are the choke points, such as bridges or tunnels? Where are the blind alleys or dead-end streets? Are there factories, chemical plants, or other places that store hazardous materials? Where are the construction sites that might present obstacles? Are there flat, open areas such as playing fields and parks that would cut your travel time? Where are the hospitals, police stations, churches, and any other buildings where zombies might be attracted to hiding humans? One city map would be essential, an additional guidebook even better, but firsthand knowledge is the best.

B. Never Use Four-Wheeled Vehicles

The chances of finding a continuously open street from one end of a city to the other are practically nil. Unless you have a constant stream of up-to-the-second information about such a route, don't even think of attempting to find one with your car, truck, or SUV. A motorbike will allow you to skirt blocked roads. Its noise, however, cancels this advantage. By traveling on foot or bicycle, you have the advantage of speed, stealth, and versatility in this concrete maze.

C. Use Freeways

If the outbreak has moved from active battle to full infestation, the safest route will be by freeway. Since the 1950s, freeways have been built through every large and medium-sized city in the United States. Their layouts are generally straight, decreasing travel time. Long sections are lined with tall fences or are suspended above ground, which makes it almost impossible for ghouls to reach you. If they do find an on-ramp or breach the fences, you will still have the speed to either ride away (on your bike or motorcycle) or simply run. Four-wheeled vehicles are, again, not an option, as every freeway will undoubtedly be jammed by static vehicles. Many will contain zombies—bitten humans who attempted to flee the city, succumbed to their wounds, and reanimated while still belted into their seats. Examine each vehicle before approaching, and watch for those with open or broken windows. Keep your machete handy for the sudden grasping hand. Be extremely cautious when using firearms, silenced or otherwise. Remember you are walking among a minefield of full or partially filled fuel tanks. One stray bullet or a single spark, and the living dead will be the least of your problems.

D. Remain Above Ground

Storm drains, subways, sewers, and other types of underground structures can shield you from the hordes above. However, as on freeways, you run the risk of being cornered by zombies already lurking in the area. Unlike freeways, you do not have the luxury of hopping over a wall or jumping from an overpass. If confronted, there may be no place to run. Traveling below ground also ensures permanent darkness, already one strike against you. The acoustics of most tunnels are far better than what you find above ground. While this may not allow zombies to get a fix on your position, it will set off a chain reaction throughout your subterranean passage. Unless you have expert knowledge of the system—unless you helped design, build, or maintain it—don't go anywhere near it.

E. Watch for Friendly Fire

Even if a city or section of it has been declared "overrun" (completely taken by zombies), there may still be pockets of humanity. These survivors will undoubtedly shoot first and identify their attackers later. To avoid friendly fire, be on the lookout for gatherings of zombies. This could indicate a still-raging battle. Also, look for piles of dead bodies. They could mark the kill zone of a sniper from a nearby stronghold. Listen for gunfire, try to determine its location, and give it a wide berth. Look and listen for other signs such as smoke, lights in windows, human voices, or the sound of machinery. Again, watch for the bodies. Mounds of corpses, especially those facing one direction, denote a concerted attempt by the undead to reach an objective. The fact that they fell in the same place could mean that a well-trained sniper picked them off from a fixed range. If you feel yourself close to humans, do *not* attempt to contact them. Making recognizable noises or shouting, "Don't shoot!" along the way will only attract the undead.

F. Enter by Dawn, Leave by Dusk

Unless the city is too large to traverse by daylight, never stop and rest within its limits. As has been said before, the perils suffered by rural nocturnal travel multiply a hundredfold in an urban setting. If you find yourself entering a city with only several hours of daylight remaining, retreat back into the countryside for the night. If you find yourself near a city's limits with only minutes to sundown, keep going until you are well clear before stopping to make camp. This is the one time when traveling by night is acceptable. The countryside in darkness is always safer (relatively) than the city in broad daylight.

G. Sleep with an Escape

Some cities may be logistically impossible to cross in one day. Especially now, with urban sprawl and "in-fill" (the development of land between two urban centers), it is becoming more difficult to define a city's limits. In these cases, it will be necessary to find a suitable place to sleep or, at least, rest for the following day. Look for buildings, preferably no more than four stories, situated close to (but not touching) each other. A building with a flat roof and only one entrance is your best temporary shelter. First, ensure that you can jump safely from one roof to another. Second, seal the door to your roof. If that proves impossible, barricade it with items that will make the greatest possible noise if broken. Third, always have a long-term escape plan as well as a short-term one. If zombies do stumble onto the roof, waking you in time to jump to the next roof, possibly the next one, and finally making it to the street, what then? Without a long-term escape plan, all you will have done is jumped into the proverbial fire.

ALTERNATE MEANS OF TRANSPORTATION

1. BY AIR

Statistics have shown that flying is the safest way to travel. When escaping an infested area, this could not be more true. Time en route compresses to minutes. Terrain and other physical barriers become insignificant. The need for food, supplies, practically every lesson of this chapter, fades as you soar well above the heads of teeming ghouls. However, traveling by air does have its disadvantages. Depending on the type of aircraft and the conditions in question, these disadvantages could cancel any perk of taking to the air.

A. Fixed-Wing Aircraft

For speed and availability, nothing beats the standard airplane, assuming at least one person in your group knows how to fly one. Fuel will literally be a matter of life and death. If your journey requires a refueling stop, make sure you know its exact location and can be *assured* of a safe arrival. In the first stages of outbreaks, many private citizens have taken off in their private planes with no knowledge of their destination. Many crashed, while others tried to refuel at infested areas. In one case, a former stunt pilot flew his plane out of the danger zone, ran out of fuel, and attempted to parachute to safety. By the time he touched down, every zombie within a ten-mile radius had seen his plane crash and were slowly approaching his position. (The result was reported by another pilot.) Pontoon aircraft negates this potential hazard (provided you remain over water). However, ditching in the middle of a lake or ocean may leave you safe from ghouls but not from nature. Read accounts of World War II pilots who spent weeks in life rafts after being shot down, and you may want to think twice before climbing into your amphibious bird.

B. Helicopter

The ability to land on any structure, at any time, presents a giant leap above fixed-wing aviation. Running out of fuel is not a death sentence, as you do not need an airstrip to land. But what if you come down in a hostile environment? The noise alone will announce your presence. Apply the same rules of fixed-wing aircraft concerning refueling.

C. Balloon

One of the most primitive flying machines is actually one of the most efficient. A balloon, either hot-air or helium, can remain aloft for weeks. The disadvantage, however, is a lack of propulsion. Balloons depend largely on wind and thermal currents to carry them. Unless you have extensive experience, heading off in a balloon may do little more than leave you hanging helplessly above hostile ground.

D. Airship

They may look ridiculous, they may be almost impossible to find, but if you're looking to travel by air, nothing is better than a helium-filled dirigible. These blimps, perfected during World War I and well on their way to replacing airplanes, were almost abandoned after the Hindenburg disaster of 1937. Today they exist as little more than floating billboards or airborne cameras for sporting events. During an infestation, however, they combine the longevity of a balloon with the mobility and all-terrain landing ability of a helicopter. Airships have been used four times during zombie outbreaks—once for escape, once for study, and twice for search-and-destroy missions. All were resounding successes.

2. BY WATER

Boats, in almost any form, have been found to be the safest form of transport during an attack. As stated previously, although zombies do not use their lungs and can travel underwater, they lack the coordination to swim. For this reason, traveling by boat has many of the same advantages as flying. Many times, people escaping across some body of water have looked down to see ghouls looking up at them from the bottom. Even if the keel of their boat is less than an inch out of the zombie's reach, the humans inside have nothing to fear. Studies have shown that over-water escapes have a survival ratio five times that of land. Because most of the United States is riddled with rivers and canals, transport is theoretically possible for hundreds of miles. In some cases, humans using boats as artificial islands on lakes or ponds have existed for weeks while the shores swarmed with living dead.

A. Types of Propulsion

1. Motor: Fossil fuel allows not only greater speed but unmatched control in any type of waterway. The obvious drawback, however, is its finite supply. Again, either make sure you have enough fuel for the entire voyage or know exactly where safe, plentiful stocks are kept. Another problem is, as can be expected, noise. Traveling at slower speeds will conserve fuel but also alert every zombie within earshot of the bank (a slow engine makes as much noise as a fast one). Fossil-fueled engines do have their place. In a pinch, they can provide an extra burst of power. Use them only when necessary, and always be careful.

2. Sail: Wind is a consistent source of energy. Harnessing it will allow you to travel without the worry of rationing fuel. Other than the flapping of loose sails, wind-powered craft have the noise signature of floating kelp—almost zero. Unfortunately, wind is also highly unpredictable. A calm day could leave you stranded; a strong gale could cause you to capsize. Nine times out of ten, the wind will not be blowing in the right direction. Even if it is, slowing or stopping won't be as easy as turning off the engine. Any novice can pilot a motorboat like a Boston whaler, but sailing requires skill, patience, intelligence, and

years of practice. Remember this before you run to the nearest day sailor, hoist the jib, and find the wind blowing directly toward the living dead.

3. Muscle: What could be simpler than rowing? With a little practice, anyone can propel, and maneuver, his own craft. Here the greatest disadvantage is as simple as humanity: We tire. This should be taken into account when planning your seaborne journey. How far do you have to go? How many people are traveling with you? Even with taking turns at the oars, can you reach your destination before everyone is exhausted? Unless you have a backup motor or sail, be careful when planning journeys that are entirely dependent on human muscle. Remember, humans require rest; zombies do not. Why put yourself in a situation that pits our greatest weakness against their greatest strength?

GENERAL RULES:

The worst thing you can do when stepping into a boat is believe that the danger is over. This false sense of security has caused the death of hundreds of people, victims who could have easily been survivors if they had kept their guard up and their minds working. Escaping by water is no different than by air or land. Warnings must be heeded, rules must be followed, and lessons must be learned inside and out for a safe and successful voyage.

1. **KNOW YOUR WATERWAY:** Are there any locks? What about dams, bridges, rapids, or waterfalls? As on land, detailed knowledge of the waterways you will encounter is essential before starting your journey.

2. **STAY IN DEEP WATER:** Preferably deeper than twelve feet. Any shallower, and a zombie may be able to reach up to your boat. Many escapees have been lost over the side to subsurface ghouls, particularly in murky water. Others have lost parts of their propellers or a section of a rudder by hitting submerged zombies.

3. **DON'T SKIMP ON SUPPLIES:** Many people believe that traveling down a river or canal removes the need for packed rations. After

all, why not just fish and drink the water right below you? Sadly, the days of *Huckleberry Finn,* when rivers were clean and bountiful, are long since gone. After decades of industrial dumping, most rivers are in no shape to support life. Even without artificial pollutants, many rivers and lakes carry enough bacteria from human and animal waste to cause life-threatening ailments. The upshot: Always carry enough food and fresh water for the journey's duration. A level-three filter pump should also be used for cooking and bathing.

4. **WATCH YOUR ANCHOR LINE!:** Too often, people feeling secure in their boat have stopped at night, dropped anchor, and dozed off. Some of these people never awoke. Zombies walking on the bottom can hear a boat approaching as well as the sound of an anchor hitting the mud. Upon finding the chain, they can use it to climb all the way up to your boat. Always leave at least one person on watch for this, and be prepared to cut your line at the first sign of trouble.

ON THE ATTACK

In July 1887, the South Island of New Zealand was the scene of a small outbreak at a farmhouse near Omarama. Although the initial stages of the attack are unknown, reports state that by dusk, a group of fourteen armed men dispatched three zombies in the surrounding countryside, then converged on the house for what was to be an easy mop-up. One man was sent to reconnoiter the house. He entered; screams, moans, and shots were heard; then nothing. Another man was sent in. At first all was quiet. He was seen leaning out of an upstairs window, shouting that he had found a half-eaten body but nothing else. Suddenly a decomposing arm appeared behind him, grabbed his hair, and pulled him inside. The others raced in to help him. No sooner had they entered the house when five zombies attacked from all directions. Long hand weapons such as axes and scythes were useless in tight quarters. The same was true of long-barreled rifles. Wild pistol shots accidentally killed three men outright and wounded another two. At the height of the melee, one of the survivors panicked, raced from the house, grabbed a lantern, and threw it through a window. A subsequent search found only charred skeletons.

This chapter is designed to help plan a civilian search-and-destroy mission. As has been stated before, various government agencies will have their own equipment and doctrine (hopefully) for dealing with such unconventional warfare. If they show up, great. Sit back, relax, and watch your tax dollars hard at work. But as has also been stated before, what if those we pay and expect to protect us are nowhere to be found? In this case, responsibility for eradicating the undead menace is up to you and those you can convince to join you. Every rule, every tactic, every tool and weapon in this section have been carefully tailored for just such a contingency. All have been taken from actual combat. All have been tested and proven battle-ready for that moment when retreat has ended and the time has come to hunt the hunters.

GENERAL RULES:

1. **COLLECTIVE RESPONSE:** As with any other type of combat, undead warfare should never be a solo mission. As stated before, in Western—particularly American—culture, there is the myth of the individual superbeing. One man or woman, well-armed and highly skilled, with nerves of steel, can conquer the world. In truth, anyone believing this should simply strip naked, holler for the undead, then lay down on a silver platter. Not only will going it alone get you killed—it may also create one more zombie. Working together, always together, has shown to be the only successful strategy for annihilating an undead army.

2. **KEEP DISCIPLINE:** If you take nothing else from this chapter, if correct armament, equipment, communication, and tactics seem a silly waste of time, if only one tool goes with you into battle against the living dead, let it be strict, unwavering, unquestionable discipline. A self-controlled group, regardless of numbers, can inflict infinitely more damage on an undead enemy than any well-armed mob. Since this book is written for civilians, not military personnel, discipline of this caliber is difficult to come by. When selecting your team, make sure that the men and women under

your command understand your instructions. Use clear, concise language. Do not resort to military or other coded jargon unless your team are all familiar with its meaning. Make sure there is *one* leader, acknowledged and respected by the entire group. Make sure there are no personal differences or, at the very least, that they are left far behind. If these demands mean thinning your ranks, so be it. Your team should and must function as one. If not, a plethora of nightmarish possibilities awaits. Large, well-equipped groups have been utterly destroyed when their members have panicked, scattered, or turned on each other. Forget what you've seen in movies about loose bands of locals, beer and shotguns in hand, protecting humanity from the zombie menace. In real life, such a gaggle would be little more than a gun-toting buffet.

3. **BE ALERT:** Maybe you're elated from a successful fight; maybe you're tired from days without sleep; maybe hours upon hours of fruitless searching have left you mind-numbingly bored. For whatever reason, *never* let your guard down. The undead could be anywhere, their sounds muffled, their signs ignored. No matter how safe the area seems, be alert, be alert, be alert!

4. **USE GUIDES:** Not every battle will occur on home turf. Before entering an area unfamiliar to you or your group, recruit someone with local knowledge. He or she can point out all the hiding places, all the obstacles, all the escape routes, and so on. Groups without guides have been known to accidentally trigger disasters by failing to know that a gas main was within their firing line or that toxic chemicals were stored in the building they had set ablaze. Successful armies throughout history have always employed locals from the territory they sought to conquer. Armies that have entered blind have usually met with defeat.

5. **HAVE A BASE, HAVE SUPPORT:** A team should never go into battle without having established a safe zone. This area should be

well outside the target area. It should be manned by a support group with all the necessary facilities to keep you fighting. It should be easily defensible should the tide of battle turn. Fortress, hospital, supply dump, combat information center—all of these should spring to mind when you order your group to "return to base."

6. **USE DAYLIGHT:** It is no accident that most horror films take place at night. Darkness has always inspired horror for one simple reason: Homo sapiens are not designed for nocturnal activity. Our lack of night vision and poor hearing and sense of smell make us creatures of the day. Although zombies are no more skilled at night fighting than we are, it has been proven that the margin of safety always drops when confronting them after dark. Daylight not only allows greater visibility but also bestows a psychological lift upon your people.

7. **PLAN YOUR ESCAPE:** How many zombies are you going up against? Unless you have an *exact* figure, make sure an escape route is always chosen, scouted, and under guard. Too often, over-confident hunters have sauntered into infested areas only to be overwhelmed by numbers they never considered. Make sure your escape path is clear, close by, and above all, clear of any obstacles. If numbers permit, leave several members of your group to keep this escape passage open. Retreating groups have sometimes been trapped when their escape route was blocked by a mass of walking dead.

8. **LET THEM COME TO YOU:** More than any other, this tactic allows the living to fully exploit their advantage of intelligence. A human army, knowing an attack is coming, will wait patiently, and safely, on the defense. This is why in conventional human warfare, an attacker always needs at least a three-to-one numerical advantage to ensure success. Not so with the undead. Because zombies

are driven simply by instinct, they will attack no matter what the situation. This gives you the advantage of simply waiting near an infested area and letting them come to you. Make as much noise as you can, light bonfires, even send one or two fast scouts in to lure them out. When the dead come, you will be in a position of "aggressive defense," ready to kill the majority before going in to mop up. Because this tactic has been proven the most effective, different examples of its execution will be discussed later in this chapter.

9. **KNOCK!:** Before entering a room, locked or otherwise, always listen for activity inside. A zombie could be on the other side of the door—docile, quiet, ready to move at the first sign of prey. How is this possible? Maybe bitten humans succumbed behind their locked doors. Maybe they were put there by other, uninformed humans who believed they were protecting their loved ones. For whatever reasons, the chances of this scenario are at least one in seven. If at first you hear nothing, make some noise. This will either galvanize any silent ghouls or confirm that the room is empty. No matter what, be on your guard.

10. **BE THOROUGH:** In the early stages of an outbreak, people tend to capture, not kill, zombies they have known in mortal life. When the captors have either fled or been devoured, restrained zombies may remain for years, able to repeat the cycle if released. After an area has been swept for ghouls, sweep it again. Then, sweep it again. Zombies could be anywhere—in sewers, attics, basements, cars, air ducts, crawl spaces, even inside walls or under mounds of debris. Pay particular attention to bodies of water. Zombies wandering at the bottom of lakes, rivers, even reservoirs have been known to surface well after an area has been declared safe. Follow the instructions later in this chapter for proper aquatic search-and-destroy.

11. **MAINTAIN COMMUNICATION:** Remaining linked to every member of your group is one of the most vital factors in a successful mission. Without proper communication, hunters can become separated, overrun, or accidentally shot by their own people (as in conventional warfare, this happens more than is generally acknowledged). Small, two-way radios—even the inexpensive brands marketed in electronics stores—are the best way to remain in contact. Walkie-talkies are also preferable to cell phones in that their signals do not depend on satellites, relays, or any other external aids.

12. **KILL AND LISTEN:** After a skirmish, always be wary of secondary zombie groups. The moment a ghoul is put down, cease all activity and listen to the world around you. Chances are that if any zombies are within earshot, they have overheard the battle and are moving in on your position.

13. **DISPOSE OF ALL BODIES:** Once the area is truly secure, burn both the bodies of the undead and those in your party who have fallen. First, this erases the chance of infected human corpses reanimating as zombies. Second, it prevents the health risk associated with any type of rotting flesh. Freshly slain humans provide an attractive meal for birds, scavenging animals, and, of course, other zombies.

14. **INCENDIARY CONTROL:** When using fire, make sure you keep in mind the larger implications. Can you control the blaze? If not, the fire will endanger your group. Is the zombie threat serious enough to warrant destroying great amounts of personal property? The answer may seem obvious, but why burn down half a town to kill three zombies that could be destroyed by rifle fire? As stated previously, fire can be as powerful an enemy as it is an ally. Use it only when necessary. Make sure your team can easily escape a wild blaze. Make sure you know where all explosive and poison-

ous chemicals are stored and if their destruction could endanger your team. Make sure you practice with your incendiary tools (blowtorch, Molotov, flare, etc.) before entering a combat zone so you know what they are capable of. Be aware of flammable fumes such as a leaking gas main. Even without resorting to fire as a weapon, the danger of these fumes, spilled chemicals, leaking fuel tanks on automobiles, and a host of other hazards are enough to prohibit smoking during any search-and-destroy mission.

15. **NEVER GO OFF ALONE!:** There may be times when it seems wasteful to send an entire team to do one person's job. Wouldn't five individuals cover more ground than a group all bunched together? In terms of time and efficiency, yes. For safety, the priority of any zombie sweep, staying together is mandatory. A separated individual could easily be surrounded and consumed. Even worse, hunters have come up against walking dead who only hours before were members of their own party!

WEAPONS AND GEAR

Arming and equipping a civilian, antizombie team should follow the same pattern as a military unit. Each person should have a standard "kit" in addition to certain items required for the whole team.
Every member should carry:

- Primary firearm (rifle or semiautomatic carbine)
- Fifty rounds of ammunition
- Cleaning kit
- Secondary weapon (preferably a pistol)
- Twenty-five rounds of ammunition
- Hand-to-hand weapon (large or small)
- Knife
- Flashlight

- Two emergency flares
- Signaling mirror
- Two-way radio
- Two ways of making fire (matches, lighter, etc.)
- Full quart canteen
- Daily rations
- Personal mess kit
- Hiking or combat boots
- Two pairs of socks
- Bedroll or pad

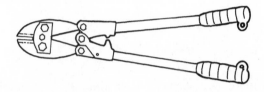

Each group (ten people or fewer) should have:

- Two silent weapons (could be carried as secondary weapons)
- Three explosive devices
- Two grappling hooks
- 500 feet of rope (nylon construction, $7/16''$ diameter, tensile strength 6,500 lbs., load absorption 1,450 ft./lb.)
- Two pairs of binoculars (minimum 50mm lenses/10X power)
- Two crowbars (could be carried as hand-to-hand weapons)
- Two bolt cutters
- Tool kit (must include: hammer-claw and ball-peen 4 oz., diagonal 4'' pliers with spring, 4–6'' longnose pliers with cutter, Phillips screwdrivers [3'', 4'', and stubby], slot screwdriver [4–5''], jeweler's screwdrivers set, 12'' × ½'' hacksaw, 3M electrical tape, adjustable wrench, hand drill with 2–5mm bit set)
- Ax or hand hatchet (could be carried as hand-to-hand weapon)
- Medical kit (must include: bandages, cotton rolls/balls, two arm

slings, scissors, medical tape, Merthiolate vials, antiseptic swab sticks, antiseptic and cleaning towelettes, bacterial soap, sterile gauze/eye pads, petrolatum, sterile lancets)

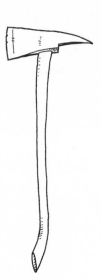

- Three gallons extra potable water
- Two maps (immediate zone/surrounding area)
- Two compasses
- Extra batteries for all electronic devices
- Ten extra emergency flares
- Four compact entrenching tools (could be carried as hand-to-hand weapons)

TRANSPORTATION

Unlike the scenario described in "On the Run," the goal of this section is to help you not escape an area but sweep it. The undead are not to be avoided but attracted. Also, unlike the previous chapter, you will not be alone, and the support area should make fueling and servicing a vehicle much easier. With this in mind, using the noise from a car's engine will act like a lure. (See "Strategies," pages 138–54.) In this instance, removing the rubber from a bicycle's tires can accomplish the same result. Do not become too dependent on your vehicles. Unless applied to a specific strategy (see below), use them more as a means of getting to and from a battle site. Once in the target area, dismount and search on foot. This will allow for greater flexibility, particularly in urban areas.

TERRAIN TYPES

At first, this section might seem redundant. However, unlike "On the Run," which teaches how to use terrain to escape, this will teach you how to use it to hunt. This time you are not simply passing through your environment as quickly, quietly, and easily as possible. As a hunter, you are here to reclaim this land—hold it, sweep it, cleanse it until every trace of the undead is gone. This section includes only information necessary to do just that.

1. FOREST
When hunting, watch for freshly eaten carcasses. Try to determine if the predator was an animal or a zombie. Also, use the trees to extend your visibility: Each one can serve as a lookout post or sniper platform. Set fires only as a last-ditch effort.

2. PLAINS
Vast, open areas provide great visibility, allowing full use of long-range sharpshooting weapons. One team of five with adequately sighted rifles and plenty of ammunition can clear several square miles in the course of a single day. Of course, great visibility allows the undead to see you as readily as you see them. Hunter groups operating on plains or prairie have reported being sighted and stalked by ghouls from as far as ten miles away. Another slight but still potential

danger is posed by the odd zombie who may be lying in the tall grass. Undead who have lost their legs or had their spinal columns severed can remain undetected until it is too late. If your team is traveling through tall grass, travel slowly, watch the ground, and listen for any rustling or moans.

3. FIELDS

Unsuspecting hunters have chased zombies through a field only to be grabbed by another one lurking inches away! Unless you are ordered to protect the harvest, or the food itself is of vital importance, this is one case in which fire should be used first. Although almost every other word in this book stresses the control of incendiary warfare, common sense dictates that no human life is worth an acre or two of maize.

4. TUNDRA

One potential danger, not experienced in other environments, is that of a multigenerational outbreak. Because of cold weather's preservative ability, zombies may remain frozen for decades. When thawed, they will join the ranks of the recently reani-

mated and, in some cases, can re-infect an entire area. Frozen tundra, more than any other environment, requires not only a tireless search but a heightened alert status during the next year's spring thaw.

5. HILLS

Rolling terrain can be as treacherous and pose as great a threat from zombies as it can from any human enemy. If possible, always take the high ground and hold it. This allows greater visibility for you. As crazy as this sounds, remember that ghouls have limited dexterity. Apply this fact to their climbing skills, and what you have is a mass of zombies struggling unsuccessfully to get up the slope while you pick them off one by one.

6. DESERT

The problems discussed in "On the Run" are doubled when operating in a desert. Unlike the escapee, your team of hunters will be out during the brightest, hottest, most excruciating part of the day. Make sure each hunter is well supplied with water and antisunstroke accessories. Combat, unlike travel, will require more energy and therefore increase the risk of dehydration. Do not ignore the signs. One incapacitated member can cripple an entire team, allowing the undead to quickly turn the tables on you. Losing touch with your supply base, becoming isolated even for a day, takes on a whole new meaning in this life-threatening environment.

7. URBAN

If the goal were only to kill zombies, an urban area could simply be bombed or burned to the ground. That would "secure" it, but where would the survivors live with their homes a pile of rubble? Urban combat is the most difficult for a variety of reasons. For starters, it takes the longest amount of time because every building, every room, every subway tunnel, every car, every sewer pipe, every nook and cranny of this massive maze must be searched. Chances are, given a city's importance, your civilian group will be working side by side with government forces. If this is not the case, however, be extremely cautious. Always think conservatively when it comes to team members, time, and resources (food, water, ammo). Cities have a way of swallowing them all up.

8. JUNGLE

This is a close-combat nightmare. Sniper rifles and other long-range weapons such as crossbows will be next to useless. Equip your team with carbines and/or shotguns. Machetes must be carried by each hunter, both for clearing foliage and for hand-to-hand combat. Use of fire will not be an option because the intense moisture will dampen most attempts to start one. Keep your team together at all times, be hyperalert, and listen carefully to the sounds of nearby wildlife. As with forests and swamps, they will be your only warning system.

9. SWAMP

Many of the aspects of jungle warfare can apply to marshes as well. They may not always be as hot or as dense, but this does not mean they are any safer. Pay close attention to the water. All equipment and tac-

tics applied to subaquatic warfare and discussed later will most likely be employed in this scenario as well.

STRATEGIES

1. LURE AND DESTROY

Use one or more vehicles, large pickup trucks, or SUVs to enter an infested area. Once inside, make as much noise as possible to draw the undead to you. Exit the area slowly, matching the speed of your pur-

suers. Like the Pied Piper, you will soon acquire a tail of zombies, a grisly parade slouching after you. At this point, sharpshooters posted at the back of the vehicles can proceed to take them down. The pursuing ghouls will not realize what is happening, as their primitive brains will not notice that their comrades are falling all around them. Continue to lead them from the area, thinning their ranks until none are left. Use this tactic in urban zones (when the roads are clear) or where natural environments allow long vehicular journeys.

2. THE BARRICADE

This tactic works similarly to "Lure and Destroy," only instead of leading the undead on for miles, your bait will draw them to a fixed position. This position could be constructed of debris, hastily erected barbed wire, wrecked cars, or your own vehicles. From the fixed position, your team will stand its ground, killing the zombies before they can overrun the barricade. In this instance, incendiary devices are ideal. Chances are, that the approaching zombies will be tightly packed by the time they reach your position. Molotovs or (and only in this one case) a flamethrower would utterly destroy their ranks. Barbed wire or other similar obstacles should be used to slow an advance and further concentrate targets. If incineration is not an option, simple marksmanship will accomplish the same task. Make sure your distances are measured and your rounds are expended wisely. Always watch your flanks. If possible, make sure the zone of approach is narrow and contained. Always have your escape route ready, but keep control of the team to avoid a premature retreat. Use the Barricade tactic in urban areas or those that provide great visibility. Specifically exclude jungles, swamps, or thick forests.

3. THE TOWER

Find an area high above ground (a tree, building, water tower, etc.). Stock this position with enough ammunition and basic supplies for a protracted battle (longer than one full day). Once all these tasks have been accomplished, do everything you can to attract the dead. As they

gather around your position, begin the slaughter. Be careful when using incendiaries, as fire may spread to the tower or smoke may become a health risk.

4. MOBILE TOWER
Drive a garbage truck, semi, or other tall vehicle into the heart of an infested area. Establish a kill zone with good visibility, park, and commence the attack. The advantages of this tactic include never being shackled to an existing tower, already luring the dead with your vehicle's engine, and (provided your cabin is always clear) a guaranteed means of escape.

5. THE CAGE
If you don't believe in cruelty to animals, don't try this on a sweep. It basically involves placing an animal in a cage, positioning your team within weapons range of that cage, then picking off the zombies that come to devour said animal. Of course, several factors need to be con-

sidered for this tactic to work. The live bait must be loud enough to attract any nearby ghouls. The cage must be strong enough to resist an attack and anchored well enough to resist being pushed. Your team needs to be hidden so as not to attract zombies to its position. They must also take care not to hit and kill the caged animal. Silent, dead bait will quickly foil the cage strategy. Environments least suited to a cage approach are those with little or no cover for your team. Avoid its use in plains, tundra, or open desert.

6. THE TANK

Obviously, any civilian group will not have access to a real tank or armored personnel carrier. What might be available is an armored car, the type used to transport valuable commodities. In this case, the commodity will be your team. Using a "tank" is very similar to the cage tactic in that your goal is to attract the zombies to a specific location, then dispose of them with rifle fire. But unlike the cage, your team members within the tank's cabin are not simply live bait. Firing slits enable them to add another level of firepower to those of the external snipers. Be aware, however, of the possibility that undead may tip your armored car on its side.

7. THE STAMPEDE

Of all hunting methods used against the dead, this is perhaps the most theatrical. Basically, the "process" involves dividing your party into teams, boarding a number of motor vehicles, driving through the infested area, and running over every zombie they find. Despite the image of a modern-day stampede, from which this tactic gets its name, it has been all but abandoned by knowledgeable hunting groups. Hitting a ghoul with a vehicle rarely results in a kill. More likely, the animated corpse is left crippled, crawling around with a shattered spinal column and useless legs. Always plan to follow up your "high-speed chase" with hours of mopping up by a team of dismounted hunters. If you do decide on the stampede tactic, use it in plains, desert, tundra, and other wide-open areas. Urban zones present too many obstacles, such as wrecked cars or abandoned barricades. Too often, stampeding hunters have found their paths blocked and their situation radically reversed. Avoid swamps or wetlands entirely.

8. MOTORIZED SWEEP

Almost the polar opposite of a Stampede, the Motorized Sweep is a slow, calm, methodical approach. Your hunters, traveling in large, powerful, well-protected vehicles, at speeds no greater than ten miles an hour, patrol the infested area. Sharpshooters pick off the undead, one shot at a time, until none are left standing. Trucks work best because they offer snipers an easier, safer vantage point from the roof. Although this tactic reduces the mop-up time of a Stampede, each body will still have to be inspected and disposed of. Open areas are ideal for the Motorized Sweep, although the slower speed involved allows limited use of this tactic in urban areas. As with all motorized vehicles, avoid dense and/or tropical areas. Once again, as with the Stampede, you will still need to plan for an extensive mopping-up period. Taking potshots from the roof of your Chevrolet Suburban will not get that last zombie at the bottom of the pond, locked in a closet, wandering the sewers, or lurking in a basement.

9. AIRBORNE SWEEP

What could be safer than attacking your enemy from the air? With several helicopters, couldn't your team cover more ground in less time with no risk at all? In theory, yes; in practice, no. Any student of conventional warfare will acknowledge the need for ground troops, no matter how superior an air force is. This applies tenfold for hunting the undead. Forget using air attacks in urban, forest, jungle, swamp, or any other canopied terrain. Chances are your kill rate will drop to under 10 percent. Forget also the idea of a clean, painless sweep, even in a high-visibility zone. Your team will still have to mop up no matter how secure it appears. Air support does have its uses, especially in forward spotting and transport. Planes or helicopters, scouting in open areas, can provide zombie location data for multiple hunter teams simultaneously. Blimps have the advantage of lingering over the infested area all day, providing a constant stream of information and warning against possible ambushes. Helicopters can provide immediate assistance to those in trouble, lifting one team to the aid of another. Be cautious, however, about using your "eye in the sky," so far ahead of the group. Mechanical failures could cause a forced landing in highly infested areas. Not only would the chopper crew be endangered—so would any team member attempting to rescue them.

What about parachuting hunters into an infested zone? This theory has been suggested many times although never put into practice. It is daring, it is courageous, it is heroic, and it is utterly insipid! Forget being injured on impact, tangled in trees, blown off course, lost on landing—forget all the possibilities associated with normal parachute jumps in regular peacetime conditions. If you want to know the true danger of an airborne attack against zombies, try dropping a square centimeter of meat on a swarming anthill. Chances are, that meat will never touch the ground. In short, air support is just that: "support." People who believe it to be a war-winner have no business planning, orchestrating, or participating in any conflict with the living dead.

10. THE FIRESTORM

Provided the blaze can be controlled, the area in question is suitably flammable, and property protection is not an issue, nothing works better than an artificial blaze. Zone boundaries must be clearly delineated. Set a simultaneous fire to the entire perimeter so that the flames march steadily inward. Do not allow for an escape route, no matter how narrow. Keep watch for zombies that may have wandered through the flames. In theory, the storm will herd the dead into a tight perimeter, incinerating them in minutes. Mopping up will still be required, however, especially in urban areas, where basements and other rooms may have shielded zombies from the flames. As always, use caution, and be ready to deal with fire as a secondary enemy.

11. UNDERWATER BATTLES

Never forget the possibility of ghouls stumbling into nearby water before you declare an area secure. Too often humans have repopulated "cleared" zones only to be attacked days, weeks, even months later by zombies who have just recently found their way back to dry land. Because the undead can exist, operate, even kill in a liquid environment, hunting them may require occasional underwater warfare. This can be extremely hazardous, as water is not the natural environment for humans. The obvious problems of breathing and lack of communication, mobility, and visibility make an underwater zone the most difficult for hunting the undead. Unlike escaping by water, in which you have the advantage over them, searching and sweeping this alien environment will tip the balance firmly in a zombie's favor. This does not mean that an under-water hunt is impossible. Far from it. Ironically, its difficulty has been known to keep hunters more alert and focused than in more familiar environments. The following general rules apply to any successful subaquatic hunt.

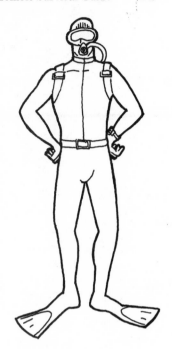

A. Know Your Zone

How deep is the body of water in question? How wide? Is it landlocked (pond, lake, reservoir)? If not, where are the exits to larger bodies of water? How is underwater visibility? Are there any sunken obstacles? Answer all these questions before proceeding with the hunt.

B. Scan from the Surface

Hooking on scuba gear and blindly diving into zombie-infested water is a wonderful way to mix the two childhood terrors of being eaten and drowning. Never submerge before thoroughly searching the area from shore, dock, or boat. If murky conditions or extreme depth prevent the use of naked eyesight, artificial means can always be employed. Sonar devices, common echo rangers found in civilian fishing boats, can easily detect something as large as a human body. Surface scans do not always confirm whether a zone is infested or clear. Underwater obstacles such as trees, rock formations, or sunken debris can obscure a

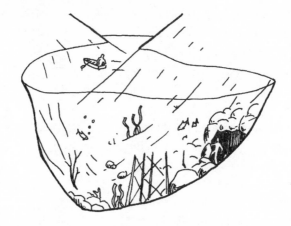

zombie's shape. If even a single one turns up, however, the next rule should be observed.

C. Consider Drainage

Why place your team in a hostile environment if that environment can be removed? Ask yourself the question: Is it possible to just empty the body of water? If so, even if it costs more time and effort than a submarine hunt, by all means proceed. Most of the time, however, this is not a viable option. To eliminate the menace below, your team will have to follow it down.

D. Find an Expert

Are any of your team licensed scuba divers? Have any of them ever worn scuba gear? How about simply snorkeling while on vacation? Sending inexperienced men and women underwater could kill them all even before they make contact with zombies. Drowning, asphyxiation, nitrogen narcosis, and hypothermia are only a few of the numerous ways that air-breathing animals such as ourselves can meet their fate beneath the waves. If time permits—for instance, if zombies are cornered in a landlocked body of water—find someone to either train and lead your team, or even to undertake the mission on his own. But if you believe that zombies have fallen into a river and could wind up near another town soon, waiting for the experts is not an option. Be ready to take the plunge, but be ready for the consequences.

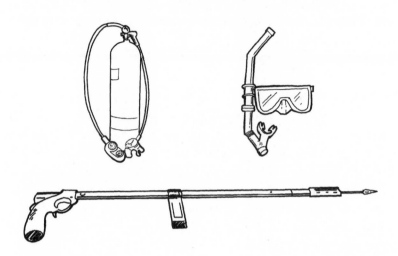

E. Prepare Your Gear

As with land warfare, the right equipment and weapons will be crucial to your survival. The most common respiratory aid is scuba (Self-Contained Underwater Breathing Apparatus). If none is available, jury-rigged compressors and rubber hoses provide a workable if not perfect substitute. Handheld searchlights are a necessity. Even in the clearest water, zombies could be lurking in sheltered, darkened nooks. Spear guns should always be thought of as a primary weapon. Their ability for skull penetration from a safe distance is shared by no other aquatic weapon. Another powerful device is the diver's "bang stick," essentially a twelve-gauge shotgun shell at the end of a metal pole. Both these weapons are rare, however, in all but coastal areas. In their absence, look for nets, hooks, or homemade harpoons.

F. Integrated Attack

Nothing is more frightening than surfacing from an underwater sweep to find zombies waiting on your boat! Always work in concert with surface units. If your team consists of ten people, take five underwater and leave the rest "on the roof." This will allow for a quick rescue if the tide of battle turns. A surface group can also aid in scouting, killing, and calling in reinforcements from land. As a general rule of all combat strategies, the more dangerous the environment, the more support is necessary.

G. Observe Wildlife

We have already established that birds and animals can signal the approach of zombies. The same is true for fish. It has been proven that aquatic wildlife can detect even minute traces of Solanum-infected flesh as it floats off a zombie's body. Once they do they consistently and immediately flee the area. Underwater hunters have always reported zones completely devoid of fish right before encountering an underwater zombie.

H. Killing Methods

Do not discount any of these tactics as fantastic or unreliable. As ludicrous as some of them may sound, all have been repeatedly tested in antizombie, underwater combat. All have shown remarkable success.

1. Sniping: Substitute a speargun for a rifle and water for air, and it is basically the same tactic. As a speargun requires less range than a rifle, the diver will find himself in greater danger. If the first shot misses, never reload on the spot! Swim to a safe distance, lock in another spear, then re-engage your target.

2. Spearfishing: This is used if a head shot proves too difficult. Attach a metal line to the end of the spear, and aim for the ribcage. Once the zombie is skewered, your surface team can haul it up for disposal. Keep in mind that these zombies still have the ability to attack. If possible, try for a head shot from a rifle the second they break the surface. This will require great coordination between a diver and the surface team. One past foul-up resulted in an unwary team hauling what they

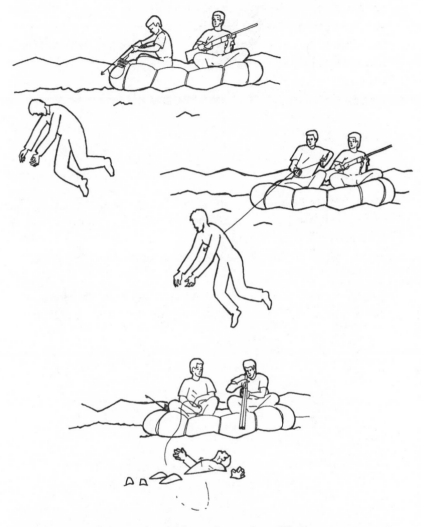

believed was a destroyed zombie to the surface. Their screams were not heard by the incompetent diver below.

3. Hook and Line: Attach a harpoon to a section of rope. Use it to spear the targeted zombie, then have your surface team haul it up. Boat or meathooks, fastened to the end of the harpoon, decrease the chances

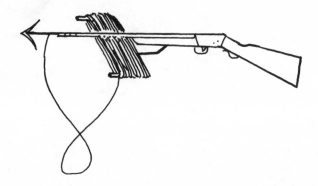

of losing your target during the ascent. If the water is clear and shallow enough, the process of harpooning could be conducted entirely from aboard a boat. Again, as with the spearfishing, the "reeled-in" ghoul must be disposed of before it comes close enough to strike.

4. Netting: Surface teams will be your primary source of attack, with divers acting only as scouts. Fish or cargo nets should be dropped on

the targeted ghoul, then used to bring them to the surface. One major advantage of netting is that the zombies you haul aboard should be too tangled in the net to strike out at you. Of course, "should" is a very dangerous word. Many a hunter was fatally wounded by zombies that "should" have been easy kills.

I. Specific Rules
Think of bodies of water as different types of terrain. Each will have its own set of conditions and can be as different from one another as a desert is from a swamp. About the only thing some bodies of water have in common is the H_2O that covers them. You already have one deadly enemy to contend with. Don't make another one.

1. Rivers: Constant currents can be both a blessing and a curse. Depending on the strength of its currents a river can wash any and all zombies well away from the initial infested area. Ghouls that fall into the Mississippi near Winona, Minnesota, could easily wash ashore a week later in downtown New Orleans. This creates a sense of urgency not found with landlocked pools. If possible, set up nets at the narrowest points. Monitor them carefully, and exercise extreme caution when sending divers in to investigate. A strong current can carry them right into the waiting arms and open mouths of their "targets."

2. Lakes and Ponds: Because they are landlocked (generally), there is little chance for zombies to escape from a lake or a pond. Any undead wandering back to shore could be sighted and killed. Those remaining submerged will be eventually fished out and destroyed. The lack of any current makes them an ideal location for divers. Lakes and ponds that freeze over present a multigenerational problem. If they freeze solid, the submerged will become entombed for the winter, making them almost impossible to find. If only the surface freezes, zombies could still prowl the water's dark depths.

3. Swamps: These are easily the most frustrating places for an underwater hunt. Their murky waters make diving next to impossible. Their root-riddled bottoms confound echo sounders. In most cases, their shallow bottoms make it easy for a zombie to simply reach up and either grab a hunter or capsize his boat. Hunting in large numbers with extensive use of searchlights and probing poles is the only proven method for sweeping this environment. After one of these arduous campaigns, you will know why so many tales of terror have their origin in the swamp.

4. Oceans: Unless the area in question is a harbor or other semi-enclosed area, forget about any successful hunts in the open seas. There is simply too much space for a real sweep, with depths beyond the reach of all but the rarest and most expensive submersibles. As problematic as this is for aggressive hunting, the threat posed by these undersea undead will probably be negligible. Most will simply wander the ocean floor, never seeing dry land again, until they eventually decay to nothing. This does not mean, however, that the threat should be ignored. Once it has been confirmed that zombies have been washed out to sea, determine the deep-water currents in that area and if—and where—they might take the undead close to land. All coastal inhabitants should be warned and a system of surveillance maintained for some time after that. Unlikely as it sounds, zombies have been known to slouch out of the surf months after an outbreak and on beaches thousands of miles away.

So let's assume that you have followed all these instructions correctly. The battle is over, the area is secure, the victims have been mourned, the zombies have been burned. Hopefully, this will be the last time you will ever have to raise your hand to undead flesh. But what if it isn't? What if your struggle was merely one small theater of a greater, all-out war between the living and the dead? What if, heaven forbid, it is a war humanity loses?

LIVING IN AN UNDEAD WORLD

What if the unthinkable happened? If zombie hordes grew large enough to dominate the entire planet? This would be a Class 4 or doomsday outbreak, in which humanity is driven to the brink of extinction. Improbable? Yes. Impossible? No. Governments of any type are nothing more than a collection of human beings—human beings as fearful, shortsighted, arrogant, closed-minded, and generally incompetent as the rest of us. Why would they be willing to recognize and deal with an attack of walking, bloodthirsty corpses when most of humanity isn't? Of course, one could argue that logic such as this might stand up in the face of a Class 1 or even Class 2 outbreak, but the threat posed by even a few hundred zombies would surely be enough to galvanize our leaders into action. How could they not? How could those in power, especially in such a modern, enlightened age as ours, ignore the spread of a deadly disease until it reached plague proportions? Just look at the world governments' response to the AIDS epidemic, and you will have your answer. But what if the "authorities" did recognize the threat for what it is—and were unable to control it? Massive economic recession, world war, civil unrest, or natural disasters could easily distract government resources from a rapidly growing outbreak. Even in perfect conditions, containing anything larger than a Class 2 outbreak is extremely difficult. Imagine trying to quarantine a large city like Chicago or Los Angeles. Of the millions attempting to escape, how many of those would already be bitten, spreading the infection far beyond the quarantined area?

But wouldn't the vast oceans that make up the majority of our planet save us? Wouldn't those in Europe, Africa, Asia, and Australia be safe from a festering outbreak in North America? Perhaps. This is assuming all borders are sealed, all air traffic has ceased, and every world government is aware of and working to stop the outbreak. Even so, with the undead ranks already in the tens of millions, is it possible to stop every aircraft with an infected passenger, every ship with an infected crewman? Is it possible to patrol every inch of coastline to watch for a waterborne ghoul? At this point, sadly, the answer is no. Time is on the side of the undead. With each day, their ranks will swell, making containment and extermination more and more difficult. Unlike its human counterparts, an army of zombies is completely independent of support. It will not require food, ammunition, or medical attention. It will not suffer from low morale, battle fatigue, or poor leadership. It will not succumb to panic, desertion, or out-and-out mutiny. Like the virus that gave it life, this undead force will continue to grow, spreading across the body of this planet until there is nothing left to devour. Where would you go? What would you do?

THE UNDEAD WORLD

When the living dead triumph, the world degenerates into utter chaos. All social order evaporates. Those in power, along with their families and associates, hole up in bunkers and secure areas around the country. Secure in these shelters, originally built for the Cold War, they survive. Perhaps they continue the façade of a government command structure. Perhaps the technology is available to communicate with other agencies or even other protected world leaders. For all practical purposes, however, they are nothing more than a government-in-exile. With the total collapse of law and order, small bands of individuals emerge to assert their authority. Looters, bandits, and common thugs prey on the survivors, taking what they want and indulging in whatever pleasure they can find. It is common at the end of any civilization to have one last massive party. As perverse as it sounds, orgies of people believing that this day is their last spring up all around the nation.

What police and military forces are left serve as protection for the government in hiding, desert in an attempt to save their families, or degenerate into bandits themselves. A total collapse in communication and transportation sweeps the globe. Isolated cities become open battlegrounds, with scattered groups of citizens fighting to defend barricaded areas from both ghouls and human renegades. Neglected machines eventually break down or, in some cases, blow up. Reactor meltdowns and other industrial accidents are common, polluting the landscape with toxic chemical by-products. The countryside flourishes with zombies. With cities picked clean of humans, the undead fan out in search of prey. Country homes and suburban neighborhoods are torn to shreds as citizens flee, attempt to stand and fight, or wait helplessly for the slouching multitudes to engulf them. The carnage is not limited to humans: The air is thick with the shrieks of farm animals trapped in pens, or even family pets trying bravely to protect their masters.

As time passes, the fires die, the explosions cease, the screams fade. Fortified areas begin to run low on supplies, forcing the occupants to face their undead attackers during foraging missions, evacuations, or battles driven by desperate insanity. Casualties will continue to mount as many well-protected and well-supplied but weak-willed humans take their own lives out of sheer despair.

The looters previously mentioned fare no better than any other human. These modern-day barbarians became such because of their disrespect for law, their hatred of organization, their choice of destruction over creation. Their nihilistic, parasitic existence feeds off the riches of others instead of producing their own. This mentality prevents them from settling down and building a new life. They are always on the run, fighting off the undead no matter where they stop. Even if they succeed in fending off this external threat, their need for anarchy eventually leads them to turn on each other. Many of these societies will be held together by the strong personality of a chieftain. Once he or she is gone, there will be nothing to hold the group together. A disbanded gang of thugs, wandering aimlessly through hostile ground, cannot survive forever. After several years, little will be left of these ruthless human predators.

It is difficult to say what will happen to the remnants of government. This will depend greatly on which country we are talking about, what resources it had before the crisis, and what type of government it was. A society living for ideals such as democracy or religious fundamentalism stands a greater chance of survival. These survivors will not need to depend on the personal magnetism (or intimidation) of a single individual. Some Third World dictator might hold his minions together only as long as he survives. As with the barbarian gangs, his demise, or even a simple display of weakness, could spell the end for the entire "government."

But no matter what happens to the surviving humans, there will always be the walking dead. With glazed eyes and gawking mouths, their putrid forms will cover the earth, hunting all living things within their grasp. Some species of animals will undoubtedly face extinction. Others who are able to escape this fate may find ways to adapt and even thrive in a radically changed ecosystem.

This post-apocalyptic world will appear as a devastated landscape: burned-out cities, silent roads, crumbling homes, abandoned ships rusting offshore, gnawed and bleached bones scattered over a world now ruled by machines of walking dead flesh. Fortunately, you will not see this, because before it happens, you will be nowhere near!

STARTING OVER

In "On the Defense," you learned how to prepare a space for what could be a long siege until rescue. In "On the Run," you learned how to travel for what could be great distances until reaching safety. Now it is time to imagine and prepare for a worst-case scenario. In this scenario, you and your closest friends and family must be able to escape all civilization, find a remote, uninhabited corner of our planet (there are more than you think), and rebuild your life from scratch. Imagine a group of shipwrecked survivors on an island, or a human colony on a new planet. This must be your mind-set to survive. No one is coming for you, no rescue planned. There are no friendly forces to run to, no battle lines to hide behind. The old life is gone forever! The new one, in terms of both quality and duration, will be entirely up to you. As horrifying as this prospect sounds, remember that humans have been adapting and rebuilding since the beginning of our history. Even today, when society appears to have softened us beyond redemption, the will to survive is deep within our genes. Ironically, in a worst-case scenario, your greatest challenge will be dealing with day-to-day life and not the living dead. In fact, if your survival strategy works perfectly, you may never even see a zombie. Your goal is to create a safe little microcosm of the world, equipped with everything you will need to not only survive but maintain a modicum of civilization.

And when is the best time to start? Immediately! An all-out war might never happen. It might be years away. But what if it's soon? What if a Class 1 outbreak has already begun and is going unchecked? What if a Class 2 or even Class 3 outbreak has begun in a totalitarian country where the press is highly censored? If so, an all-out war could be months away. In all probability, this is not the case. But is it any reason not to be prepared? Unlike stocking up for a siege, preparing to re-create a tiny corner of civilization takes a tremendous amount of time. The more you have, the better off you will be. Does this mean you should give up your entire life and do nothing but prepare for the end of the world? Of course not. This text was prepared to coincide with the average citizen's conventional lifestyle. Minimum preparation, however, should take no less than 1,500 hours. Even if spread over the course of several years, this is a formidable amount of time. If you believe you can accomplish everything by "cramming" at the eleventh hour, by all means, don't lift a finger now. But you may think twice about beginning to build your ark once it has already started raining.

GENERAL RULES:

1. **ASSEMBLE A GROUP:** As detailed in previous chapters, collective response is always preferable to an individual attempt. A group will extend your financial resources, allowing for the purchase of a greater amount of land and equipment. As with a siege, a greater variety of skills will also be available. Unlike a siege, in which you will be lucky with whatever talents you find, preparing for a worst-case scenario allows the time to train members of your party in whatever skills are required. For example, how many blacksmiths do you know? How many doctors can find medicines in the wild? How many real urban dwellers know anything about farming? Specialization also allows for quicker preparation (a team scouts potential land while another acquires equipment, etc.). During the crisis, one or several members of your group could be sent ahead to the designated safe zone to prepare it if the situation gets worse. Of course, there are potential dangers. Unlike the relatively short sieges of protected areas, this long-term survival may lead to social problems unknown in modern society. People who believe help is eventually coming are much more likely to remain loyal than those who know the future is what they make it. Discontent, mutiny, even bloodshed are always a possibility. As is the mantra of this manual, be prepared! Take several classes on leadership and group dynamics. Books and lectures on basic human psychology are always a must. This knowledge will be instrumental in choosing your members and governing them later. To reiterate earlier statements, making a group of individuals cooperate over a long period of time is the hardest task on earth. However, when successful, this group will be capable of anything.

2. **STUDY, STUDY, STUDY!:** To say you will be starting from square one is inaccurate. Our ancestors were in this position because knowledge took so long to discover, accumulate, and exchange. Your great advantage over the first sentient apes will be thousands of years of experience right at your fingertips. Even if you were to find yourself in some desolate, hostile environment with no tools whatsoever, the knowledge stored in your brain would still put you light-years ahead of the most well-equipped Neanderthal. In addition to general survival manuals, you should also add works on other worst-case scenarios. Many books have been published concerning wilderness survival in a nuclear war. Make sure these are as up-to-date as possible. Stories of true-life survival will also be a great help. Accounts of shipwrecks, plane crashes, even early European colonists will contain a treasure trove of dos and don'ts. Learn about our ancestors and how they adapted to their environment. Fictional accounts, as long as they are based in fact, may also be helpful, such as *The Life and Adventures of Robinson Crusoe*. Absorbing all these stories, both true and fictional, will help you realize you are not the first to attempt such an endeavor. Knowing that "it's been done" should be a calming influence as you embark upon your new life.

3. **WEAN YOURSELF OFF LUXURY ITEMS:** Most of us dream of a simpler yet more nutritious diet. "I'm cutting down on coffee," "I need to have less sugar," "I'm trying to eat more leafy greens" are phrases we either speak or hear frequently in everyday life. Living through a Class 4 outbreak would leave you with little choice. Even in ideal conditions, it would be impossible to grow or produce every food and chemical you now enjoy. To go from so much to zero overnight would be a significant shock to your system. Instead, begin to cut down on the foods and luxury items you will not have in your new home. Obviously, you will need to know what this new environment is and what you will be able to produce there. Even without going down a long list now, common sense

will dictate exactly what you can and cannot live without. For example, as much as you love them, tobacco and alcohol are not part of human physiology. Cravings for vitamins, minerals, and sugar can be satisfied with natural foods. Even certain medications such as light pain relievers can be supplemented with skills like acupressure, various massage techniques, or even simple meditation. All of these suggestions might sound a little too foreign or "crunchy granola" for our practical, Western society. Remember though that many of these diet and healing techniques originated not with Northern California burnouts but with Third World societies where resources were and are scarce. Always keep in mind how spoiled Americans are in comparison to the rest of the planet. Studying the so-called "less fortunate" might give you some insight into how to handle problems with simpler, if not as comfortable, means.

4. **REMAIN VIGILANT:** Implementing plans for a Class 4 outbreak should begin during the early stages of a Class 1. At the first sign of an outbreak (bizarre homicides, missing persons, unusual diseases, contradictory press, government involvement), contact all members of your group. Begin discussing your plans for evacuation. Make sure none of the laws have changed concerning travel, permits, equipment licenses, etc. If the outbreak expands to Class 2, prepare to move. Catalog and pack all your gear. Send a scouting party ahead to prepare the safe zone. Begin the first stage of your alibi. (If it's a funeral of a loved one, let it drop now that the loved one is ill.) Be ready to leave at a moment's notice. Once the outbreak expands to Class 3, get out!

5. **TO THE ENDS OF THE EARTH!:** You may be tempted to remain in your home or your newly constructed defensive zombie fortress permanently instead of heading for the wilderness. This is not recommended. Even if you lived in some sort of compound that is well-stocked and well-protected, with the means of pro-

ducing food and water for decades to come, the chances of survival would be marginal. Urban zones will, in the immediate future, become the center of vicious combat between the living and the dead. Even if your fortress survived these street battles, it would eventually fall victim to extreme military measures, such as saturation bombing. As discussed previously in "On the Defense," urban centers are the most likely areas for industrial accidents, large fires, and so on. Simply put: Stay in the city, and you stand little or no chance for survival. Suburban and even settled country areas will fare no better. As the numbers of living dead increase, they will almost certainly find your dwelling. A siege that begins with dozens of zombies will turn into hundreds, thousands, then hundreds of thousands in a short time. Once they find you, they will never leave. If anything, their moans, the collective shriek of several thousand zombies, will alert others hundreds of miles away. Theoretically, you could find yourself besieged by more than a million zombies.

Of course, it may not come to that. If your fortress is in the Midwest, Great Plains, or even Rocky Mountains, the chances of a million-zombie siege are small (though not impossible!). In these places, however, there is a greater possibility of bandits. We will not know exactly what these brigands of the future will look like—whether they will travel on motorcycles or horses, carrying swords or military firepower. What is certain is that they will always be on the lookout for loot. As time goes by, this might mean women. Later it could mean children for slavery or new warriors. And, as if the threat of zombies were not bad enough, these ruffians could eventually look to their fellow humans as a last-ditch source of food. If they discover your compound, they will attack. Even if you repel an assault, one survivor is enough to put your fortress on the map forever. Until these gangs eventually self-destruct, you will always be their target. So when you run, it must be far away from all civilization. Not just far enough where the only thing you see is a road. There must be *no* road, no power or telephone lines—nothing! It must be on the fringes of the globe, a place uninhabited by humans. It must be far enough away to make zombie migration difficult, make a bandit raid impractical, and make the risk of industrial fallout or military strikes insignificant. Short of flying to another planet or colonizing the bottom of the ocean, it must be as far as you can get from the centers of humanity.

6. **KNOW YOUR LOCATION:** When it comes time to flee, don't just pack up the Jeep, head north, and hope you find some nice safe nook in the Yukon. When planning to escape the living dead, *especially* in an uninhabited part of the world, you must know *exactly* where you are going. Spend time studying the most up-to-date maps. Older maps may not have roads, pipelines, outposts, or other structures listed. When choosing your location, make sure the following questions are answered:

   A. Is it remote—at least several hundred miles from any civilization?

   B. Does it have a source of fresh water for not only you but any animals you decide to bring? Remember that you will require water for a multitude of purposes, including drinking, washing, cooking, and farming.

C. Does it have the capacity to produce food? Is the soil good enough for growing? What about animal grazing or fishing? Will foraging produce enough *consistent* sustenance without being depleted?

D. Does it have any natural defenses? Is it atop a high peak or surrounded by cliffs or rivers? During an attack by the living dead or human bandits, will the terrain aid you or your enemy?

E. What are its natural resources? Are there building materials such as wood, stone, or metal? What about fuel such as coal, oil, peat, or again, wood? How much building material would you need to bring with you in order to construct a compound? How much of the local flora has medicinal properties?

All these questions must be answered before you even begin to consider a permanent refuge. Building materials and natural defenses are negotiable. Food, water, and extreme distance are *not!* Without any of those three essential elements, you seriously compromise your long-term survival. When choosing your new home, make a list of at least five possible places. Visit them all, preferably in their harshest season. Camp at least a full week with primitive gear and zero outside contact. Only then should you make your decision about which is best suited to your needs.

7. **BECOME AN EXPERT:** Research your potential new home thoroughly. Read every book, every article, every sentence written about it. Examine every map and photograph. The type of terrain you choose will have its own specific survival manuals. Purchase and study them all. In addition, study the accounts of earlier, indigenous peoples who lived in similar environments. Again, visit the site many times, and during every season. Spend at least several weeks there, exploring and camping in every sector. Get to

know each tree and rock; every sand dune or ice floe. Calculate the most efficient source of food production (farming, fishing, hunting, gathering) and how many humans the land can support with this method. The answer will be vital in choosing the size of your group. If legally possible, purchase the land. This will allow you (resources permitting) to begin construction of an actual dwelling. It may not be your permanent domicile, but it should at least be something that can shelter you during construction of your future compound. If small and functional, it should serve as a storage shed for pre-stocked supplies. If large and comfortable, it could serve as a second home or vacation getaway. Many people during the Cold War built vacation homes that also served as potential escapes from nuclear holocaust. Familiarize yourself with the nearest local population. If they speak a different language, learn it, as well as local customs and personal history. Their knowledge and expertise should complement your book-learned education on the environment. *Never* tell the locals why you are there. (More on that later.)

8. **PLAN YOUR ROUTE:** Follow the rules relating to this section in "On the Run." Then multiply them by a hundred. Not only will you face the dangers of closed roads and natural barriers, but you will be crossing a landscape crawling with zombies, bandits, and all the chaotic elements of an imploding society. And all this is before a state of emergency is declared! Once that happens, all your previous problems will pale next to the threat of your own military. Unlike simply fleeing a zombie-infested zone, you will not have the luxury of choosing from a variety of possible destinations. There can only be one, and you will have to reach it to survive. As has been stated many times before: *Advance planning can never be taken for granted!* It should even be a factor in choosing your location. For example, a remote oasis in the middle of the Sahara Desert sounds great, but how will you get there if the airlines stop flying? Even an island several miles off the coast could

seem as far as the Sahara if you don't have a boat. All the lessons of "On the Run" will apply to this scenario. What it does not cover is the international perspective. What if, say, you buy a piece of land in the wilds of Siberia, and the airlines are still flying—but Russia has closed its borders? This does not mean you shouldn't choose a place in Siberia, but make sure you've set up the means (legal or otherwise) to enter the country.

9. **PLANS B-C-D-E!:** What if your first means of transportation doesn't work? What if the road or waterway is blocked? What if you discover that your safe haven has been overrun by zombies, bandits, the military, or other refugees? What if a thousand more things go wrong? Have backup plans. Map out potential hazards in your path and develop individual, tailor-made ways to counter them. Alternate vehicles, routes, even a backup safe area that, while it may not be as ideal or prepared as the first, will at least keep you alive long enough to think up a new strategy.

10. **LIST YOUR GEAR, BE READY TO SHOP:** Any competent disaster-survival manual should catalog everything you will need to begin a new life. Always maintain three detailed and up-to-date lists: 1. What you absolutely need to survive. 2. Equipment to help build and expand your dwelling and surroundings. 3. If not all the comforts of home, at least a close approximation. If finances permit, purchase all your items immediately. If not, know where to purchase them. Check prices and locations frequently. Keep track of suppliers that have moved and locate substitutes for those that have gone out of business. Always have at least two backup options in case your primary supplier runs out of stock. Make sure the suppliers are within several hours' driving distance at most. Do *not* depend on catalogs or on-line purchases. So-called "express" freight is unreliable enough in normal circumstances. What would it be like in an emergency? Keep all this information with your list. Adjust it accordingly. Always have a cash reserve for the bare

essentials (the total amount will depend on the prices of your gear). Even before the situation spirals out of control, checks and credit cards will not compare to the comfort of paper money.

11. **CONSTRUCT DEFENSES:** Nothing is more important than those structures that aid in your protection. Once you have established your group in a quiet corner of the wilderness, begin fortifying it immediately. You never know when the odd zombie will stumble into your camp, attracting others with its moans. Formulate detailed plans for your defense. The layout should be scouted and building materials either purchased or designated from the terrain. Everything, including building materials, tools, and supplies, should already be in place by the time you arrive, so there is nothing left to do but build. Remember: Your defenses must protect you not only from zombies but from bandits as well. Also remember that those human attackers will, at least in the beginning, possess firearms and perhaps explosives. If they succeed in breaching your defenses, always have a fallback position prepared. This secondary defense could be a fortified house, a cave, or even another wall. Keep it maintained and ready for action. A strong fallback position could be the turning point in an otherwise hopeless battle.

12. **PLAN AN ESCAPE ROUTE:** What if during an attack, your defenses are breached? Make sure everyone knows the escape

route's location and can get there on his or her own. Ensure that emergency supplies and weapons are packed and ready at all times. Designate a rally point for your fleeing group, a place to reassemble if scattered during an attack. Deserting your new "home" will not be psychologically or emotionally simple, especially after all the time and energy you have spent building it. People around the world who live in precarious situations will tell you how hard this can be. As attached as you may become to this place you now call home, it will always be better to cut and run than die defending it. An alternate location should also be chosen well before you land in your new home. It should be far enough away that zombies or raiders cannot track you from one place to another. It should also be close enough that an overland trek is possible under the harshest conditions (you never know when you might have to abandon your first base). Again, it must be chosen *before* the outbreak. Scouting for a new home or anything else after an outbreak won't be easy (see following section).

13. **BE ON GUARD:** Once you are settled in, defenses built, dwellings erected, crops planted, labor divided, by no means should you ever truly relax. Lookouts should be posted at all times. Keep them camouflaged and equipped with a reliable way to alert the others. Make sure the means of alarm will not alert the attackers as well. Designate a secure perimeter outside your fixed defenses. Keep that perimeter patrolled both day and night. People venturing outside the compound should never do so alone, and never unarmed. Those within camp should always be within several seconds of the weapons locker, ready for battle in case of attack.

14. **REMAIN CONCEALED:** Although the topography of your location should minimize the chances of discovery, you never know when a zombie or raider will venture close to your camp. Make sure no lights can be seen at night. Make sure the smoke

from your fires is extinguished before daybreak. If the area's natural elements do not already camouflage your compound, do so artificially. Practice "noise discipline" at all hours of the day and night. Yell only when necessary. Insulate your communal buildings so that music, conversion, and other sounds will not escape. During new construction and day-to-day maintenance, post additional scouts at the outer limit of the potential noise range. Remember that the slightest sound may be carried on the wind and can betray your position. Always determine which way the wind is blowing, either in the direction of possible inhabitants (the direction you came from) or across a known safe area (a large body of water, deep desert, etc.). If your power source is noisy (e.g., a fossil-fuel generator), make sure it is insulated and used sparingly. Such a constant state of heightened vigilance will be difficult at first. As time goes by, it will become second nature. Life was lived in this fashion for centuries from medieval Europe to the steppes of central Asia. Most of humanity's history has been the story of small islands of order in an ocean of chaos, people scratching to survive with the constant threat of invasion always hanging above their heads. If they could survive in this manner for countless generations, then, with a little practice, so can you.

15. **REMAIN ISOLATED:** Do *not* give in to curiosity under *any circumstances*. Even an expert scout, highly trained in the art of stealth, can accidentally lead armies of undead back to the compound. If your scout is captured and tortured by brigands, the bandits may learn of your location. Beyond the more dramatic threat of zombies or bandits, there is always the risk of your scout contracting some conventional disease and infecting the rest of the population (with few medicines at your disposal, an epidemic of any kind could be devastating). Staying put does not mean staying ignorant of the outside world. Dynamo- or solar-powered radios are a perfectly safe means of gathering information. But listen only! Transmitting will reveal your position to anyone with even

the crudest direction-finding equipment. As much as you trust those in your group, it would not be a bad idea to keep all transmitters, flares, and other signaling devices under lock and key. A moment's weakness could doom your entire existence. Your leadership training will be the best instruction on how to handle such a delicate matter.

TERRAIN TYPES

Examine a map of the world and find the best land and mildest climate. Overlay it with the densest population, and you will see a perfect match-up. Early humans knew what to look for when they began to build communities: moderate weather, fertile soil, plentiful fresh water, and a bounty of natural resources. These prime spots became the first centers of humanity, expanding outward into the modern population centers we know today. It is this way of thinking, this perfectly logical thought process, that you will have to completely abandon when choosing your new home. Back to the map. Say you find a place that looks immediately attractive. Chances are that several million people will be thinking the same thing when their time comes to flee. Combat this thinking with the slogan "harsher is safer," and to be as safe as possible, you will have to find the harshest, most extreme places on Earth. You will have to find an area that looks so unattractive, so inhospitable, that the last thing you would ever want to do is call it home. The following list of environments is provided to aid you in making an informed choice. Supplementary texts will give you more detailed information concerning their exact weather patterns, available food, water, natural resources, and so on. What this section demonstrates is how they relate to all the factors associated with an undead world.

1. DESERT
Second only to the polar regions, this is one of the harshest and, therefore, safest environments in the world. Despite what we see in movies,

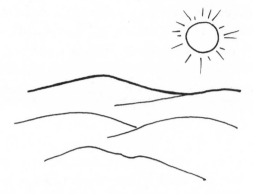

deserts are rarely oceans of sand. Rocks can easily be broken and shaped for building comfortable homes and, more important, defensive walls. The more remote your camp is, the greater chance it will have of avoiding raiders. These renegade scavengers will not be interested in riding across any deep desert where they know no major outposts exist. What would be the point? Even if some tried, the intense heat and lack of water would probably kill them off before they even reached your camp. Zombies, on the other hand, would not suffer from this problem. Heat and thirst are not part of the equation. The dry air would retard their already-slowed decomposition. If the chosen desert is situated between populated areas, such as those in the American Southwest, there will be a very real chance of some discovering your compound. Unless you build your fortification on top of a hill or large rock formation, the flat terrain will increase the need for artificial defenses.

2. MOUNTAINS

Depending on their location and elevation, this environment offers excellent defense against the living dead. The steeper the slope, the harder it will be for them to climb. If the mountain in question has no roads or wide paths, human bandits might also be deterred. Although high elevation allows a better view of the surrounding countryside, it also makes camouflage more difficult. Visual-concealment measures must be a top priority, especially where lights and smoke are concerned. Another drawback of the strategic high ground is its distance from usable resources. Commuting to level ground for food, water, and building materials will compromise your security. Consequently, the mountaintop you choose may not be the highest or easily defended but must contain all you need to survive.

3. JUNGLE

The opposite of deserts, jungles or tropical rainforests will provide all the water, food, and building materials you need as well as a host of medicinal vegetation, burning fuel, and instant camouflage. The thick foliage acts as a noise buffer, insulating sounds that would travel miles in the open. Unlike what we saw in "On the Attack," where the terrain will work against a team of hunters, the absence of visibility and muddy earth are perfectly suited for a defensive posture. Bandit groups can be easily ambushed and destroyed. Individual zombies can be dispatched without alerting others. There are, of course, negatives associated with this equatorial ecosystem. Moisture breeds life, which includes millions of species of bio-organisms. Disease will be a constant threat. Any cuts or scrapes could turn rapidly gangrenous. Food will decompose much more quickly than in drier climates. Metal gear must be watched for rust. Any clothing not rubberized or otherwise treated will rot, literally, off your back. Mold will be everywhere. The local insect population will be your most constant enemy. Some will be mere nuisances; some may have painful, even fatally venomous stings. Some will carry horrible diseases such as yellow fever, malaria, or dengue fever. One positive natural aspect of jungle survival is that the intense moisture, coupled with the multitude of microscopic organic life, accelerates undead decomposition. Field tests have shown at least a 10 percent higher decay rate in jungle-bound zombies. In certain cases, the percentage has been as high as 25! What all these factors equal out to is an environment with many natural hardships but one extremely well-suited to worst-case survival.

4. TEMPERATE FORESTS

This worldwide zone is easily the most comfortable for long-term survival. However, with such attractive land will come a host of problems. The wilds of Northern Canada are sure to be crowded with refugees. Caught unprepared, these panicked mobs will surely flee north. For at least the first year, they will roam the wilderness, stripping the land of food, turning to violence to obtain equipment, perhaps even turning to cannibalism in the cold winter months. Brigands will no doubt be among them or will follow in the later years when some decide to attempt a safe settlement. And of course, there is always the zombie threat. Temperate forests are still relatively close to civilization, as well as being dotted with outposts of humanity. Ghoul encounters would be ten times as likely as under normal circumstances. With an influx of refugees, the chances of the undead simply following them north is almost a given. Remember also, the problem of zombies freezing in the winter and thawing in the summer. Choose an area only if it is isolated by natural boundaries: mountains, rivers, and so on. Anything less— even if it seems far from humanity—will be too much of a risk. Do not believe that the vast expanse of Siberia will be any safer than Northern Canada. Remember, to the south of this thinly peopled wilderness are both India and China, the two most populous nations on Earth.

5. TUNDRA

Refugees will not consider these seemingly barren lands capable of supporting life. Those who try will perish without large stores of supplies, elaborate equipment, or extensive knowledge of the environment. Bandits will also be hard-pressed to survive. In all probability, none will venture this far north. The living dead may reach your camp, however. Those that have migrated north following fleeing refugees, or former refugees now reanimated as zombies, may detect your presence and signal others. Their numbers will not be great and can be handled by those in your group. All the same, build your defenses strong and keep constant vigilance. As with temperate forests, be prepared for zombie activity to follow the seasons.

6. POLAR

This environment is, without a doubt, the harshest on the planet. Extremely low temperatures with a high wind chill can kill an exposed human in seconds. Building materials will consist mainly of ice and snow. Fuel will be scarce. Medicinal or any other type of plants are unheard of. Food is plentiful but takes skill and experience to obtain. Even in summer, hypothermia will be a constant danger. Every day will be spent on the fringe of existence. One mistake regarding food, clothing, shelter, even hygiene could mean certain death. Many people have heard of Allariallak, the Inuit whose life in the frozen Hudson Bay region was documented in the film *Nanook of the North*. Few know that "Nanook" starved to death a year after that documentary was shot. This is not to say that life in the polar regions is an impossibility. People have been doing it successfully for thousands of years. What it will take is ten times the knowledge and determination to even attempt a life at the top or bottom of the world. If you are not ready to spend at least one winter practicing under these conditions, do *not* try it when the time to flee comes. So why go? Why risk death from such a hostile environment when the goal is to stay alive? The truth is that the environment should be your *only* worry. Refugees and bandits will never make it that far. The chance of zombies randomly wandering that far north are one in 35 million (a proven calculated statistic). As with temperate forests and tundra, you do run the risk of an odd ghoul freezing and thawing in its travels. If you are camped near a coastline, watch for one possibly brought ashore by the current or a derelict-infested ship. Coastlines also leave you vulnerable, in the beginning, to pirates. (More on this concerning islands.) Maintain some means of static defense and always keep alert, although the need for both is relatively less than for any other environment.

7. ISLANDS

What could be safer than land surrounded on all sides by water? Zombies can't swim. Doesn't that mean living on an island is the obvious choice for a worst-case scenario? To some degree, yes. Its geographical isolation does negate the possibility of mass zombie migration, something that must be taken into account when billions will be prowling every continent on the globe. Even islands a few miles offshore will save you from the writhing, clamoring hordes. For this reason alone, islands are always a preferable choice. However, just because you decide to live on a rock surrounded by water does not guarantee your survival. Offshore islands will be the obvious choices for refugees. Anyone with a boat or raft will make for them. Ruffians will use them as bases from which to conduct raids on the mainland. Offshore islands may also be destroyed by industrial accidents, some well inland that dump pollution into nearby rivers. To avoid these immediate dangers, choose an island accessible only by a sturdy craft and expert navigation. Look for one without a good natural harbor or too many accessible beaches. This will make it less attractive to other seaborne refugees attempting the same strategy as you. (Remember, purchasing an island will keep people away only *before* the crisis! No starving, frantic refugee ship is going to obey a "keep out" sign.) Look for islands with high cliffs and, if possible, wide, dangerous reefs.

Even with these natural boundaries, construct defenses and maintain concealment. Dangers are still out there! Pirates, in the beginning phases of the crisis, may cruise from island to island, hoping to scavenge what they can from survivors. Always keep a lookout for their ships on the horizon. Zombies, too, may come in many forms. With the world completely infested, many will certainly find themselves roaming the floors of our oceans. There is the possibility, slight though it may be, of one lumbering up the underwater slope that leads to your little coastline. Others still wearing lifejackets from mortal life may be carried to your island by the current. Then there is the chance of a zombie-infested ship, and in a worst-case scenario, there could be one wrecking on your shore and spilling its deadly cargo. No matter what, do not destroy your means of escape. Drag your boat onto the beach or keep it camouflaged offshore. Losing it will mean turning your fortress into a prison.

8. LIVING BY SEA

It has been suggested that, with the right vessel and crew, a group could survive a worst-case scenario entirely at sea. Theoretically, this is possible, but the odds of its success are astronomical. In the short run, many people will take to water in everything from two-person sailboats to 80,000-ton freighters. They will survive on what they have brought aboard, scavenging the world's infested ports, catching fish, and distilling fresh water if possible. Pirates in fast, armed private boats will roam the seas. These modern-day buccaneers already exist today, robbing freighters and yachts along many Third World coastlines and even strategic choke points. In a worst-case scenario, their numbers will swell to several thousand, and their targets will not be exclusive. As military ports become overrun, warships not supporting ground operations will set sail for safer anchorage. In these remote atoll bases, the world's navies will wait for the crisis to pass, and wait, and wait.

After several years, time and the elements will take their toll on these ad-hoc seaborne populations. Ships relying on fossil fuel will eventually run dry, doomed to drift helplessly. Some attempting to scavenge from abandoned ports and fuel depots may meet their end as zombie food. As medicines and vitamins run out, diseases such as scurvy will begin to take their toll. Rough seas will destroy many vessels. Pirates will eventually burn themselves out through infighting, clashes with victims who choose not to be victimized, and encounters with the occasional living dead. This last contingency will also lead to raider infection, increasing the danger of seaborne undead. Derelict, zombie ghost ships will float aimlessly across the world's oceans, their moans carrying on salty wind. This wind will eventually erode delicate machinery, including those that purify water and generate power. Within several years, only a few dedicated sailing ships will ride the waves. All others will be sunk, wrecked, reanimated, or will have simply dropped anchor in some remote beach, determined to make a go of it on land.

Anyone even entertaining the idea of a seaborne existence must have the following assets:

A. At least ten years of experience at sea, either in commercial or military service. Simply owning a cabin cruiser for that amount of time does not qualify.

B. A sturdy, wind-powered craft, at least one hundred feet or more with equipment constructed mainly of nonorganic, noncorrosive material.

C. The ability to distill fresh water on a constant basis without relying on rain! Not only must your system and device be simple, easy to maintain, and resistant to rust, but you must also have a backup system aboard.

D. The ability to catch and prepare food without the use of non-renewable fuel. In other words, no propane stove.

E. Complete knowledge of every aquatic plant and animal. All vitamins and minerals obtained on land can be replaced by a seaborne substitute.

F. Full emergency equipment for everyone in your group should the need to abandon ship arise.

G. Knowledge of the location of a safe haven. All boats need a port, no matter how primitive. It could be a collection of rocks off Canada or some barren atoll in the Pacific. No matter what it is, unless you know where your port in a storm is, you are, literally and figuratively, sunk.

With all these in place, it might be easier to simply compromise your living conditions. Use your boat as a movable home as you forage from small island to island, or coastline to coastline. This will be a more comfortable, safer existence than on the open sea. Even so, keep a watch for zombies in shallow water, and always, *always,* watch your anchor line! Theoretically, this type of life is possible, but it is not recommended.

DURATION

How long will you have to endure this primitive existence? How long before the walking dead simply crumble to dust? How long before life can return to even a semblance of normality? Sadly, there is no exact figure. The first zombie to rise will, unless it is frozen, embalmed, or otherwise preserved, completely decompose after five years. However, by the time the undead have world domination, ten years might have already passed. (Remember, you will be fleeing when the war begins, not at its end.) When zombies truly dominate the planet, and there are no more fresh humans to infect, it will truly take five years for the majority of them to rot away. Dry climate and freezing will preserve many, keeping them functional for, potentially, decades. Bandits, refugees, and other survivors like yourself may become further prey, adding a newer but smaller generation to the older, decaying horde. By the time these turn to dust, the only undead left will be those preserved artificially or constantly refrozen with each winter. These you will have to watch for decades to come. Your children and even your children's children will have to be wary of them. But when will it be safe to come out?

Year 1: A state of emergency is declared. You flee. Your defenses are built; your compound is established. Labor is divided. A new life begins. All this time, you monitor radio and television broadcasts, keeping a close watch on the unfolding conflict.

Year 5–10: Somewhere within this time period, the war ends. The dead have won. The signals stop. You assume that the entire world is overrun. You continue your life, keeping a close eye on defense as bandits and refugees might begin to enter your zone.

Year 20: After two decades of isolation, you consider sending a scouting party. Doing so will risk discovery. If the party does not return by a fixed date, you assume they have been lost, perhaps even divulged your location. You stay hidden. Do *not* send out another search party, and prepare for battle. Another party will not be sent out for at least five years. If the scouts do return, their findings will determine your next course of action.

Your scouts will discover a new world in which one of three scenarios prevails:

1. Zombies still roam the earth. Between those artificially preserved and those freezing with each winter, millions continue to exist. Although they may be infrequent, one per two square miles, they are still the planet's dominant predator. Almost all humanity is gone. Those who survive remain in hiding.

2. Few undead remain. Decomposition and constant warfare have taken their toll. Perhaps every hundred or so miles, a lone zombie will be spotted. Humanity has begun to make a comeback. Pockets of survivors have banded together and are striving to rebuild society. This could take many forms, from a harmonious collective of law-abiding citizens to the chaotic, feudal society of barbarians and warlords. The latter would be reason enough to stay hidden. There is the possibility, no matter how slight, that all or some governments-in-exile will eventually show their faces. Armed with the remnants of military and police, equipped with stored technology and archived know-how, they attempt, successfully, to set humanity on a slow but steady course to re-establishing global dominance.

3. Nothing has survived. Before eventually rotting away, the living dead have cleaned out all vestiges of humanity. Refugees have been devoured. Bandits have either killed one another off or succumbed to ghoul attacks. Survivor camps have fallen to attack, disease,

internal violence, or simple ennui. It is a silent world, devoid of zombie or human activities. Apart from the wind rustling in leaves, the surf breaking upon shore, and the chirps and calls of what wildlife remain, the earth has found an eerie peace not known for millions of years.

No matter what the human (or undead) situation, the animal kingdom will go through its own metamorphosis. Any creatures unable to escape will be devoured by the living dead. This will lead to the near-extinction of many species of grazing animals, the chief diet of large predators. Birds of prey will also face starvation, as will carrion birds (remember that even after a zombie is killed, the flesh remains poisonous). Even insects, depending upon their size and speed, may find themselves the target of roving zombies. It is difficult to say what forms of wildlife will inherit the earth. What can be said is that an undead world will have as much, if not a greater, impact on the global ecosystem as the last ice age.

THEN WHAT?

Post-apocalyptic fiction usually shows the survivors of a new age reclaiming their world in dramatic steps, such as retaking an entire city. While this makes for exciting imagery, especially in moving pictures, it does not represent a safe or efficient means of re-colonization. Instead of marching across the George Washington Bridge to repopulate Manhattan, a safer, smarter, more conservative stance will be to either expand your existing living space or migrate to a better, if still relatively isolated area. For example, if you have made your home on a small island, the best choice would be to land on a larger, previously inhabited island, clean out what zombies are left, and reclaim the abandoned structures as your new home. On land, the equivalent would be to migrate from, for example, the deep desert or frozen tundra to the nearest abandoned town. Worst-case survival manuals, as well as many historical texts, will be your best guide to a complete rebuilding. What they may not instruct you to do, and what you must do, is make sure that your new, more civilized home is secure! Remember: Yours is the only government, the only police force, the only army around. Safety will be your responsibility, and although the immediate danger may have passed, it must never be taken for granted. No matter what you will find, and no matter what challenges you will face, take heart in the knowledge that you have survived a catastrophe not seen since the extinction of the dinosaurs, a world ruled by the living dead.

RECORDED ATTACKS

This is not a list of all zombie attacks throughout history. This simply chronicles all attacks for which the information has been recorded, survived, and been released to the author of this book. Accounts from societies with an oral history have been more difficult to acquire. Too often these stories have been lost when their societies have fragmented as a result of war, slavery, natural disasters, or simply the corruption of international modernization. Who knows how many stories, how much vital information—perhaps even a cure—has been lost through the centuries. Even in a society as information-savvy as our own, only a fraction of total outbreaks is reported. This is due, in some part, to various political and religious organizations that have sworn to keep all knowledge of the living dead secret. It is also due to ignorance of a zombie outbreak. Those who suspect the truth but fear for their credibility will, in most cases, withhold the information. This leaves a short but well-documented list. Note: These events are listed in the chronological order of their occurrence, not discovery.

60,000 B.C., KATANDA, CENTRAL AFRICA

Recent archaeological expeditions discovered a cave on the banks of the Upper Semliki River that contained thirteen skulls. All had been crushed. Near them was a large pile of fossilized ash. Laboratory analysis determined the ash to be the remains of thirteen Homo sapiens. On the wall of the cave is a painting of a human figure, hands raised in a threatening posture, eyes fixed in an evil gaze. Inside its gaping mouth is the body of another human. This find has not been accepted as a genuine zombie incident. One school of thought argues that the crushed skulls and burned bodies were a means of ghoul disposal, while the cave drawing serves as a warning. Other academics demand some type of physical evidence, such as a trace of fossilized Solanum. Results are still pending. If Katanda's authenticity is confirmed, it raises the question of why there was such a large gap between this first outbreak and the one that followed.

3000 B.C., HIERACONPOLIS, EGYPT

A British dig in 1892 unearthed a nondescript tomb. No clues could be found to reveal who the person who occupied it was or anything about his place in society. The body was found outside the open crypt, curled up in a corner and only partially decomposed. Thousands of scratch marks adorned every surface inside of the tomb, as if the corpse had tried to claw its way out. Forensic experts have revealed that the scratches were made over a period of several years! The body itself had several bite marks on the right radius. The teeth match those of a

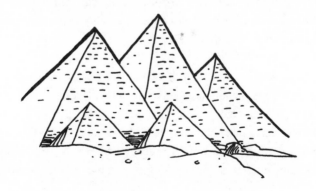

human. A full autopsy revealed that the dried, partially decomposed brain not only matched those infected by Solanum (the frontal lobe was completely melted away) but also contained trace elements of the virus itself. Debate now rages as to whether or not this case prompted late Egyptian specialists to remove the brains from their mummies.

500 B.C., AFRICA

During his voyage to explore and colonize the continent's western coast, Hanno of Carthage, one of Western civilization's most famous ancient mariners, wrote in his sea log:

On the shores of a great jungle, where green hills hide their crowns above the clouds, I dispatched an expedition inland in search of sweet water. . . . Our soothsayers warned against this action. In their eyes was a cursed land, a place of demons abandoned by the gods. I ignored their warnings and paid the highest price. . . . Of the thirty and five men sent, seven returned. . . . The survivors sobbed a tale of monsters from the jungles. Men with fangs of snakes, claws of leopards, and eyes burning with the fires of hell. Bronze blades cut their flesh but drew no blood. They feasted upon our sailors, their wails carried on the wind . . . our soothsayers warned of the wounded survivors, claiming they would bring sorrow on all they touched. . . . We hastened to our ships, abandoning those poor souls to this land of man-beasts. May the Gods forgive me.

As most readers know, much of Hanno's work is controversial and debated among academic historians. Given that Hanno also describes a confrontation with large, ape-like creatures he dubbed "Gorillas" (actual gorillas have never inhabited that part of the continent), it can be inferred that both these incidents were a product either of his imagination or those of later historians. Even with this in mind, and disregarding the obvious exaggerations of snake's fangs, leopard's claws, and burning eyes, Hanno's basic description does closely resemble the walking dead.

329 B.C., AFGHANISTAN

An unnamed Macedonian column built by the legendary conqueror Alexander the Great was visited many times by Soviet Special Forces during their own war of occupation. Five miles from the monument, one unit discovered the ancient remains of what is believed to be Hellenic Army barracks. Among other artifacts, there was a small bronze vase. Its inlaid pictures show: (1) one man biting another; (2) the victim lying on his deathbed; (3) the victim rising up again; and back to (1) biting another man. The circular nature of this vase, as well as the pictures themselves, could be evidence of an undead outbreak either witnessed by Alexander or related to him by one of the local tribes.

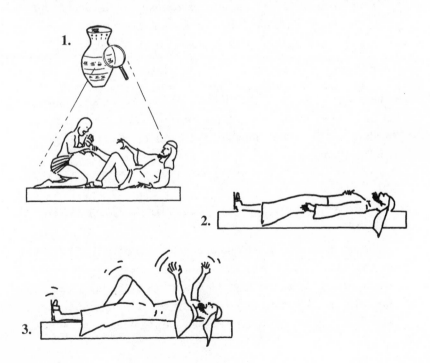

212 B.C., CHINA

During the Qin Dynasty, all books not relating to practical concerns such as agriculture or construction were ordered burned by the emperor to guard against "dangerous thought." Whether accounts of zombie attacks perished in the flames will never be known. This obscure section of a medical manuscript, preserved in the wall of an executed Chinese scholar, might be proof of such attacks:

> *The only treatment for victims of the Eternal Waking Nightmare is complete dismemberment followed by fire. The patient must be bodily restrained, his mouth filled with straw then bound securely. All limbs and organs must be removed, avoiding contact with any bodily fluids. All must be burned to ash then scattered at least twelve li in all directions. No other remedy will suffice as the sickness has no cure . . . the desire for human meat, unquenchable. . . . If victims are encountered in numbers, with no hopes of restraining them, immediate decapitation must be used . . . the Shaolin spade being the swiftest weapon for this task.*

There is no mention of the "Eternal Waking Nightmare" victims as actually being dead. Only the section about craving the flesh of the healthy, and the actual "treatment," suggest a presence of zombies in ancient China.

121 A.D., FANUM COCIDI, CALEDONIA (SCOTLAND)

Although the source of the outbreak is unknown, its events are well-documented. The local barbarian chieftains, believing the undead to be simply insane, sent more than 3,000 warriors to "end this mad uprising." The result: More than 600 warriors were devoured, the rest wounded and eventually transformed into walking dead. A Roman merchant named Sextus Sempronios Tubero, who was traveling through this province at the time, witnessed the battle. Although not realizing that the walking dead were just that, Tubero was observant enough to notice that only the decapitated zombies ceased to be a threat. Barely escaping with his life, Tubero reported his findings to Marcus Lucius Terentius, commander of the nearest military garrison in Roman Britannia. Less than a day away were well over 9,000 zombies. Following the stream of refugees, these ghouls continued to migrate south, moving steadily toward Roman territory. Terentius had only one cohort (480 men) at his disposal. Reinforcements were three weeks away. Terentius first ordered the digging of two seven-foot-deep, inwardly narrowing ditches that eventually straightened to form a straight, mile-long corridor. The result looked similar to a funnel opening into the north. The bottoms of both trenches were then filled with *bitumen liquidum* (crude oil: common for heating lamps in this part of Britannia). As the zombies approached, the oil was ignited. All ghouls falling into the trench were trapped in its deep confines and incinerated. The remainder were forced into the funnel, where no more than 300 could stand abreast. Terentius ordered his men to draw swords, raise shields, and advance on the enemy. After a nine-hour battle, every zombie had been decapitated, the still-snapping heads rolled into the ditches for cremation. Roman casualties numbered 150 dead, no wounded (the legionnaires killed any bitten comrade).

Ramifications from this outbreak were both immediately and historically important. Emperor Hadrian ordered all information regarding the outbreak to be compiled in one comprehensive work. This manual not only detailed a zombie's behavioral pattern and instructions on efficient methods of disposal, it recommended overwhelming numerical force "to deal with the inevitable panic of the general populace." A copy of this document, known simply as "Army Order XXXVII," was distributed to every legion throughout the empire. For this reason, outbreaks in areas under Roman rule never reached critical numbers again and were therefore never reported in detail. It is also believed that this first outbreak prompted the building of "Hadrian's

Wall," a structure that effectively isolated Northern Caledonia from the rest of the island. This is a textbook Class 3 outbreak, and easily the largest on record.

140–41 A.D., THAMUGADI, NUMIDIA (ALGERIA)

Six small outbreaks among desert nomads were recorded by Lucius Valerius Strabo, Roman governor of the province. All outbreaks were crushed by two cohorts from the III Augusta Legionary base. Total zombies dispatched: 134. Roman casualties: 5. Other than the official report, a private journal entry by an army engineer records a significant discovery:

> *A local family remained imprisoned in their home for at least twelve days while the savage creatures scratched and clawed fruitlessly at their bolted doors and windows. After we dispatched the filth and rescued the family, their manner looked near to insane. From what we could gather, the wails of the beasts, day after day, night after night, proved to be a merciless form of torture.*

This is the first known recognition of psychological damage caused by a zombie attack. All six incidents, given their chronological proximity, make a credible case for one or more ghouls from earlier attacks "surviving" long enough to reinfect a population.

156 A.D., CASTRA REGINA, GERMANIA (SOUTHERN GERMANY)

An attack by seventeen zombies left a prominent cleric infected. The Roman commander, recognizing the signs of a newly turned zombie, ordered his troops to destroy the former holy man. Local citizens became enraged, and a riot ensued. Total zombies dispatched: 10, including the holy man. Roman casualties: 17, all from the riot. Civilians killed by Roman crackdown: 198.

177 A.D., NAMELESS SETTLEMENT NEAR TOLOSA, AQUITANIA (SW FRANCE)

A personal letter, written by a traveling merchant to his brother in Capua, describes the assailant:

> *He came from the wood, a man stinking of rot. His gray skin bore many wounds, from which flowed no blood. Upon seeing the screaming child, his body seemed to shake with excitement. His head turned in her direction; his mouth opened in a howling moan.... Darius, the old legionary veteran, approached ... pushing the terrified mother aside, he grabbed the child with one arm, and brought his gladius around with the other. The creature's head fell to its feet, and rolled downhill before the rest of his body followed.... Darius insisted they wear leather coverings as they pitched the body into the fire ... the head, still moving in a disgusting bite, was fed to the flames.*

This passage should be taken as the typical Roman attitude toward the living dead: no fear, no superstition, just another problem requiring a practical solution. This was the last record of an attack during the Roman Empire. Subsequent outbreaks were neither combated with such efficiency nor recorded with such clarity.

700 A.D., FRISIA (NORTHERN HOLLAND)

Although this event appears to have taken place on or about 700 A.D., physical evidence comes in the form of a painting recently discovered in the vaults of the Rijksmuseum in Amsterdam. Analyses of the materials themselves fix the date listed above. The picture itself shows a collection of knights in full armor, attacking a mob of ragged men with gray flesh, arrows and other wounds covering their bodies, and blood dripping from their mouths. As the two forces clash in the center of the frame, the knights bring their swords down to decapitate their enemies. Three "zombies" are seen in the lower right-hand corner, crouching over the body of a fallen knight. Some of his armor has been pulled off, one limb ripped from his body. The zombies feed on the exposed flesh. As the painting itself is unsigned, no one has yet to determine where this work came from or how it ended up in the museum.

850 A.D., UNKNOWN PROVINCE IN SAXONY (NORTHERN GERMANY)

Bearnt Kuntzel, a friar on his pilgrimage to Rome, recorded this incident in his personal diary. One zombie wandered out of the Black Forest to bite and infect a local farmer. The victim reanimated several hours after his demise and turned on his own family. From there, the outbreak spread to the entire village. Those who survived fled into the lord's castle, not realizing that some among them had been bitten. As the outbreak spread even farther, neighboring villagers descended in a mob toward the infested zone. Local clergy believed that the undead had been infected by the spirit of the devil and that holy water and incantations would banish the evil spirits. This "holy quest" ended in a massacre, with the entire congregation either devoured or turned to living dead themselves.

In desperation, neighboring lords and knights united to "purify the devil's spawn with fire." This ramshackle force burned every village and every zombie within a fifty-mile radius. Not even uninfected humans survived the slaughter. The original lord's castle, inhabited by people who had shut themselves in with the undead, had by then been

transformed into a prison of more than 200 ghouls. Because the inhabitants had barred the gates and raised the drawbridge before succumbing, the knights could not enter the castle to purify it. As a result, the
fortress was declared "haunted." For over a decade afterward, peasants
passing nearby could hear the moans of the zombies still within.
According to Kuntzel's figures, 573 zombies were counted and more
than 900 humans were devoured. In his writings, Kuntzel also tells of
massive reprisals against a nearby Jewish village, their lack of "faith"
blamed for the outbreak. Kuntzel's work survived in the Vatican
archives until its accidental discovery in 1973.

1073 A.D., JERUSALEM

The story of Dr. Ibrahim Obeidallah, one of the most important pioneers in the field of zombie physiology, typifies the great strides forward and tragic steps back in science's attempt to understand the
undead. An unknown source caused an outbreak of fifteen zombies in
Jaffa, a city on the coast of Palestine. Local militia, using a translated
copy of Roman Army Order XXXVII, successfully exterminated the
threat with a minimum of human casualties. One newly bitten woman
was taken under the care of Obeidallah, a prominent physician and
biologist. Although Army Order XXXVII called for the immediate
decapitation and burning of all bitten humans, Obeidallah convinced
(or perhaps bribed) the militia to allow him to study the dying woman.
A compromise was reached in which he was permitted to move
the body, and all his equipment, to the city jail. There, in a cell, under
the law's watchful eye, he observed the restrained victim until she
expired—and continued to study the corpse while it reanimated. He
performed numerous experiments on the restrained ghoul. Discovering
that all bodily functions necessary to sustain life were no longer functioning, Obeidallah scientifically proved that his subject was physically dead yet functioning. He traveled throughout the Middle East,
gathering information on other possible outbreaks.

Obeidallah's research documented the entire physiology of the living dead. His notes included reports on the nervous system, digestion, even the rate of decomposition in relation to the environment. This work also included a complete study of the behavioral patterns of living dead, a remarkable achievement if actually true. Ironically, when Christian knights stormed Jerusalem in 1099, this amazing man was beheaded as a worshiper of Satan, and almost all of his work was destroyed. Sections of it survived in Baghdad for the next several hundred years, with only a fraction of the original text rumored to survive. Obeidallah's life story, however, minus the details of his experiments, survived the crusaders' slaughter, along with his biographer (a Jewish historian and former colleague). The man escaped to Persia, where the work was copied, published, and gained modest success in various Middle Eastern courts. A copy remains in the National Archives in Tel Aviv.

1253 A.D., FISKURHOFN, GREENLAND

Following the great tradition of Nordic exploration, Gunnbjorn Lundergaart, an Icelandic chieftain, established a colony at the mouth of an isolated fjord. There were reported to be 153 colonists in the party. Lundergaart sailed back to Iceland after one winter, presumably to procure supplies and additional colonists. After five years, Lundergaart returned to find the island compound in ruins. Of the colonists, he found just three dozen skeletons, the flesh picked clean from the bones. It is also reported that he encountered three beings, two women and one child. Their skin was a mottled gray, and bones stuck through the flesh in places. Wounds were evident, but no traces of blood could be observed. Once sighted, the figures turned and approached Lundergaart's party. Without responding to any verbal communication, they attacked the Vikings and were immediately chopped to pieces. The Norseman, believing the entire expedition was cursed, ordered the burning of all bodies and artificial structures. As his own family were among the skeletons, Lundergaart ordered his men to kill him as well, dismember his body, and add it to the flames. The "Tale of Fiskurhofn," told by Lundergaart's party to traveling Irish monks, survives in the national archives in Reykjavik, Iceland. Not only is this the most accurate account of a zombie attack within ancient Nordic civilization, it may also explain why all Viking settlements within Greenland mysteriously vanished during the early fourteenth century.

1281 A.D., CHINA

The Venetian explorer Marco Polo wrote in his journal that during one visit to the emperor's summer palace of Xanadu, Kublai Khan displayed a severed zombie head preserved in a jar of clear alcoholic fluid (Polo described the fluid as "with the essence of wine but clear and biting to the nose"). This head, the Khan stated, had been taken by his grandfather, Genghis, when he returned from his conquests in the West. Polo wrote that the head was aware of their presence. It even watched them with nearly decomposed eyes. When he reached out to touch it, the head snapped at his fingers. The Khan chastised him for

this foolish act, recounting the tale of a low-ranking court official who had tried the same thing and had been bitten by the severed head. This official later "seemed to die within days but rose again to attack his servants." Polo states that the head remained "alive" throughout his stay in China. No one knows the fate of this relic. When Polo returned from Asia, his story was suppressed by the Catholic Church and therefore does not appear in the official publication of his adventures. Historians have theorized that, since the Mongols reached as far as Baghdad, the head may be one of the original subjects of Ibrahim Obeidallah, which would entitle the head to the record of the best-preserved, oldest "living" relic of a zombie specimen.

1523 A.D., OAXACA, MEXICO

The natives tell of a sickness that darkens the soul, causing a thirst for the blood of their brothers. They tell of men, women, even children whose flesh have become gray with rot and possess an unholy smell. Once darkened, there is no method of healing, save death, and that can only be achieved through fire, since the body becomes resistant to all arms of man. I believe this to be a tragedy of the heathen, for, without their knowledge of Our Lord Jesus Christ, there was indeed no cure for this illness. Now that we have blessed their masses with the light and truth of His love, we must strive to seek these darkened souls, and cleanse them with all the force of Heaven.

This text was, supposedly, taken from the accounts of Father Esteban Negron, a Spanish priest and student of Bartolome de las Casas, previously edited from the original works and recently discovered in Santo Domingo. Opinions vary on the authenticity of this manuscript. Some believe it to be a part of a Vatican order to suppress all information on the subject. Others believe it to be an elaborate hoax along the lines of the "Hitler diaries."

1554 A.D., SOUTH AMERICA

A Spanish expedition under the command of Don Rafael Cordoza penetrated the Amazon jungle in search of the fabled El Dorado, the City of Gold. Tupi guides warned him not to enter an area known as "The Valley of Endless Sleep." In it, they cautioned, he would find a race of creatures who moaned like wind and thirsted for blood. Many men had entered this valley, said the Tupi. None ever returned. Most of the conquistadors were terrified by this warning and begged to return to the coast. Cordoza, believing that the Tupi had fabricated this story in order to hide the golden city, pushed his expedition forward. After dark, the camp was attacked by dozens of walking dead. What transpired that night is still a mystery. The passenger manifest from the *San Varonica,* the ship that carried Cordoza from South America to Santo Domingo, has shown that he was the only survivor to reach the coast. Whether he fought to the end or simply abandoned his men, no one knows. A year later, Cordoza reached Spain, where he provided a full account of this attack to both the Royal Court in Madrid and the Holy Office in Rome. Accused of squandering crown resources by the Royal Court, and of speaking blasphemous acts by the Vatican, the conquistador was stripped of his title and died in obscure poverty. His story is a compilation of fragments from many texts concerning this period in Spain's history. No original work has been discovered.

1579 A.D., THE CENTRAL PACIFIC

During his circumnavigation of the globe, Francis Drake, the pirate who later became a national hero, stopped at an unnamed island to restock his supplies of food and fresh water. The natives warned him not to visit a small, nearby cay that was inhabited by "the Gods of the Dead." According to custom, the deceased and terminally ill were placed on this island, where the gods would take them, body and soul, to live on forever. Drake, fascinated by their story, decided to investigate. Observing from aboard ship, he watched as a native shore party placed the body of a dying man on the island's beach. After blowing several calls from a conch shell, the natives retreated to the sea. Moments later, several figures staggered slowly out of the jungle. Drake watched them feed on the corpse before slouching out of sight. To his amazement, the half-eaten body rose to its feet and hobbled after them. Drake never spoke of this incident during his life. The facts were discovered in a secret journal he kept hidden until his death. This journal, passing from one personal collector to another, eventually found its way into the library of Admiral Jackie Fischer, the father of the modern Royal Navy. In 1907 Fischer had it copied and gave it to several of his friends as a Christmas gift. Along with exact coordinates, Drake proclaimed this landmass "the Isle of the Damned."

1583 A.D., SIBERIA

A scouting party for the infamous Cossack Yermak, lost and starving in the frozen wild, was sheltered by an indigenous, Asiatic tribe. Once they had recovered their strength, the Europeans repaid the kindness by declaring themselves the rulers of the village, and settled down for the winter until Yermak's main force arrived. After feasting for several weeks on the village's stored food, the Cossacks now turned their hunger upon the villagers themselves. In a savage act of cannibalism, thirteen people were eaten, while the others fled into the wilderness. The Cossacks went through this new source of food within days. In desperation, they turned to the village burial ground, where, it was believed, the freezing temperatures had preserved any fresh corpses. The first body exhumed was a woman in her early twenties, who had been buried with her hands and legs bound and her mouth gagged. Once defrosted, the dead woman revived. The Cossacks were astounded. Hoping to learn how she had achieved such a feat, they removed her gag. The woman bit one Cossack on the hand. With continued shortsightedness, ignorance, and brutality, the Cossacks dismembered, roasted, and ate her flesh. Only two abstained: the wounded warrior (it was believed by his comrades that food should not be wasted on the dying) and a deeply superstitious man who believed the meat to be cursed. In a manner of speaking, he was right. All who ate the zombie's flesh died that night. The wounded man expired the next morning.

The one survivor attempted to burn the bodies. As he was preparing a funeral pyre, the bitten corpse revived. With the new zombie in hot pursuit, the lone survivor took off across the steppe. Barely an hour into the chase, the exposed zombie froze solid. The Cossack wandered for several days until he was rescued by another scouting party from Yermak. His account was documented by a Russian historian, Father Pietro Georgiavich Vatutin. The work remained obscure for several generations, housed in the remote monastery on Valam Island on Lake Ladoga. It is only now being translated into English. Nothing is known of the fate of the Asiatic villagers or even what their true identity is. The subsequent genocide against these people by Yermak left few survivors. From a scientific point of view, this account represents the first known occurrence of a zombie freezing solid.

1587 A.D., ROANOKE ISLAND, NORTH CAROLINA

English colonists, isolated from any support from Europe, sent regular hunting parties to the mainland in search of food. One of these parties disappeared for three weeks. When a lone survivor returned, he described an attack by "a band of savages . . . their putrid, worm-ridden skin impervious to powder and shot!" Although only one of the eleven-man party was killed, four of the others were savagely mauled. These men died the following day, were buried, then rose from their shallow graves within hours. The survivor swore that the remainder of his party was eaten alive by his former comrades, and that he alone escaped. The colony magistrate declared the man both a liar and a murderer. He was hanged the next morning.

A second expedition was sent to recover the bodies "lest their remains be desecrated by heathens." The five-man party returned in a state of near collapse, bite and scratch marks covering their bodies. They had been attacked on the mainland, both by the "savages" described by the now-vindicated, deceased survivor, and also by members of the first hunting party. These new survivors, after a period of medical examination, passed away within hours of each other. Burial was set for the following dawn. That night, they reanimated. Details are sketchy as to the rest of the story. One version describes the eventual infection and destruction of the entire town. Another has the Croatan Nation, recognizing the danger for what it was, rounding up and burning every colonist on the island. In a third account, these same Native Americans rescued the surviving townspeople and dispatched the undead and wounded. All three stories have appeared in fictional accounts and historical texts for the last two centuries. None presents an airtight explanation as to why the first English settlement in North America literally vanished without a trace.

1611 A.D., EDO, JAPAN

Enrique Desilva, a Portuguese merchant doing business in the islands, wrote this passage in a letter to his brother:

> *Father Mendoza, reacquainting himself with Castillian wine, spoke of a man who has recently converted to our faith. This Savage was a member of one of the most secretive orders in this exotic, barbaric land, "The Brotherhood of Life." According to the old clergyman, this secret society trains assassins for, and I speak in all sincerity, the purpose of executing demons. . . . These creatures, from his explanation, were once human beings. After their death, some unseen evil caused them to arise . . . feasting upon the flesh of the living. To combat this terror, "The Brotherhood of Life" has been formed, according to Mendoza,*

by the Shogun himself.... They are taken from an early age ... trained in the art of destruction. ... Their strange manner of unarmed battle devotes much time to avoiding manhandling by the demons, wriggling as does a snake to avoid being seized.... Their weapons, oddly shaped Oriental scimitars, are designed for the severing of heads.... Their temple, although its location remains the utmost secret, is said to possess a room where the live and still-wailing heads of destroyed monsters adorn the walls. Senior recruits, primed for their ascension into the brotherhood, must spend an entire night in this room, with nothing but the unholy objects for company.... If Father Mendoza's story is true, this land is, as we have always suspected, one of godless evil.... Were it not for the lure of silk and spice, we would do well to avoid it at all costs.... I asked the old priest where this new convert was, in order to hear the words of this tale from his own lips. Mendoza informed me that he had been found murdered almost a fortnight ago. "The Brotherhood" do not allow their secrets to be spilled, nor their members to renounce their allegiance.

Many secret societies existed in feudal Japan. "The Brotherhood of Life" does not appear in any text, past or present. Desilva does make some historical inaccuracies in his letter, such as referring to a Japanese sword as a "scimitar." (Most Europeans did not bother with learning any aspects of Japanese culture.) His description of the wailing heads is also an inaccuracy as a severed zombie head could not produce any noise without a diaphragm, lungs, and vocal cords. If his story is true, however, it would explain why there have been few reported outbreaks in Japan as opposed to the rest of the world. Either Japanese culture has produced an effective wall of silence surrounding its outbreaks or the Brotherhood of Life accomplished its mission. Either way, there were no reports of outbreaks in connection with Japan until the mid-twentieth century.

1690 A.D., THE SOUTHERN ATLANTIC

The Portuguese merchantman *Marialva* left Bissau, West Africa, with a cargo of slaves bound for Brazil. It never reached its destination. Three years later, in the middle of the South Atlantic, the Danish vessel *Zeebrug* spotted the drifting *Marialva*. A boarding party was dispatched for the purpose of salvage. They found, instead, a cargo hold of undead Africans still chained to their bunks, writhing and moaning. There was no sign of the crew, and each of the zombies had at least one bite taken from its body. The Danes, believing this ship to be cursed, rowed hastily back to their vessel and reported their findings to the captain. He immediately sank the *Marialva* with cannon fire. Because there is no way of knowing exactly how the infestation came aboard, all that is left to us is speculation. No lifeboats were found aboard. Only the captain's body was found, locked in his cabin, with a self-inflicted pistol wound to the head. Many believe that, since the Africans were all chained, the initial infected person must have been a member of the Portuguese crew. If this is true, the unfortunate slaves would have to have endured watching their captors devour or infect one another after their slow transformation into living dead, the virus having worked its way through their systems. Even worse is the awful likelihood that one of these crewmembers attacked and infected a chained slave. This new ghoul, in turn, bit the chained, screaming person next to him. On and on down the line, until the screams were eventually quiet and the entire hold was filled with zombies. Imagining those at the end of the line, seeing their future creeping steadily closer, was enough to conjure the worst nightmares.

1762 A.D., CASTRIES, ST. LUCIA, THE CARIBBEAN

The story of this outbreak is still told today, both by Caribbean islanders and Caribbean immigrants in the United Kingdom. It serves as a powerful warning, not just of the power of the living dead but of humanity's frustrating inability to unite against them. An outbreak of indeterminate source began in the poor white area of the small, overcrowded city of Castries on the island of St. Lucia. Several free black and mulatto residents realized the source of the "illness" and attempted to warn the authorities. They were ignored. The outbreak was diagnosed as a form of rabies. The first group of infected people were locked in the town jail. Those who suffered bites while trying to restrain them were sent home without treatment. Within forty-eight hours, all of Castries was in chaos. The local militia, not knowing how to stem the onslaught, was overrun and consumed. The remaining whites fled the city to the outlying plantations. Because many of them had already been bitten, they eventually spread the infection throughout the entire island. By the tenth day, 50 percent of the white population was dead. Forty percent, more than several hundred individuals, were prowling the island as reanimated zombies. The remainder had either escaped by whatever seacraft they could find or remained holed up in the two fortresses at Vieux Fort and Rodney Bay. This left a sizable force of black slaves who now found themselves "free" but at the mercy of the undead.

Unlike the white inhabitants, the former slaves possessed a deep cultural understanding of their enemy, an asset that replaced panic with determination. Slaves on every plantation organized themselves into tightly disciplined hunting teams. Armed with torches and machetes (all firearms had been taken by the fleeing whites) and allied with the remaining free blacks and mulattoes (St. Lucia contained small but prominent communities of both), they swept the island from north to south. Communicating by drum, the teams shared intelligence and coordinated battle tactics. In a slow, deliberate wave, they cleared St. Lucia in seven days. Those whites still within the forts refused to join the struggle, as their racial bigotry matched their cowardice. Ten days after the last zombie was dispatched, British and French colonial troops arrived. Instantly, all former slaves were placed back in chains. Any resisters were hanged. As the incident was recorded as a slave uprising, all free blacks and mulattoes were either enslaved or hanged for aiding in the supposed rebellion. Although no written records were kept, an oral account was passed down to the present day. A monument is rumored to exist somewhere on the island. No resident will testify to its location. If one can take a positive lesson from Castries, it is that a group of civilians, motivated and disciplined, with only the most primitive arms and basic communication, is a formidable match for any zombie attack.

1807 A.D., PARIS, FRANCE

A man was admitted to Château Robinet, a "hospital" for the criminally insane. The official report filed by Dr. Reynard Boise, chief administrator, states: "The patient appears incoherent, almost feral, with a insatiable lust for violence. . . . With jaws that snap like a rabid dog, he successfully wounded one of the other patients before being restrained." The story that followed consists of the "wounded" inmate receiving minor treatment (bandaging his wounds and a dose of rum), then being placed back in a communal cell with more than fifty other men and women. What followed days later was an orgy of violence. Guards and doctors, too frightened by the screams emanating from the cell, refused to enter until a week had passed. By this time, all that remained were five infected, partially devoured zombies, and the scattered parts of several dozen corpses. Boise promptly resigned his position and retired to private life. Little is known of what happened to the walking dead, or the original zombie that was brought to the institution. Napoleon Bonaparte himself ordered the hospital to be closed, "purified," and turned into a convalescent home for army veterans. Also, nothing is known of where the first zombie came from, how he contracted the disease, or, in fact, if he had infected anyone else before being sent to Château Robinet.

1824 A.D., SOUTHERN AFRICA

This excerpt was taken from the diary of H. F. Fynn, a member of the original British expedition to meet, travel, and negotiate with the great Zulu king Shaka.

The kraal was abuzz with life. . . . The young nobleman stepped forward into the center of the cattle pen. . . . Four of the king's greatest warriors brought forth a figure, carried and restrained by the hands and feet . . . a bag fashioned of royal cowhide covered his head. This same hide covered the hands and forearms of his guards, so their flesh never touched that of the condemned. . . . The young nobleman grabbed his assegai [four-foot stabbing spear] and leapt into the pen. . . . The King shouted his order, commanding his warriors to hurl their charge into the kraal. The condemned struck the hard earth, flailing about like a drunken man. The leather bag slipped from his head . . . his face, to my horror, was frighteningly disfigured. A large knob of flesh had been gouged from his neck as if torn by some ungodly beast.

His eyes had been plucked out, the remaining chasms staring into hell. From neither wound flowed the smallest drop of blood. The King raised his hand, silencing the frenzied multitude. A stillness hung over the kraal; a stillness so complete, the birds themselves appeared to obey the mighty King's order. . . . The young nobleman raised his assegai to his chest and uttered a word. His voice was too meek, too soft to reach my ears. The man, the poor devil, however, must have heard the solitary voice. His head turned slowly, his mouth widened. From his bruised and torn lips came a howl so terrifying, it shook me to my very bones. The monster, for now I was convinced it was a monster, slouched slowly towards the nobleman. The young Zulu brandished his assegai. He stabbed forward, embedding the dark blade in the monster's chest. The demon did not fall, did not expire, did not hint that its heart had been pierced. It simply continued its steady, unrelenting approach. The nobleman retreated, shaking like a leaf in the wind. He stumbled and fell, earth sticking to his perspiration-covered body. The crowd kept their silence, a thousand ebony statues staring down at the tragic scene. . . . And so Shaka leapt into the pen and bellowed "Sondela! Sondela!" The monster immediately turned from the prone nobleman to the King. With the speed of a musket ball, Shaka grabbed the assegai from the monster's chest and drove it through one of the vacant eye pouches. He then twirled the weapon like a fencing champion, spinning the blade tip within the monster's skull. The abomination dropped to its knees, then toppled forward, burying its abhorrent face in the red soil of Africa.

The narrative abruptly ends here. Fynn never explained what happened to the doomed nobleman or the slain zombie. Naturally, this rite of passage ceremony presents several burning questions: What is the origin of the use of zombies in this way? Did the Zulus have more than one ghoul on hand for this purpose? If so, by what means did they come by them?

1839 A.D., EAST AFRICA

The travel diary of Sir James Ashton-Hayes, one of the many incompetent Europeans seeking the source of the Nile, reveals the probability of a zombie attack, and an organized, culturally accepted response to it.

He came to the village early that morning, a young Negro with a wound in his arm. Obviously the little savage had missed his spear shot and the intended dinner had kissed him goodbye. As humorous as this was to behold, the events that followed struck me as utterly barbaric. . . . Both the village witch doctor and the tribal chief examined the wound, heard the young man's story, and nodded some unspoken decision. The injured man, through tears, said goodbye to his wife and family . . . obviously in their custom, physical contact is not permitted, then knelt at the feet of the chief. . . . The old man took hold of a large, iron-tipped cudgel then brought it crashing down upon the doomed man's head, stoving it in like a giant black egg. Almost immediately, ten of the tribe's warriors flung down their spears, unsheathed their primitive cutlasses, and uttered a bizarre chant, "Nagamba ekwaga nah eereeah enge." That said, they simply headed out across the Savanna. The body of the unfortunate savage was then, to my horror, dismembered and burned while the women of the tribe wailed to the pillar of smoke. When I asked our guide for some sort of explanation, he merely shrugged his diminutive frame and responded, "Do you want him to rise again, this night?" Queer sort of folk, these savages.

Hayes neglects to say exactly what tribe this was, and further study has revealed all his geographical data to be woefully inaccurate. (Small wonder he never found the Nile.) Fortunately, the battle cry was later identified as *"Njamba egoaga na era enge,"* a Gikuyu phrase meaning, "Together we fight, and together we win or die." This gives historians a clue that he was at least in what is today modern Kenya.

1848 A.D., OWL CREEK MOUNTAINS, WYOMING

Although this is probably not the first U.S. zombie attack, it is the first to be recorded. A group of fifty-six pioneers, known as the Knudhansen Party, disappeared in the Central Rockies on their way to California. One year later, a second expedition discovered the remains of a base camp believed to be their last resting place.

Signs of a battle were obvious. All manner of broken gear lay strewn among charred wagons. We also discovered the remains of at least five and forty souls. Among their many wounds, each shared a common breakage of the skull. Some of these holes appeared to have been caused by bullets, others by blunt instruments such as hammers or even rocks. . . . Our guide, an experienced man with many years in these wilds, believed this not to be the work of wild Indians. After all, he argued, why would they have murdered our people without taking both horse and oxen? We counted skeletons of all animals and found him to be correct. . . . One other fact we found most distressing was the number of bite wounds found on each of the deceased. As no animals, from the howling snow wolf to the tiny ant, touched the carcasses, we ruled out their complicity in this matter. Stories of cannibalism were ever present on the frontier, but we were horrified to believe such tales of godless savagery could be true, especially after such horrific tales of the Donner Party. . . . What we could not fathom, however, was why they would turn on each other so quickly when supplies of food had still not run out.

This passage came from Arne Svenson, a schoolteacher turned pioneer and farmer, of the second expedition. This story in itself does not necessarily prove there was a Solanum outbreak. Solid evidence would surface, but not for another forty years.

1852 A.D., CHIAPAS, MEXICO

A group of American treasure hunters from Boston, James Miller, Luke MacNamara, and Willard Douglass, traveled to this remote jungle province for the purpose of pillaging rumored Mayan ruins. While staying in the town of Tzinteel, they witnessed the burial of a man claimed to be "a drinker of Satan's blood." They saw that the man was bound, gagged, and still alive. Believing this to be some sort of barbaric execution, the North Americans succeeded in rescuing the condemned man. Once the chains and gag were removed, the prisoner immediately attacked his liberators. Gunfire had no effect. MacNamara was killed; the other two were lightly wounded. One month later, their families received a letter dated the day after the attack. Within its pages, the two men related the details of their adventure, including a sworn statement that their murdered friend had "come back to life" following the attack. They also wrote that their superficial bite wounds were festering and that a horrible fever had set in. They promised to rest for a few weeks in Mexico City for medical treatment, then return to the United States as soon as possible. They were never heard from again.

1867 A.D., THE INDIAN OCEAN

An English mail steamer, *RMS Rona,* transporting 137 convicts to Australia, anchored off Bijourtier Island to aid an unidentified ship that appeared stranded on a sandbar. The shore party discovered a zombie whose back had been broken, dragging itself across the ship's deserted decks. When they tried to offer help, the zombie lurched forward and bit off one of the sailor's fingers. While another seaman sliced the zombie's head off with his cutlass, the others took their injured comrade back to the ship. That night, the wounded sailor was placed in his bunk and given a draught of rum and a promise by the ship's surgeon to check on him at dawn. That night, the fresh zombie reanimated and attacked his shipmates. The captain, in a panic, ordered the cargo hold boarded up, sealing the convicts in with the ghoul, and continued on course for Australia. For the rest of the voyage, the hold echoed with screams that melted into moans. Several of the crew swore they could hear the agonizing squeaks of rats as they were eaten alive.

After six weeks at sea, the ship anchored at Perth. The officers and crew rowed ashore to inform the magistrate what had happened. Apparently, no one believed the stories of these sailors. A contingent of regular troops were sent for, if for no other reason than to escort the prisoners off. *RMS Rona* remained at anchor for five days, waiting for these troops to arrive. On the sixth day, a storm broke the ship's anchor chain, carried it several miles up the coastline, and smashed it against a reef. Townspeople, and the ship's former crew, found no evidence of the undead. All that remained were human bones and tracks leading inland. The story of the *Rona* was common among sailors in the late nineteenth and early twentieth centuries. Admiralty records list the ship as lost at sea.

1882 A.D., PIEDMONT, OREGON

Evidence of the attack comes from a relief party, sent to investigate the small silver-mining town after two months of isolation. This group found Piedmont in shambles. Many houses had been burned. Those still standing were riddled with bullet holes. Strangely, these holes showed that all shots had been fired from inside the houses, as if the battles had all taken place within their walls. Even more shocking was the discovery of twenty-seven mangled and half-eaten skeletons. An early theory regarding cannibalism was discarded when the town's warehouses were found to contain enough food supplies for an entire winter. When investigating the mine itself, the relief party made its final and most terrifying discovery. The entry shaft had been blasted shut from the inside. Fifty-eight men, women, and children were found, all dead from starvation. The rescuers determined that enough food to last several weeks had been stored and eaten, suggesting that these people had been entombed for much longer than that. Once a thorough count of all corpses, mangled and starved, had been made, at least thirty-two townsfolk could not be accounted for.

The most widely accepted theory is that, for some reason, a ghoul or group of ghouls emerged from the wilderness and attacked Piedmont. After a short, violent battle, the survivors carried what food they could to the mine. After sealing themselves in, these people presumably waited for a rescue that never came. It is suspected that, before the decision was made to retreat to the mine, one or more survivors attempted to trek through the wilderness to the closest outpost for help. Since no record of this exists and no bodies have ever been found, it is logical to assume that these proposed messengers either perished in the wild or were consumed by the undead. If zombies did exist, their remains have never been recovered. No official cover-up followed the Piedmont incident. Rumors ranged from plague, to avalanche, to infighting, to attacks by "wild Indians" (no Native Americans lived in or anywhere near Piedmont). The mine itself was never reopened. The Patterson Mining Company (owner of the mine and the town) paid compensation of $20 to each relative of the residents of Piedmont in exchange for their silence. Evidence of this transaction appeared in the company's accounting logs. These were discovered when the corporation declared bankruptcy in 1931. No subsequent investigation followed.

1888 A.D., HAYWARD, WASHINGTON

This passage describes the appearance of North America's first professional zombie hunter. The incident began when a fur trapper named Gabriel Allens stumbled into town with a deep gash on his arm. "Allens spoke of a soul who wandered like a man possessed, his skin as gray as stone, his eyes fixed in a lifeless stare. When Allens approached the wretch, he let out a hideous moan and bit the trapper on his right forearm." This passage comes from the journal of Jonathan Wilkes, the town doctor who treated Allens after his attack. Little is known about how the infestation spread from this first victim to the other members of the town. Fragments of data suggest the next victim was Dr. Wilkes, followed by three men who attempted to restrain him. Six days after the initial attack, Hayward was a town under siege. Many hid themselves in private homes or the town church while the zombies relentlessly attacked their barricades. Although firearms were plentiful, no one recognized the need for a head shot. Food, water, and ammunition were rapidly consumed. No one expected to hold longer than another six days.

At dawn on the seventh day, a Lakota man named Elija Black arrived. On horseback, with a U.S. Army cavalry saber, he decapitated twelve ghouls within the first twenty minutes. Black then used a charred stick to draw a circle around the town's water tower before climbing to the top. Between yells, an old army bugle, and his tethered horse for bait, he managed to attract every walking dead in town toward his position. Each one that entered the circle received a head shot from his Winchester repeater. In this careful, disciplined manner, Black eliminated the entire horde, fifty-nine zombies, in six hours. By the time the survivors realized what had happened, their savior was gone. Later accounts have pieced together the background of Elija Black. As a fifteen-year-old boy, he and his grandfather had been hunting when they came upon the Knudhansen Party massacre. At least one member had been infected earlier and, once turned, had attacked the rest of the group. Black and his grandfather destroyed the other zombies with tomahawk strikes to the head, decapitation, and fire. One of the "survivors," a thirty-year-old woman, explained how the infestation spread and how over half of the now-reanimated party had wandered into the wilderness. She then confessed that her wounds and those of the others were an incurable curse. Unanimously, they begged for death.

After this mass mercy killing, the old Lakota revealed to his grandson that he had hidden a bite wound suffered during the battle. Elija Black's last kill of the day would be his own grandfather. From then on, he devoted his life to hunting down the remaining zombies of the Knudhansen Party. With each encounter, he grew in knowledge and experience. Although never reaching Piedmont, he had dispatched nine of the town's zombies that had wandered into the wilderness. By the time of Hayward, Black had become, in all probability, the world's leading field scholar, tracker, and executioner of the undead. Little is known of the remainder of his life or how it eventually ended. In 1939, his biography was published both in book form and a series of articles that appeared in English newspapers. As neither version has survived, it is impossible to know exactly how many battles Black fought. A dedicated search is under way to track down lost copies of his book.

1893 A.D., FORT LOUIS PHILIPPE, FRENCH NORTH AFRICA

The diary of a junior officer in the French Foreign Legion relates one of the most serious outbreaks in history:

Three hours after dawn he came, a lone Arab on foot, on the brink of death from sun and thirst. . . . After a day's rest, with treatment and water, he related the story of a plague which turned its victims into cannibalistic horrors. . . . Before our expedition to the village could be mounted, lookouts on the south wall spotted what appeared to be a herd of animals on the horizon. . . . Through my glasses, I could see they were not beasts but men, their flesh absent of color, their clothes worn and tattered. As the wind shifted, it brought to us, first a withering groan, then not long afterward, the stench of human decay. . . . We guessed these poor wretches to be on the heels of our survivor. How they managed to traverse such a distance without food nor water, we could not say. . . . Calls and warnings produced no response. . . . Bursts from our cannon did nothing to scatter them. . . . Long-

range rifle shots seemed to have no effect! . . . Corporal Strom was immediately dispatched on horseback to Bir-El-Ksaib while we shut the gates and prepared for an attack.

The attack turned into the longest recorded undead siege. The legion-naires were unable to grasp the fact their attackers were dead, wasting their ammunition on shots to the torso. Accidental head shots were not enough to convince them of this successful tactic. Corporal Strom, the man sent for help, was never heard from again. It is assumed that he met his fate from hostile Arabs or the desert itself. His comrades inside the fort remained besieged for three years! Fortunately, a supply cara-van had just arrived. Water was already available from the well that prompted the building of the fort. Pack animals and horses were even-tually slaughtered and rationed as a last-ditch effort. All this time, the undead army, well over five hundred, continued to surround the walls. The diary reports that, over time, many were brought down by home-made explosives, improvised Molotov cocktails, and even large stones hurled over the parapet. It was not enough, however, to break the siege. Incessant moaning drove several men insane and led two of them to commit suicide. Several attempts were made to leap over the wall and run for safety. All who tried were surrounded and mauled. An attempted mutiny further thinned their ranks, bringing the total num-ber of survivors to only twenty-seven. At this time, the unit's com-manding officer decided to try one more desperate plan:

All men were equipped with a full supply of water and what little food remained. All ladders and staircases leading up to the para-pets were destroyed. . . . We assembled on the south wall and began to call to our tormentors, gathering almost all right at our gates. Colonel Drax, with the courage of a man possessed, was lowered into the parade ground, where he lifted the bolt himself. Suddenly, the stinking multitude swarmed into our fortress. The colonel made sure he provided them with enough bait, leading the wretches across the parade ground, through the barracks and mess

*hall, across the infirmary . . . he was hoisted to safety just in time,
a severed, rotting hand clasped tightly to his boot. We continued to
call to the creatures, booing and hissing, jumping about like wild
monkeys, only now we were calling to those creatures within our
own fort! . . . Dorset and O'Toole were lowered to the north
wall . . . they sprinted to the gate and pulled it shut! . . . The creatures inside, in their mindless rage, did not think to simply pull
them open again! Pushing as they did against the inward opening
gates, they only succeeded in trapping themselves further!*

The legionnaires then dropped to the desert floor, dispatched the few
zombies outside the walls in vicious hand-to-hand combat, then
marched over 240 miles to the nearest oasis, at Bir Ounane. Army
records do not tell of this siege. No explanation is given why, when regular dispatches stopped arriving from Fort Louis Philippe, no inves-
tigative forces were sent. The only official nod to anyone involved in
the incident is the court-martial and imprisonment of Colonel Drax.
Transcripts of his trial, including the charges, remain sealed. Rumors of
the outbreak continued to populate the Legion, the Army, and French
society for decades. Many fictional accounts were written about "the
Devil's Siege." Despite their denial of the incident, the French Foreign
Legion never sent another expedition to Fort Louis Philippe.

1901 A.D., LU SHAN, FORMOSA

According to Bill Wakowski, an American sailor serving with the
Asiatic fleet, several peasants from Lu Shan rose from their beds and
proceeded to attack the village. Because of Lu Shan's remoteness and
lack of wire communication (telephone/telegraph), word did not reach
Taipei until seven days later.

*These American missionaries, Pastor Alfred's flock, they thought
that it was God's punishment on the Chinamen for not taking in*

His word. They knew faith, and the Holy Father would chase the devil out of them. Our skipper, he ordered them to stay put until he could muster an armed escort. Pastor Alfred wouldn't hear of it. While the old man wired for help, they headed up the river. . . . Our shore party and a platoon of Nationalist Troops reached the village just about midday . . . bodies, or pieces of them, were everywhere. The ground was all sticky. And the smell, God almighty, that smell! . . . When those things came out of the mist, disgusting creatures, human devils. We plugged them at less than a hundred yards. Nothing worked. Not our Krags, not our Gattling . . . Riley just kind of lost his marbles, I guess. Fixed his bayonet and tried to skewer one of the beasties. About a dozen others swarmed around him. Quick like lightning they tore my buddy limb from limb. They gnawed his flesh right down to the bone! It was a grisly sight! . . . And here he comes, little bald witch doctor or monk, or whatever you call him . . . swinging what looked like a flat shovel with a quarter moon blade on the back . . . must have been ten, twenty corpses at his feet . . . he runs over, chattering all crazy, pointing to his head then theirs. The Old Man, Lord knows how he reckoned what the Chinaman was babbling about, ordered us to aim for the beasties' heads. . . . We drilled them point blank. . . . Picking through the bodies, we discovered among the Chinamen were a few white men, our missionaries. One of our guys found a monster whose spine had been snapped by a round. It was still alive, flapping its arms, snapping its bloody teeth, letting out that God Awful moan! The Old Man recognized it as Pastor Alfred. He said the Lord's Prayer, then shot the padre in the temple.

Wakowski sold his full account to the pulp magazine *Tales of the Macabre,* an act that resulted in his immediate discharge and imprisonment. Upon release, Wakowski refused any further interviews. To this day, the U.S. Navy denies the story.

1905 A.D., TABORA, TANGANYIKA, GERMAN EAST AFRICA

Trial transcripts state that a native guide referred to only as "Simon" was arrested and charged with the decapitation of a famous white hunter, Karl Seekt. Simon's defense counsel, a Dutch planter named Guy Voorster, explained that his client believed he had actually committed a heroic act. According to Voorster:

Simon's people believe that a malady exists that robs the life force from a man. In its place is left the body, dead yet still living, without sense of self or surroundings and with only cannibalism as its drive. . . . Furthermore, the victims of this undead monster will rise from their own graves to devour even more victims. This cycle will be repeated, again and again, until none is left upon our Earth but these horrible flesh-eating monstrosities. . . . My client tells that the victim in question returned to his base camp two days behind schedule, his mind delirious and an unexplained wound on his arm. Later that day he expired. . . . My client then describes Herr Seekt rising from his deathbed to set his teeth upon the rest of his party. My client used his native blade to decapitate Herr Seekt and incinerate his head in the campfire.

Mr. Voorster quickly added that he was not in agreement with Simon's testimony and submitted it only to prove that the man was insane and should not be executed. As an insanity defense applied only to white men and not Africans, Simon was sentenced to death by hanging. All records of the trial still exist, albeit in terrible condition, in Dar es Salaam, Tanzania.

1911 A.D., VITRE, LOUISIANA

This common American legend, told in bars and high school locker rooms throughout the Deep South, has its roots in documented historical fact. On Halloween night, several Cajun youths took part in a "dare" to stay in the bayou from midnight till dawn. Local custom told of zombies originally descended from a plantation family that prowled the swamp, consuming or reanimating any humans who crossed their path. By noon the next day, none of the teenagers had returned from their dare. A search party was formed to comb the swamp. They were attacked by at least thirty ghouls, their ranks including the youths. The searchers retreated, unwittingly leading the undead back to Vitre. While townsfolk barricaded themselves in their homes, one citizen, Henri De La Croix, believed that dousing the undead with molasses would bring millions of insects to devour their flesh. The scheme failed, and De La Croix barely escaped with his life. The undead were doused again, this time with kerosene, and set ablaze. Without realizing the full consequences of their actions, Vitre residents watched in horror as the burning ghouls set fire to everything they touched. Several victims, trapped in barricaded buildings, burned to death while the others fled into the swamp. Several days later, rescue volunteers counted a total of fifty-eight survivors (the town's previous population being 114). Vitre itself had completely burned to the ground. Figures vary as to the number of undead versus human casualties. When Vitre casualties were added to the amount of zombie corpses found, at least fifteen bodies are unaccounted for. Official government records in Baton Rouge explain the attack as "riotous behavior from the Negro population," a curious explanation as the town of Vitre was entirely white. Any proof of a zombie outbreak comes from private letters and diaries that exist among the survivors' descendants.

1913 A.D., PARAMARIBO, SURINAM

While Dr. Ibrahim Obeidallah might have been the first to expand humanity's scientific knowledge of the undead, he was (thankfully) not the last. Dr. Jan Vanderhaven, already respected in Europe for his study of leprosy, arrived in the South American colony to study a bizarre outbreak of this familiar disease.

The infected souls show symptoms similar to those around the globe: festering sores, mottled skin, flesh decomposing in its appearance. However, all similarities with the conventional affliction end here. These poor souls appear to have gone completely mad. . . . They display no signs of rational thought nor even recognition of anything familiar. . . . They neither sleep nor take water. They reject all food except that which is alive. . . . Yesterday a hospital orderly, for sheer sport, and against my orders, flung an injured rat into the patients' holding cell. One of them promptly grabbed the vermin and swallowed it whole. . . . The infected display almost rabid hostility. . . . They snap at all who approach, teeth bared like animals. . . . One patient's visitor, an influential woman who defied all hospital protocols, was subsequently bitten by her infected husband. Despite all known methods of treatment, she succumbed rapidly to the wound, passing later that day. . . . The body was returned to the family plantation. . . . Against my pleadings, an autopsy was denied out of concern for decorum. . . . That night the corpse was reported stolen. . . . Experiments with alcohol, formalin, and heating tissue to 90 degrees centigrade have erased the possibility of bacteria. . . . I must therefore deduce that the agent can only be contagious living fluid . . . dubbed "Solanum."

("Contagious living fluid" was a common term before the later adoption of the Latin word *virus*.) These excerpts come from a 200-page, year-long study done by Dr. Vanderhaven on this new discovery. In this study, he documents a zombie's tolerance to pain, apparent lack of respiration, slow rate of decomposition, lack of speed, limited agility, and absence of healing. Because of the violent nature of his subjects and the apparent fear of the hospital orderlies, Vanderhaven was never able to get close enough to do a full autopsy. For this reason, he was unable to discover that the living dead were just that. In 1914, he returned to Holland and published his work. Ironically, it earned him neither praise nor ridicule in the scientific community. His story, like many others of the day, was eclipsed by the outbreak of the First World War. Copies of the work lay forgotten in Amsterdam. Vanderhaven returned to practicing conventional medicine in the Dutch East Indies (Indonesia), where he subsequently died of malaria. Vanderhaven's major breakthrough was the discovery of a virus as the culprit behind a zombie's creation and he was, notably, the first person to ascribe the name "Solanum" to the virus. Why he chose this term is unknown. Although his work was not celebrated by his European contemporaries, it is now widely read all over the world. Unfortunately, one country put the good doctor's findings to devastating use. (See "1942–45 A.D., Harbin," pages 220–22.)

1923 A.D., COLOMBO, CEYLON

This account comes from *The Oriental,* an expatriate newspaper for Britons living in the Indian Ocean colony. Christopher Wells, a copilot for British Imperial Airways, was rescued from a life raft after fourteen days at sea. Before dying of exposure, Wells explained that he had been transporting a corpse discovered by a British expedition to Mount Everest. The corpse had been a European, his clothing of a century earlier, with no identifying documents. As he was frozen solid, the expedition leader had decided to fly him to Colombo for further study. While en route, the corpse thawed, reanimated, and attacked the airplane's crew. The three men managed to destroy their assailant by crushing his skull with a fire extinguisher (as they did not realize what they were dealing with, the attempt may have been to simply incapacitate the zombie). While safe from this immediate danger, they now had to contend with a damaged aircraft. The pilot radioed a distress signal but had no time to send a position report. The three men parachuted into the ocean, the crew-chief not realizing that a bite he sustained would have dire consequences later. The following day, he expired, reanimated several hours later, and immediately attacked the other two men. While the pilot wrestled with the undead assailant, Wells, in a panic, kicked both of them overboard. After relating—some

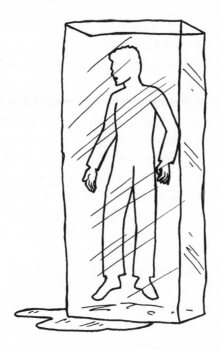

would say confessing—his story to the authorities, Wells lapsed into unconsciousness and died the next day. His story was reported as the ravings of a sunstroke maniac. A subsequent investigation produced no evidence of the plane, the crew, or the alleged zombie.

1942 A.D., THE CENTRAL PACIFIC

During Japan's initial advance, a platoon of Imperial Marines was sent to garrison Atuk, an island in the Caroline chain. Several days after landing, the platoon was attacked by a swarm of zombies from the inland jungle. Initial casualties were high. Without any information about the nature of their attackers or the correct means of destruction, the marines were driven to a fortified mountaintop on the north end of the island. Ironically, as the wounded were left to die, the surviving marines spared themselves the danger of taking infected comrades with them. The platoon remained stranded in their mountaintop fortress for several days, lacking food, low on water, and cut off from the outside world. All this time, the ghouls were besieging their position, unable to scale the steep cliffs but preventing any chance of escape. After two weeks of imprisonment, Ashi Nakamura, the platoon sniper, discovered that a head shot was fatal to a zombie. This knowledge allowed the Japanese to finally combat their attackers. After dispatching the surrounding ghouls with rifle fire, they advanced into the jungle for a complete sweep of the island. Eyewitness accounts have the commanding officer, Lieutenant Hiroshi Tomonaga, decapitating eleven zombies with nothing but his officer's Katana (an argument for the use of this weapon). A postwar examination and comparison of records have shown that Atuk is in all probability the same island that Sir Francis Drake described as "the Isle of the Damned." Tomonaga's own testimony, given to American authorities after the war, states that once radio communication with Tokyo had been reestablished, the Japanese High Command sent specific instructions to capture, not kill, any remaining zombies. Once this was accomplished (four ghouls had been successfully bound and gagged), the Imperial Submarine I-58 was dispatched to retrieve the undead prisoners. Tomonaga confessed his lack of knowledge of what happened to the four zombies. He and his men were ordered not to discuss their experience, under penalty of death.

1942–45 A.D., HARBIN, JAPANESE PUPPET STATE OF MANCHUKUO (MANCHURIA)

In his 1951 book *The Sun Rose on Hell,* former U.S. Army Intelligence officer David Shore details a series of wartime biological experiments conducted by a unit of the Japanese military known as "Black Dragon." One experiment, dubbed "Cherry Blossom," was organized specifically for the breeding and training of zombies into an army. According to Shore, when Japanese forces invaded the Dutch East Indies in 1941–42, a copy of Jan Vanderhaven's work was discovered in a medical library in Surabaya. The work was sent to Black Dragon headquarters in Harbin for further study. Although a theoretical plan was ordered, no sample of Solanum could be found (proof that the ancient zombie-killing "Brotherhood of Life" had done its job too well). All this changed six months later with the incident on Atuk Island. The four restrained zombies were delivered to Harbin. Experiments were performed on three of them, and one was used specifically to breed other zombies. Shore states that Japanese "dissidents" (anyone who disagreed with the military regime) were used as guinea pigs. Once a "platoon" of forty zombies had been reanimated, Black Dragon operatives attempted to train them like obedient drones. This met with dismal results: Bites turned ten of the sixteen instructors into zombies. After two years of fruitless attempts, the decision was made to release the force of the now fifty zombies against the enemy no matter what condition they were in. Ten ghouls were to be parachuted over British forces in Burma. The plane was hit by antiaircraft fire before reaching its target, exploding into a fireball that destroyed all traces of its undead cargo. A second attempt was made to deliver ten zombies by submarine to the American-held Panama Canal zone (it was hoped that the ensuing chaos would interrupt Atlantic-built, Pacific-bound American warships). The submarine was sunk en route. A third attempt was made (again by submarine) to release twenty zombies into the ocean off the West Coast of the United States. Halfway across the Northern Pacific, the submarine's captain radioed that the zombies had broken free of their restraints and were attacking the crew, and that he had no choice but to scuttle the boat. As the war drew to a close, a fourth and final attempt was made to parachute the remaining zombies onto a nest of Chinese guerrillas in Yonnan Province. Nine of the parachuted zombies were dispatched by head shots from Chinese snipers. The sharpshooters did not realize the importance of their shots. Their orders had *always* been to go for the head. The final zombie was captured, restrained, and taken to Mao Zedong's personal headquarters for further study. When the Soviet Union invaded Manchukuo in 1945, all records and evidence of the "Cherry Blossom" project disappeared.

Shore states that his book is based on the eyewitness accounts of two Black Dragon operatives, men whom he personally debriefed after they surrendered to the U.S. Army in South Korea at the end of the war. At first Shore found a publisher for his book, a small, independent company known as Green Brothers Press. Before it reached the shelves, the government ordered all copies confiscated. Green Brothers Press was directly charged by Senator Joseph McCarthy with publishing "obscene and subversive material." Under the weight of legal fees, the company filed for bankruptcy. David Shore was charged with violating national security and sentenced to life imprisonment at Fort Leavenworth, Kansas. He was pardoned in 1961 but died of a heart attack two months after his release. His widow, Sara Shore, retained a secret and illegal copy of his manuscript until her death in 1984. Their daughter, Hannah, just recently won a lawsuit for the right to republish it.

1943 A.D., FRENCH NORTH AFRICA

This excerpt comes from the debriefing of P.F.C. Anthony Marno, tail-gunner on a U.S. Army B-24 bomber. Returning from a night raid against German troop concentrations in Italy, the aircraft found itself lost over the Algerian desert. Low on fuel, the pilot saw what looked like a human settlement below and ordered his crew to bail out. What they found was Fort Louis Philippe.

It looked like something out of a kiddie's nightmare. . . . We open the gates, there wasn't no bar on it or nothing. We walk into the courtyard, and there was all these skeletons. Mountains of them, no kidding! Just piled up everywhere, like a movie. Our skipper, he just kinda shakes his head and says, "Sorta feel like there should be buried treasure here, you know?" Good thing none of them bodies was in the well. We managed to fill up our canteens, grab some supplies. There wasn't no food, but who'd want it anyway, you know?

Marno and the rest of his crew were rescued by an Arab caravan fifty miles from the fort. When questioned about the place, the Arabs would not respond. At the time, the U.S. Army had neither the resources nor the interest in investigating some abandoned ruin in the middle of the desert. No later expedition was ever mounted.

1947 A.D., JARVIE, BRITISH COLUMBIA

A series of articles in five separate newspapers recount the bloody events and individual heroism associated with this small Canadian hamlet. Little is known of the source of the outbreak. Historians suspect the carrier was Mathew Morgan, a local hunter who returned to town one night with a mysterious bite on his shoulder. By dawn of the next morning, twenty-one zombies were prowling the streets of Jarvie. Nine individuals were completely consumed. The remaining fifteen humans barricaded themselves in the sheriff's office. A lucky shot by an embattled citizen had proved what a bullet to the brain could do. By this point, however, most of the windows were boarded up, so no one was able to aim their weapons. A plan was hatched to crawl out to the roof, make it to the telephone-telegraph office, and signal the authorities in Victoria. The survivors made it halfway across the street when the nearby ghouls noticed them and gave chase. One member of the group, Regina Clark, told the others to continue while she held off the undead. Clark, armed only with a U.S. M1 carbine, led the zombies into a blind alley. Eyewitnesses insist that Clark did this on purpose, herding the undead into a confined space to allow her no more than four targets at one time. With cool aim and an astounding reload time, Clark dispatched the entire mob. Several eyewitnesses observed her emptying one fifteen-round clip in twelve seconds without missing a single shot. Even more astounding is that the first zombie she dispatched was her own husband. Official sources label the event "an unexplainable display of public violence." All newspaper articles are based on Jarvie's citizens. Regina Clark declined to be interviewed. Her memoirs remain a guarded secret of her family.

1954 A.D., THAN HOA, FRENCH INDOCHINA

This passage is taken from a letter written by Jean Beart Lacoutour, a French businessman living in the former colony.

> *The game is called "Devil Dance." A living human is placed in a cage with one of these creatures. Our human has with him only a small blade, perhaps eight centimeters at most. . . . Will he survive his waltz with the living corpse? If not, how long will it last? Bets are taken for these and all other variables. . . . We keep a stable of them, these fetid gladiators. Most are turned from the victims of a failed match. Some we take from the street . . . we pay their families well. . . . God have mercy on me for this unimaginable sin.*

This letter, along with a sizable fortune, arrived in La Rochelle, France, three months after the fall of French Indochina to Ho Chi Minh's Communist guerrillas. The fate of Lacoutour's "Devil Dance" is unknown. No further information has been uncovered. One year later, Lacoutour's body arrived in France, badly decomposed, with a bullet in the brain. The North Vietnamese coroner's explanation was suicide.

1957 A.D., MOMBASA, KENYA

This excerpt was taken from an interrogation by a British Army officer of a captured Gikuyu rebel during the Mau Mau uprising (all answers come secondhand through a translator):

Q: How many did you see?
A: Five.
Q: Describe them.
A: White men, their skin gray and cracked. Some had wounds, bite marks on parts of their bodies. All had bullet holes in their chests. They stumbled, they groaned. Their eyes had no sight. Their teeth were stained with blood. The smell of carrion announced them. The animals fled.

An argument erupts between the prisoner and the Mosai interpreter. The prisoner grows silent.

Q: What happened?
A: They came for us. We drew our lalems (Mosai weapon, similar to a machete) and sliced off their heads, then buried them.
Q: You buried the heads?
A: Yes.
Q: Why?
A: Because a fire would have given us away.
Q: You were not wounded?
A: I would not be here.
Q: You were not afraid?
A: We only fear the living.
Q: So these were evil spirits?

The prisoner chuckles.

Q: Why are you laughing?

A: Evil spirits are invented to frighten children. These men were walking death.

The prisoner gave little information for the rest of his interrogation. When asked if there were more zombies out there, he remained silent. The entire transcript appeared in a British tabloid later that year. Nothing was made of it.

1960 A.D., BYELGORANSK, SOVIET UNION

It had been suspected, since the end of the Second World War, that the Soviet troops who invaded Manchuria captured most of the Japanese scientists, data, and test subjects (zombies) involved in Black Dragon's special project. Recent revelations have confirmed these rumors to be true. The purpose of this new Soviet project was to create a secret army of walking dead to be used in the inevitable Third World War. "Cherry Blossom," rechristened "Sturgeon," was conducted near a small town in Eastern Siberia whose only other structure was a large prison for political dissidents. The location ensured not only total secrecy but also a ready supply of test subjects. Based on recent findings, we are able to determine that, for some reason, the experiments went awry, causing an outbreak of several hundred zombies. What few scientists were left managed to escape to the prison. Safe behind its walls, they settled down for what was believed to be a short siege until help arrived. None did. Some historians believe that the town's remote nature (no roads existed, and supplies had to be airlifted) prevented an immediate response. Others believed that, since the project had been started by Josef Stalin, the KGB was reluctant to inform Premier Nikita Khrushchev of its existence. A third theory holds that the Soviet leadership was aware of the disaster, had ringed the area with troops to prevent a breakout, and was watching and waiting to see the result of the siege. Inside the prison walls, a coalition of scientists, military personnel, and prisoners was surviving quite comfortably. Greenhouses were constructed; wells were dug; power was improvised both by windmills and human dynamos. Radio contact was even maintained on a daily basis. The survivors reported that, given their position, they could hold out until winter, when, hopefully, the undead would freeze solid. Three days before the first autumn frost, a Soviet aircraft dropped a crude thermonuclear device on Byelgoransk. The one-megaton blast obliterated the town, the prison, and the surrounding area.

For decades, the disaster was explained by the Soviet government as a routine nuclear test. The truth was not revealed until 1992, when information began leaking to the West. Rumors of the outbreak also surfaced among older Siberians, interviewed for the first time by Russia's newly free press. Memoirs of senior Soviet officials hinted at the true nature of the devastation. Many acknowledge that the town of Byelgoransk did exist. Others confirm that it was both a political prison and biowarfare center. Some even go so far as to admit some kind of "outbreak," although none describe exactly what broke out. The most damaging evidence came when Artiom Zenoviev, a Russian mobster and former KGB archivist, released all copies of the government's official report to an anonymous Western source (an act for which he was paid handsomely). The report contains radio transcripts, aerial photographs (both before and after), and depositions of both ground troops and the bomber's air crew, along with the signed confessions of those in command of project Sturgeon. Included with this report are 643 pages of laboratory data concerning the physiology and behavioral patterns of undead test subjects. The Russians discount the entire disclosure as a hoax. If this is true, and Zenoviev is nothing more than a brilliantly creative opportunist, then why does his list of those held responsible match official records of top scientists, military commanders, and Politburo members who were executed by the KGB one month to the day after Byelgoransk was incinerated?

1962 A.D., UNIDENTIFIED TOWN, NEVADA

Details of this outbreak are surprisingly sketchy, given that it occurred within a relatively settled part of the planet within the latter half of the twentieth century. According to fragments of secondhand eyewitness accounts, scraps of yellowed newsprint, and a suspiciously vague police report, a small outbreak of zombies attacked and besieged Hank Davis, a local farmer, and three hired hands in a barn for five days and nights. When state police dispatched the ghouls and entered the barn, they found all the occupants dead. A subsequent investigation determined that the four men killed one another. More specifically, three men were slain, while the fourth took his own life. No concrete reason is given for this occurrence. The barn was more than safe from attack, and a small stock of food and water was only half depleted. The present theory is that the zombie's incessant moaning, coupled with feelings of total isolation and helplessness, led to a complete psychological breakdown. No official explanation was given for the outbreak. The case is "still under investigation."

1968 A.D., EASTERN LAOS

This story was related by Peter Stavros, a substance-abuse patient and former Special Forces sniper. In 1989, while under psychological evaluation at a V.A. hospital in Los Angeles, he related this story to the attending psychiatrist. Stavros stated that his team was on a routine search-and-destroy mission along the Vietnamese border. Their intended target was a village suspected of being a staging area of the Pathet Lao (Communist guerrillas). Upon entering the village, they discovered the inhabitants were in the midst of their own siege against several dozen walking dead. For unknown reasons, the team leader ordered his team to withdraw, then called in an air strike. Sky raiders armed with napalm plastered the area, destroying both the living dead and the human survivors. No documented evidence exists to corroborate Stavros' story. The other members of his team are either dead, missing in action, missing within the United States, or simply declined to be interviewed.

1971 A.D., NONG'ONA VALLEY, RWANDA

Jane Massey, wildlife journalist for *The Living Earth*, was sent by her magazine to document the lives of endangered silverback gorillas. This excerpt ran as a small anecdote among the larger and more popular story of rare and exotic primates:

> *As we passed a steep valley, I saw the movement of something in the foliage below. Our guide saw it too and encouraged us to pick up the pace. At that moment I heard something pretty rare for that part of the world: complete silence. No birds, no animals, not even insects, and we're talking some pretty loud insects. I asked Kengeri, and he just told me to keep it down. From down in the valley, I could hear this creepy moan. Kevin [the expedition's photographer] turned even whiter than usual and kept saying it must be the wind. Now, I've heard wind in Sarawak, Sri Lanka, the Amazon, and even Nepal, and that was NOT the wind! Kengeri put a hand on his machete and encouraged us to shut up. I told him I wanted to go down into the valley to check it out. He refused. When I pushed, he said, "The dead walk there" and took off.*

Massey never explored the valley or discovered the source of the moan. The guide's story could have been local superstition. The moan could have simply been the wind. However, maps of the valley reveal it to be surrounded by sheer cliffs in all directions, making it impossible for ghouls to escape. Theoretically, this valley could serve as a receptacle for tribes wishing to trap but not destroy the walking dead.

1975 A.D., AL-MARQ, EGYPT

Information concerning this outbreak comes from a variety of sources: eyewitness interviews of the town's inhabitants, nine depositions from low-ranking Egyptian military personnel, and the accounts of Gassim Farouk (a former Egyptian Air Force intelligence officer who recently emigrated to the United States), and several international journalists who have requested that their identities be kept secret. All these sources corroborate the story that an outbreak of unknown origin attacked and overran this small Egyptian village. Calls for help went unanswered, both from police from other towns and the base commander of Egypt's Second Armored Division at Gabal Garib only thirty-five miles away. In a bizarre twist of fate, the telephone operator at Gabal Garib was also an Israeli Mossad agent who passed the information along to IDF headquarters in Tel Aviv. The information was discounted as a hoax by both the Mossad and the Israeli General Staff and would have been forgotten had it not been for Colonel Jacob Korsunsky, an aide to Prime Minister Golda Meir. An American Jew and former colleague of the late David Shore, Korsunsky was well aware of the existence of zombies and what threat they posed if left unchecked. Amazingly, Korsunsky convinced Meir to assemble a reconnaissance mission to investigate Al-Marq. By now the infestation was in its fourteenth day. Nine survivors had barricaded themselves in the town mosque with little water and no food. A platoon of paratroopers, led by Korsunsky, dropped into the center of Al-Marq and, after a twelve-hour battle, eliminated all zombies. Wild speculation surrounds the ending of this story. Some believe that the Egyptian Army surrounded Al-Marq, captured the Israelis, and prepared to execute them on the spot. Only after pleading from the survivors, who showed the soldiers the zombie corpses, did the Egyptians allow the Israelis safe passage home. Others take this possibility further, believing it to be one of the reasons for the Egyptian-Israeli détente. No hard evidence exists to substantiate this story. Korsunsky died in 1991. His memoirs, personal accounts, army communiqués, subsequent newspaper articles, and even film of the battle purportedly shot by a Mossad cameraman, have been sealed by the Israeli government. If the story is true, it does present one interesting and possibly disturbing question. Why would the Egyptian Army be convinced of the living dead's existence simply by eyewitness accounts and seemingly human corpses? Would not an intact, still-functioning specimen (or specimens) have to exist to prove such an incredible story? If so, where are those specimens now?

1979 A.D., SPERRY, ALABAMA

While on his daily rounds, Chuck Bernard, the local postal delivery man, stopped at the Henrichs farm to find that the previous day's mail had not been collected. As this had never happened before, Bernard decided to carry the mail himself up to the house. Fifty feet from the front door, he heard what sounded like gunshots, cries of pain, and calls for help. Bernard fled the scene, drove ten miles to the nearest pay phone, and called the police. When two sheriff's deputies and a paramedic team arrived, they found the Henrichs family brutally slaughtered. The only survivor, Freda Henrichs, was obviously experiencing the symptoms of advanced infection. She bit both paramedics before the deputies could restrain her. A third deputy, last to arrive and new to the force, panicked and shot her in the head. The two bitten men were brought to the county hospital for treatment and died soon afterward. Three hours later, they rose during their autopsy, attacked the coroner and his assistant, and moved out to the street. By midnight the entire town was in a panic. At least twenty-two zombies were now at large and had completely devoured fifteen people. Many survivors sought refuge in their homes. Others tried to flee the city. Three schoolchildren managed to climb to the top of a water tower. Although surrounded (several ghouls tried to scale the tower but were kicked back to the ground), these children remained safe until they were rescued. One man, Harland Lee, left his home armed with a modified Uzi submachine gun, a sawed-off, double-barreled shotgun, and two .44

magnum pistols (one a revolver, the other an automatic). Witnesses reported seeing Lee attack a group of twelve zombies, firing first his Uzi then the other weapons in turn. Each time, Lee aimed for the zombie's torso, causing extreme damage but no kills. Low on ammo, and backed against a mass of wrecked cars, Lee attempted head shots with a pistol in each hand. Because his hands were shaking too violently, Lee produced no hits whatsoever. The self-appointed town savior was quickly devoured. By morning, deputies from neighboring towns, along with state police and hastily assembled vigilante groups, had converged on Sperry. Armed with sighted hunting rifles and new knowledge of the fatal head shot (a local hunter had learned this defending his home), they quickly dispatched the threat. The official explanation (provided by the Department of Agriculture) was "mass hysteria from pesticide release in local water table." All bodies were removed by the Centers for Disease Control before civilian autopsies could be performed. The majority of radio recordings, news footage, and private photographs was immediately confiscated. One hundred and seventy-five lawsuits were filed by various survivors. Ninety-two of these cases have been settled out of court, forty-eight are still pending, and the remainder have been mysteriously dropped. One lawsuit was recently filed for access to the confiscated media footage. A court decision is said to be years away.

OCT. 1980 A.D., MARICELA, BRAZIL

News of this outbreak initially came from Green Mother, an environmental group seeking to draw attention to the plight of local Indians suffering the seizure and destruction of their land. Cattle ranchers, seeking to achieve their aims through violence, armed themselves and set out for the Indian village. While deep in the rainforest, they were attacked by another, more terrifying enemy: a horde of more than thirty zombies. All ranchers were either devoured or reanimated as walking dead. Two survivors managed to make it to the nearby town of

Santerem. Their warnings were ignored, and official reports explained the battle as an uprising by the Indian population. Three army brigades advanced on Maricela. After finding no trace of the undead, they moved into the Indian village. The incident that followed has been officially denied by the Brazilian government, as has any knowledge of an attack by walking dead. Eyewitness accounts have described the massacre as exactly that, with government troops destroying every walking being, zombie and human. Ironically, members of Green Mother deny the story as well, stating that it actually was the Brazilian government that fabricated a zombie hoax as justification for massacring the Indians. One piece of interesting evidence comes from a retired major in the Brazilian Army's Bureau of Ordnance. He recounts that, in the days leading up to the battle, nearly every flamethrower in the country was requisitioned. After the operation, the weapons were returned empty.

DEC. 1980 A.D., JURUTI, BRAZIL

This outpost, more than 300 miles downriver from Maricela, became the scene of several attacks five weeks later. Zombies rising from the water attacked fishermen in their boats or clambered ashore at several points along the bank. The result of these attacks—numbers, response, casualties—is still unknown.

1984 A.D., CABRIO, ARIZONA

This outbreak, extremely minor considering the space and people involved, barely qualifies as a Class 1. However, the ramifications represent one of the most significant events in the study of Solanum. A fire at an elementary school caused the deaths of forty-seven children, all by smoke inhalation. The only survivor, Ellen Aims, nine years old, escaped by jumping out of a broken window but suffered deep lacerations and loss of blood. Only a hurried transfusion from stored blood saved her life. Within half an hour, Ellen began to suffer the symptoms of a Solanum infection. This was not understood by the medical staff, who suspected the blood to be contaminated by other diseases. While tests were under way, the child died. In full view of the staff, witnesses, and parents, she reanimated and bit the attending nurse. Ellen was restrained, the nurse was put in quarantine, and the doctor on call relayed the details of his case to a colleague in Phoenix. Two hours later, doctors from the Centers for Disease Control arrived, escorted by local law enforcement and "nondescript federal agents." Ellen and the infected nurse were airlifted to an undisclosed location for "further treatment." All hospital records as well as the entire blood supply were confiscated. The Aims family was not allowed to accompany their child. After an entire week without news, they were informed that their daughter had "passed away" and the body had been cremated for "health reasons." This case is the first on record to prove that Solanum is transferable from stored blood. This begs the questions: Who was the donor of the infected blood, how was it taken without the subject knowing he was infected, and why was the infected donor never heard from again? Furthermore, how did the CDC hear of the Aims case so quickly (the physician in Phoenix declined to be interviewed), and why did the agency respond so quickly? Needless to say, conspiracy theories continue to orbit this case. Ellen's parents have filed a lawsuit against the CDC, for the sole purpose of having the truth revealed. Their statements were instrumental in the author's research of this case.

1987 A.D., KHOTAN, CHINA

In March 1987, Chinese dissident groups informed the West of a near disaster at the nuclear power plant in Xinjiang. After several months of denying the story, the Chinese government officially announced that there had been a "malfunction" at the facility. Within a month, the story had been changed to "attempted acts of sabotage . . . by counter-revolutionary terrorists." In August, *Tycka!*, a Swedish newspaper, published a story that a U.S. spy satellite over Khotan had photographed tanks and other armored vehicles firing point-blank into what appeared to be disorganized mobs of civilians who were attempting to enter the power plant. More photographs revealed that some of the "civilians" surrounding certain individuals were tearing them to pieces and feeding on their corpses. The U.S. government denies that its satellite produced such images, and *Tycka!* has retracted the story. If Khotan were a zombie outbreak, then more questions exist than answers. How did the outbreak start? What was the duration? How was it eventually contained? How many zombies were involved? Did they actually enter the plant? How much damage was done? Why was there not a meltdown on the scale of Chernobyl? Did any zombies escape? Have there been attacks since then? One piece of information that gives credence to the story of the outbreak comes from Professor Kwang Zhou, a Chinese dissident who has since defected to the United States. Kwang knew one soldier involved in the incident. Before being sent to a reeducation camp with all other witnesses, the young man stated that the code name for the operation was "Eternal Waking Nightmare." One question still remains, how did this initial outbreak start? After reading David Shore's book, specifically the section on how a Black Dragon zombie was captured by Chinese Communist troops, it is logical to theorize that the Chinese government had, or still has, its own version of "Cherry Blossom" and "Sturgeon," its own project to create an army of undead.

DEC. 1992 A.D., JOSHUA TREE NATIONAL MONUMENT, CALIFORNIA

Several hikers and day-trippers to this desert park reported an abandoned tent and gear just off the main road. Park rangers investigating the reports discovered a gruesome scene a mile and a half from the abandoned camp sight. A woman in her mid-twenties was found dead, her head caved in by a large rock and her body covered with human bite marks. A further investigation by the local and state police identified the victim as Sharon Parsons from Oxnard, California. She and her boyfriend, Patrick MacDonald, had been camping in the park the previous week. An all points bulletin was immediately put out on MacDonald. A full autopsy of Parsons revealed a fact that startled the attending coroner. Her body's rate of decomposition did not match that of her brain tissue. Furthermore, her esophagus contained traces of human flesh that matched MacDonald's recorded blood type. However, skin samples from under her nails matched a third party, Devin Martin, a loner and wildlife photographer who had bicycled through the park a month earlier. As he had few friends, no family, and worked freelance, Martin's disappearance was never filed. A full search of the park revealed nothing. A surveillance video from a gas station in Diamond Bar revealed that MacDonald had stopped there briefly. The clerk on duty described MacDonald as haggard, frenzied, and holding a bloody cloth over his shoulder. MacDonald was last seen heading west, toward Los Angeles.

JAN. 1993 A.D., DOWNTOWN LOS ANGELES, CALIFORNIA

An investigation is still underway regarding the earliest phase of this outbreak, including how it initially spread to the immediate area. The outbreak was first detected by a group of youths, members of a street gang known as the V.B.R., or Venice Boardwalk Reds. Their reason for entering this area of the city was to avenge the death of one of their members, murdered by a rival gang known as Los Peros Negros. Around one A.M., they entered a post-industrial, nearly abandoned area where the Peros had their hangout. The first thing they noticed was the lack of homeless people. That area was known for its large shantytown in a local vacant lot. The cardboard boxes, shopping carts, and other various paraphernalia that belonged to these vagrants lay strewn around the street, but there was no sign of the people. Paying little attention to the road, the driver of the Reds' vehicle accidentally ran over a slow-moving pedestrian. The driver lost control of his El Camino and spun into the side of a building. Before the Reds could repair their damaged vehicle or fully berate their companion for his lack of driving skill, they saw the injured pedestrian move. Despite a broken back, the victim began crawling toward the street gang. One of the Reds raised his 9mm pistol and shot the man through the chest. Not only did this act fail to stop the crawling man, but it sent a soundwave echoing across a several-block radius. The Red fired several more shots, all striking his target, all producing zero results. His last shot entered the figure's skull, ending its life. The Reds never had time to discover exactly what they had killed. Suddenly they heard a moan that seemed to come from all directions. What they had taken for shadows in streetlights was a crowd of more than forty zombies approaching from all directions.

With their car wrecked, the Reds took off down the street, literally running through the thinnest line of living dead. After several blocks they encountered, ironically, the remaining members of Los Peros Negros, also on foot after their hangout and vehicles had been overrun by the living dead. Forsaking rivalry for survival, the two gangs called a truce and set out in search of either a means of escape or a safe refuge. Although most of the buildings—well-built, windowless warehouses—would have made excellent fortresses, they were either locked or (in the case of the abandoned ones) boarded up and could not be entered. As they knew the turf better, the Peros took the lead and suggested De Soto Junior High, a small school easily within running distance. With the living dead barely minutes away, the two gangs made it to the school and broke in through a second-story window. This set off a burglar alarm which, in turn, alerted every zombie in the immediate area, swelling their ranks to more than a hundred. The alarm, however, was the only negative aspect of this formidable redoubt. In terms of a fortress, De Soto was an excellent choice. Solid concrete construction, barred and mesh-covered windows and steel-covered, solid wood doors made the two-story building easily defensible. Once inside, the group acted with commendable forethought, establishing a secondary fallback, checking all doors and windows for security, filling any receptacles they could with water, and taking stock of their own personal weapons and ammunition. As they believed the police to be a worse enemy than the living dead, both gangs used the phone to call allied street gangs instead of the authorities. None of those contacted believed what they were hearing, but promised to arrive as soon as possible anyway.

This last act was, in another ironic twist, one of the few cases of overkill ever recorded in an undead uprising. Well-protected, well-armed, well-led, well-organized, and extremely well-motivated, the gang members were able to dispatch the living dead from the upstairs windows without losing any of their own. Reinforcements (allied street gangs promising their support) did show up, unfortunately at the same time as the L.A.P.D. The result was the arrest of all those involved.

The incident was officially explained as "a shoot-out between local street gangs." Both Reds and Peros tried to relay the truth to anyone who would listen. Their story was explained as a delusion brought on by "Ice," a narcotic popular at that time. As the police and reinforcement gang members had only seen shot corpses and no walking zombies, none could be counted on as actual eyewitnesses. The bodies of the undead were removed and cremated. As almost all of them had been homeless people, none could be identified and none were missed. The original gang members involved were each found guilty of first-degree murder and sentenced to life at one of several of California's state prisons. All were murdered within a year of their incarceration, supposedly by rival gang members. This story would have ended there had it not been for an L.A.P.D. detective who has asked to remain nameless. He/she had read about the Parsons-MacDonald case several days before and was intrigued by its bizarre details. This allowed him/her to partially believe the gang members' stories. The coroner's report gave the most compelling argument. It perfectly matched

Parsons' autopsy. The final nail in the coffin was a wallet found on one of the undead, a man in his early thirties who appeared to be better dressed and groomed than the average street vagrant. The wallet belonged to Patrick MacDonald. As the owner had been shot in the face with a twelve-gauge solid slug, there was no way to positively identify him. The anonymous detective knew better than to bring the matter to his/her superiors for fear of disciplinary action. Instead, he/she copied the entire case file and presented it to the author of this book.

FEB. 1993 A.D., EAST LOS ANGELES, CALIFORNIA

At one forty-five A.M. Octavio and Rosa Melgar, the owners of a local *carnecería,* were awoken by frantic cries beneath their second-story bedroom window. Fearing that their store was being looted, Octavio grabbed his pistol and raced downstairs while Rosa telephoned the police. Crumpled near an open manhole was a quivering, sobbing man, covered in mud, dressed in tattered Department of Sanitation coveralls and bleeding profusely from the mangled stump where his right foot had once been. The man, who never identified himself, shouted repeatedly for Octavio to cover the manhole. Not knowing what else do, Octavio obliged. Before the metal cover slid into position, Octavio thought he heard a sound like distant moaning. As Rosa tied off the wounded man's leg, he half-whimpered, half-yelled that he and five other sanitation workers were inspecting a storm drain junction when they were attacked by a large group of "crazies." He described his assailants as being covered in a variety of rags and wounds, groaning rather than speaking, and approaching at a methodical limp. The man's words trailed off into an unintelligible string of phrases, grunts, and sobs before he slipped into unconsciousness. The police and paramedics arrived ninety minutes later. By this time, the wounded man was pronounced dead. As his body was driven away, the L.A.P.D. officers took statements from the Melgars. Octavio mentioned that he had heard the moaning. The officers noted this but said nothing. Six hours later, the Melgars heard on the morning news that the ambulance carrying the dead man had crashed and exploded on its way to the county hospital. The radio call from the paramedics (how the news station was able to obtain it is still a mystery) consisted mainly of panicked screams about the deceased subject tearing out of his body bag. Forty minutes after the broadcast, four police trucks, an ambulance, and a national guard truck pulled up in front of the Melgar's *carnicería*. Octavio and Rosa watched as the area was sealed off by the L.A.P.D. and a large, olive drab green tent was erected over the manhole with an identical passage running from it to the truck. The Melgars, along with a small crowd of onlookers, heard the unmistakable echo of gunfire from the manhole. Within the hour, the tent was struck, the barricade was lifted, and the vehicles quickly departed. There is little doubt that this incident was an aftershock of the downtown Los Angeles attack. Details of the government response, exactly what transpired in that underground labyrinth, may never be known. The Melgars, citing "personal legal reasons," have not made any further inquiries. The L.A.P.D. has explained the incident as a "routine health and maintenance inspection." The Los Angeles Department of Sanitation has denied the loss of any of its employees.

MAR. 1994 A.D., SAN PEDRO, CALIFORNIA

If not for Allie Goodwin, a crane operator at this Southern California shipyard, and her twenty-four-frame disposable camera, the world might have never known the true story of this zombie outbreak. An unmarked container was offloaded from the S.S. *Mare Caribe,* a Panamanian-flagged freighter out of Davao City, the Philippines. For several days it remained in the dockyard, awaiting pickup. One night, a watchman heard sounds emanating from the container. He and several security guards, suspecting it to be crowded with illegal immigrants, immediately opened the container. Forty-six zombies streamed out. Those in close proximity were devoured. Others sought shelter in warehouses, office buildings, and other facilities. Some of these structures provided adequate shelter; others became deathtraps. Four intrepid crane workers, Goodwin among them, climbed into their machines and used them to create an ad-hoc fortress of containers. This prefabricated shelter kept thirteen workers protected for the remainder of the night. The crane operators then used their machines as weapons, dropping containers on any zombie within range. By the time the police arrived (entry to the facility was barred by several locked gates), only eleven zombies remained at large. These were put down by a barrage of gunfire (including some lucky head shots). Total human casualties have been estimated at twenty. Zombie dead numbered thirty-nine. The seven unaccounted for are believed to have fallen into the water and been taken out to sea by the current.

All news stories filed claimed the incident was an attempted break-in. No government statements, on any level, were made. Dockyard management, the San Pedro Police—even the private security company that lost eight of its guards—have remained silent. The *Mare Caribe*'s crew, her captain, and even the company itself deny any knowledge of the original container, which has also mysteriously vanished. The port itself coincidentally caught fire the day after the attack. What makes this cover-up so incredible is that San Pedro is a large, busy port situated in one of the most heavily populated areas in the United States. How the government was able to suppress almost all sources of information is truly astounding. Goodwin's photos and statement have been branded a hoax by all parties involved. She was dismissed from her job on the grounds of psychological incompetence.

APR. 1994 A.D., SANTA MONICA BAY, CALIFORNIA

Three Palos Verdes residents, Jim Hwang, Anthony Cho, and Michael Kim, reported to police that they were attacked while fishing in the bay. The three men swore that Hwang had been bottom fishing when his line hooked a large, extremely heavy catch. What broke the surface was a man, naked, partially burned, partially decomposed, and still alive. The man attacked the three fishermen, grabbing Hwang and attempting to bite him on the neck. Cho pulled his friend back and Kim smashed the creature in the face with an oar. The attacker sank beneath the surface while the three fishermen headed for shore. All three were immediately subject to drug and alcohol tests by the Palos Verdes Police Department (tests that revealed no traces of either), held overnight for questioning, and released the next morning. The case is still officially "under investigation." Given the time and place of the attack, it is logical to assume that the creature was one of the original San Pedro outbreak zombies.

1996 A.D., THE LINE OF CONTROL, SRINAGAR, INDIA

This excerpt was taken from a post action report by Lieutenant Tagore of the Border Security Force:

The subject approached at a slow stagger, as if ill or intoxicated. [Through binoculars] *I could observe that he wore the full uniform of the Pakistan Rangers, odd since none were reported to be operating in this zone. At three hundred meters we ordered the subject to halt and identify himself. He would not comply. A second warning was given. Still no reply. He seemed to be moaning incoherently. At the sound of our calls his pace increased slightly. At two hundred meters he tripped the first mine, an American "Bouncing Betty." We observed the subject receiving shrapnel wounds to his upper and lower torso. He stumbled, fell on his face, then regained his footing and continued forward. . . . I deduced he wore some type of body armor. . . . This action occurred again at one hundred and fifty meters. This time the shrapnel tore the subject's jaw from his face. . . . At this range I could observe that the wound did not bleed. . . . The wind shifted in our direction. . . . We detected a putrid odor from the subject similar to decomposing meat. At one hundred meters I ordered Private Tilak [platoon sniper] to dispatch the subject. Tilak placed a direct shot through the subject's forehead. The subject dropped immediately. He did not rise, nor make any further movement.*

Subsequent reports document the recovery and initial autopsy of the body at the military hospital in Srinagar. Shortly thereafter the body was removed by the National Security Guard. No subsequent information has been released regarding their findings.

1998 A.D., ZABROVST, SIBERIA

Jacob Tailor, an acclaimed documentary filmmaker for the Canadian Broadcast Company, arrived in the small Siberian town of Zabrovst with the intention of photographing an intact, and potentially cloneable, saber-toothed tiger carcass. The body of a man in his late twenties, whose clothing matched that of a sixteenth-century cossack, had also been found. The shoot was due to take place in July, but Tailor arrived with an advance team in February to familiarize himself with the area and his subjects. Tailor believed the human corpse would not be the subject of more than a few seconds in his film, but asked that it be stored with the tiger's until his return. Tailor and his crew then returned to Toronto for a much needed rest. On June 14 a few members of Tailor's crew returned to Zabrovst to prepare their frozen subjects and the dig site for filming. That was the last time they were heard from.

When Tailor arrived by helicopter with the rest of his film crew on July 1 he found all twelve buildings at the site deserted. There were signs of violence and forced entry, including broken windows, over-turned furniture, and blood and pieces of flesh on the walls and floor. A scream brought Tailor back to the helicopter, where he found a group of thirty-six ghouls, including local villagers and the missing members of his advance team, feasting on the pilots. Tailor did not understand what he was seeing, but knew enough to run for his life.

The situation seemed grim. Tailor and his cameraman, soundman, and field researcher had no weapons, no supplies, and, being in the middle of the Siberian wasteland, nowhere to turn for help. The film-makers sought refuge in a two-story farmhouse in the village. Instead of boarding up the doors and windows, Tailor decided to destroy the two staircases. They stocked the second story with whatever food they could find and buckets of water filled from the well. An ax, a sledge-hammer, and several smaller tools were used to destroy the first stair-case. The arrival of the zombies prevented the destruction of the second one. Tailor acted quickly, taking doors from the second-story bedrooms and nailing them onto the second stairway. This created a ramp that prevented the approaching zombies from gaining any trac-tion. One by one they attempted to crawl their way up the ramp and were pushed back down by Tailor's team. This low-intensity battle went on for two days; half the group kept their attackers at bay while the other half slept (with cotton stuffed into their ears to deaden the sound of the moans).

On the third day, a freak accident gave Tailor the idea for their even-tual salvation. For fear the ghouls would grab their legs if they attempted to kick them back down the ramp, the filmmakers had resorted to shoving the zombies down with a long-handled wooden broom. The broom handle, already weak from so much use, finally snapped as it was grabbed by one of the attacking fiends. Tailor man-aged to kick the zombie back down, and watched in amazement as the sharp, broken tip of the handle, still clutched in the falling monster's hand, went right through the eye socket of a fellow ghoul. Not only had Tailor unwittingly killed his first zombie, but for the first time he realized the proper way to dispose of them. Now, instead of trying to force their attackers back down the ramp, the film crew aggressively encouraged them. Each one that came close enough to attack was given a devastating blow to the head with the team's ax. When this weapon was lost (stuck in the skull of a dead zombie), they switched to their sledgehammer. When its handle broke, they resorted to a crowbar. The battle took seven hours, but by the end the exhausted Canadian film-makers had dispatched every one of their attackers.

To this day, the Russian government has no official explanation of what occurred at Zabrovst. Any official asked about the incident will explain that it is being "looked into." However, in a country with as many social, economic, political, environmental, and military prob-lems as the new Russian Federation, there is little interest in the deaths of a few foreigners and backwoods Siberians.

Tailor, amazingly, kept his two cameras rolling throughout the entire incident. The result is forty-two hours of the most exciting footage ever recorded, digital video that the Lawson Film cannot hold a candle to. Tailor has tried, for the last few years, to have at least a portion of this footage released to the general public. All international "experts" who have viewed the video have labeled it as an expert hoax. Tailor has lost all credibility in an industry that once hailed him as one of its finest. He is now in the process of settling a divorce and several lawsuits.

2001 A.D., SIDI-MOUSSA, MOROCCO

The only evidence of an attack comes from a small article on the back page of a French newspaper:

> *Outbreak of Mass Hysteria in Moroccan Fishing Village—Sources confirm that a previously unknown neurological condi-tion has affected five residents, causing them to attack their relatives and friends in an attempt to eat their flesh. Acting on local custom, the afflicted were bound with rope and weights, taken out to sea, then dumped into the ocean. A government investigation is pending. Charges range from murder to negligent manslaughter.*

No government trial materialized, and no further reports appeared.

2002 A.D., ST. THOMAS, U.S. VIRGIN ISLANDS

A zombie—bloated, waterlogged, with skin completely dissolved—washed ashore on the northeast coast of the island. Local inhabitants were unsure of what to make of it, keeping their distance and calling for the authorities. The zombie, stumbling up on the beach, began to pursue its onlookers. Although curiosity kept them close, the crowd continued to retreat from the approaching ghoul. Two members of the St. Thomas police arrived and ordered the "suspect" to halt. When no reply came, they fired a warning shot. The zombie did not respond. One of the officers fired two rounds into its chest, producing no effect. Before another volley could be delivered, a six-year-old boy, excited by the events and not realizing the danger, ran up to the zombie and began to poke it with a stick. The walking dead immediately grabbed the child and tried to raise it to its mouth. The two officers rushed forward and attempted to wrestle the child from the zombie's grip. At that moment, Jeremiah Dewitt, a recent immigrant from the island of Dominica, stepped out of the crowd, grabbed one of the officer's sidearms and fired a round through the zombie's head. Amazingly, no human was infected by the ghoul. A criminal trial acquitted Dewitt of all charges, claiming the act was in self-defense. Photographs of the zombie corpse show it, even though decomposed horribly, to be of Middle Eastern or North African descent. The tatters of clothing and rope make a convincing case that the creature was one of those dumped into the ocean off the coast of Morocco. Theoretically, it would be possible for an undead specimen to travel with the currents across the Atlantic, although it would be the only case on record. In one of the strangest twists of outbreak cover-ups and suppression, this case has taken on celebrity status. Like Bigfoot in the Pacific Northwest or the Loch Ness Monster in Scotland, tourists can buy "St. Thomas Zombie" photographs, T-shirts, sculptures, clocks, watches, and even children's picture books at many of the shops in downtown Charlotte Amalie (the island capital). Dozens of bus drivers compete (sometimes fiercely) every day for the chance to drive newly arrived tourists from Cyril E.

King Airport to the site where the famous zombie came ashore. After the trial, Dewitt left for a new life in the United States. His friends in St. Thomas and his family in Dominica have not heard from him since.

HISTORICAL ANALYSIS

Until the late twentieth century, those who studied the living dead were convinced that the frequency of outbreaks remained constant throughout time. Societies that suffered more attacks than others appeared so only because they kept the best records. The most commonly held example was ancient Rome compared to the early Middle Ages. This theory was also used to calm "alarmists" by stating that, as humanity as a whole relied more and more on the written word, it would appear as if outbreaks were becoming more and more common. This way of thinking, although still common, has been falling into disfavor for some time. The world's population is growing. Its center has shifted from rural to urban zones. Transportation has linked the planet with increasing speed. All these factors have led to a renaissance of infectious diseases, most of which were thought to be eradicated centuries ago. Logic dictates that Solanum can flourish in such a ripe environment. Even though information is being recorded, shared, and stored as never before, it cannot hide the fact that zombie attacks are on the rise, their frequency mirroring the "development" of this planet. At this rate, attacks will only increase, culminating in one of two possibilities. The first is that world governments will have to acknowledge, both privately and publicly, the existence of the living dead, creating special organizations to deal with the threat. In this scenario, zombies will become an accepted part of daily life—marginalized, easily contained, perhaps even vaccinated against. A second, more ominous scenario would result in an all-out war between the living and the dead: a war you are now ready for.

APPENDIX: OUTBREAK JOURNAL

This space is reserved for a journal of suspicious events that could indicate a possible outbreak. (See "Detection," pages 25–27, for possible signs.) Remember: Early detection and advance preparation will ensure your best chance for survival. A sample journal entry follows.

DATE: 05/07/14

TIME: 3:51 A.M.

LOCATION: Anysmalltown, U.S.A.

DISTANCE FROM ME: Approx. 290 miles

SPECIFICS: The morning news (local, Channel 5) reported that a family was butchered and partially eaten by some kind of "maniac" or "maniacs." The bodies all looked like they'd been in a hardcore brawl: bruises, cuts, broken bones. All had big bites in their flesh. All died from gunshots to the head. They say it's a cult killing. Why? What cult? From where? And who are "they"? All the reporter said was that the explanation came from an "official source." There's a manhunt on now. I noticed that it's only police (no deputized citizens) and half of the cops were sharp-shooters. The press isn't allowed on the search because the police "can't guarantee their safety." The reporter said that the bodies were taken back to Largecity, and not the local morgue because they needed to do a "full autopsy." The hospital they are taking them to is ONLY 50 MILES AWAY!

ACTION TAKEN: Got out the checklists. Called Tom, Gregg, Henry. Meeting tonight, Gregg's place, 7:30 P.M. Sharpened the machete. Cleaned and oiled the carbine and signed up for practice at the range tomorrow before work. Filled the bike's tires with air. Called the park service just to make sure the river is at normal level. If incidents occur at the autopsy hospital, we'll take more serious steps.

DATE: _____

TIME: _____

LOCATION: _____

DISTANCE FROM ME: _____

SPECIFICS: _____
_____
_____
_____
_____
_____
_____
_____
_____
_____
_____
_____

ACTION TAKEN: _____
_____
_____
_____
_____
_____
_____
_____
_____
_____
_____
_____

DATE: _____

TIME: _____

LOCATION: _____

DISTANCE FROM ME: _____

SPECIFICS: _____
_____
_____
_____
_____
_____
_____
_____
_____
_____
_____

ACTION TAKEN: _____
_____
_____
_____
_____
_____
_____
_____
_____
_____
_____

DATE: _____

TIME: _____

LOCATION: _____

DISTANCE FROM ME: _____

SPECIFICS: _____

_____

_____

_____

_____

_____

_____

_____

_____

_____

ACTION TAKEN: _____

_____

_____

_____

_____

_____

_____

_____

_____

_____

DATE: _____

TIME: _____

LOCATION: _____

DISTANCE FROM ME: _____

SPECIFICS: _____
_____
_____
_____
_____
_____
_____
_____
_____
_____
_____

ACTION TAKEN: _____
_____
_____
_____
_____
_____
_____
_____
_____
_____
_____

DATE: _____

TIME: _____

LOCATION: _____

DISTANCE FROM ME: _____

SPECIFICS: _____
_____
_____
_____
_____
_____
_____
_____
_____
_____

ACTION TAKEN: _____
_____
_____
_____
_____
_____
_____
_____
_____
_____
_____

ACKNOWLEDGMENTS

First and foremost, thanks to Ed Victor for believing.

To David, Jan, Sergei, Jacob, Alex, Carley, Sara, Fikhirini, Rene, Paulo, and Jiang for the translations.

To Dr. Zane and his team for their field research.

To James "The Colonel" Lofton for his strategic perspective.

To Professor Sommers for the data.

To Sir Ian for the use of his library.

To Red and Steve for their help with the cartography.

To Manfred for a look through an old museum's basement.

To Artiom for your honesty and courage.

To "Joseph" and "Mary" for making a stranger feel welcome in their country.

To Chandara, Yusef, Hernan, Taylor, and Moishe for the photographs.

To Avi for the transcripts.

To Mason for the footage.

To M.W. for his illustrations.

To Tatsumi for his time and patience.

To "Mrs. Malone" for cutting through the red tape. (THANK YOU!)

To Josene for the tour.

To Tron for a drive by "the place."

To Captain Ashley and the crew of the *Sau Tome* for proving the point.

To Alice, Pyotr, Hugh, Telly, Antonio, Hideki, and Dr. Singh for the interviews.

To the boys (and girl) at the lab for "you know what."

To Annik for her brilliance with pen and sword.

And, of course, to all those who have asked to remain anonymous. The lives you have helped to save will be your greatest credit.

The end was near . . .

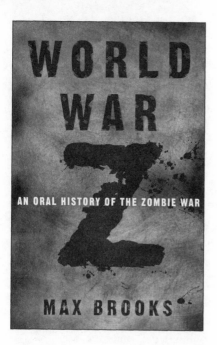

WORLD WAR Z

AN ORAL HISTORY OF THE ZOMBIE WAR

MAX BROOKS

We survived *World War Z,* but how many of us are still haunted by that terrible time? We may have (temporarily?) defeated the living dead, but at what cost? Told in the haunting and riveting voices of the men and women who witnessed the horror first-hand, *World War Z* is the only record of the plague years.

WORLD WAR Z
$14.95 PAPER
(CANADA: $21.00)
ISBN-10: 0-307-34661-7
ISBN-13: 978-0-307-34661-2

FROM **WORLD WAR Z**

It goes by many names: "The Crisis," "The Dark Years," "The Walking Plague," as well as newer and more "hip" titles such as "World War Z" or "Z War One." I personally dislike this last moniker as it implies an inevitable "Z War Two." For me, it will always be "The Zombie War," and while many may protest the scientific accuracy of the word *zombie*, they will be hard-pressed to discover a more globally accepted term for the creatures that almost caused our extinction. *Zombie* remains a devastating word, unrivaled in its power to conjure up so many memories or emotions, and it is these memories, and emotions, that are the subject of this book.

This record of the greatest conflict in human history owes its genesis to a much smaller, much more personal conflict between me and the chairperson of the United Nation's Postwar Commission Report. My initial work for the Commission could be described as nothing short of a labor of love. My travel stipend, my security access, my battery of translators, both human and electronic, as well as my small, but nearly priceless voice-activated transcription "pal" (the greatest gift the world's slowest typist could ask for), all spoke to the respect and value my work was afforded on this project. So, needless to say, it came as a shock when I found almost half of that work deleted from the report's final edition.

"It was all too intimate," the chairperson said during one of our many "animated" discussions. "Too many opinions, too many feelings. That's not what this report is about. We need clear facts and figures, unclouded by the human factor." Of course, she was right. The official report was a collection of cold, hard data, an objective "after-action report" that would allow future generations to study the events of that apocalyptic decade without being influenced by "the human factor." But isn't the human factor what connects us so deeply to our past? Will future generations care as much for chronologies and casualty statistics as they would for the personal accounts of individuals not so different from themselves? By excluding the human factor, aren't we risking the kind of personal detachment from a history that may, heaven forbid, lead us one day to repeat it? And in the end, isn't the human factor the only true difference between us and the enemy we now refer to as "the living dead"? I presented this argument, perhaps less professionally than was appropriate, to my "boss," who after my final exclamation of "we can't let these stories die" responded immediately with, "Then don't. Write a book. You've still got all your notes, and the legal freedom to use them. Who's stopping you from keeping these stories alive in the pages of your own (expletive deleted) book?"

Some critics will, no doubt, take issue with the concept of a personal history book so soon after the end of worldwide hostilities.

After all, it has been only twelve years since VA Day was declared in the continental United States, and barely a decade since the last major world power celebrated its deliverance on "Victory in China Day." Given that most people consider VC Day to be the official end, then how can we have real perspective when, in the words of a UN colleague, "We've been at peace about as long as we were at war." This is a valid argument, and one that begs a response. In the case of this generation, those who have fought and suffered to win us this decade of peace, time is as much an enemy as it is an ally. Yes, the coming years will provide hindsight, adding greater wisdom to memories seen through the light of a matured, postwar world. But many of those memories may no longer exist, trapped in bodies and spirits too damaged or infirm to see the fruits of their victory harvested. It is no great secret that global life expectancy is a mere shadow of its former prewar figure. Malnutrition, pollution, the rise of previously eradicated ailments, even in the United States, with its resurgent economy and universal health care, are the present reality; there simply are not enough resources to care for all the physical and psychological casualties. It is because of this enemy, the enemy of time, that I have forsaken the luxury of hindsight and published these survivors' accounts. Perhaps decades from now, someone will take up the task of recording the recollections of the much older, much wiser survivors. Perhaps I might even be one of them.

Although this is primarily a book of memories, it includes many of the details, technological, social, economic, and so on found in the original Commission Report, as they are related to the stories of those voices featured in these pages. This is their book, not mine, and I have tried to maintain as invisible a presence as possible. Those questions included in the text are only there to illustrate those that might have been posed by readers. I have attempted to reserve judgment, or commentary of any kind, and if there is a human factor that should be removed, let it be my own.

WARNINGS

GREATER CHONGQING, THE UNITED FEDERATION OF CHINA

[At its prewar height, this region boasted a population of over thirty-five million people. Now, there are barely fifty thousand. Reconstruction funds have been slow to arrive in this part of the country, the government choosing to concentrate on the more densely populated coast. There is no central power grid, no running water besides the Yangtze River. But the streets are clear of rubble and the local "security council" has prevented any postwar outbreaks. The chairman of that council is Kwang Jingshu, a medical doctor who, despite his advanced age and wartime injuries, still manages to make house calls to all his patients.]

The first outbreak I saw was in a remote village that officially had no name. The residents called it "New Dachang," but this was more out of nostalgia than anything else. Their former home,

"Old Dachang," had stood since the period of the Three Kingdoms, with farms and houses and even trees said to be centuries old. When the Three Gorges Dam was completed, and reservoir waters began to rise, much of Dachang had been disassembled, brick by brick, then rebuilt on higher ground. This New Dachang, however, was not a town anymore, but a "national historic museum." It must have been a heartbreaking irony for those poor peasants, to see their town saved but then only being able to visit it as a tourist. Maybe that is why some of them chose to name their newly constructed hamlet "New Dachang" to preserve some connection to their heritage, even if it was only in name. I personally didn't know that this other New Dachang existed, so you can imagine how confused I was when the call came in.

The hospital was quiet; it had been a slow night, even for the increasing number of drunk-driving accidents. Motorcycles were becoming very popular. We used to say that your Harley-Davidsons killed more young Chinese than all the GIs in the Korean War. That's why I was so grateful for a quiet shift. I was tired, my back and feet ached. I was on my way out to smoke a cigarette and watch the dawn when I heard my name being paged. The receptionist that night was new and couldn't quite understand the dialect. There had been an accident, or an illness. It was an emergency, that part was obvious, and could we please send help at once.

What could I say? The younger doctors, the kids who think medicine is just a way to pad their bank accounts, they certainly weren't going to go help some "nongmin" just for the sake of helping. I guess I'm still an old revolutionary at heart. "Our duty is to hold ourselves responsible to the people."[1] Those words still mean

---

1. From "Quotations from Chairman Maozedong," originally from "The Situation and Our Policy After the Victory in the War of Resistance Against Japan," August 13, 1945.

something to me . . . and I tried to remember that as my Deer[2] bounced and banged over dirt roads the government had promised but never quite gotten around to paving.

I had a devil of a time finding the place. Officially, it didn't exist and therefore wasn't on any map. I became lost several times and had to ask directions from locals who kept thinking I meant the museum town. I was in an impatient mood by the time I reached the small collection of hilltop homes. I remember thinking, *This had better be damned serious.* Once I saw their faces, I regretted my wish.

There were seven of them, all on cots, all barely conscious. The villagers had moved them into their new communal meeting hall. The walls and floor were bare cement. The air was cold and damp. *Of course they're sick,* I thought. I asked the villagers who had been taking care of these people. They said no one, it wasn't "safe." I noticed that the door had been locked from the outside. The villagers were clearly terrified. They cringed and whispered; some kept their distance and prayed. Their behavior made me angry, not at them, you understand, not as individuals, but what they represented about our country. After centuries of foreign oppression, exploitation, and humiliation, we were finally reclaiming our rightful place as humanity's middle kingdom. We were the world's richest and most dynamic superpower, masters of everything from outer space to cyber space. It was the dawn of what the world was finally acknowledging as "The Chinese Century" and yet so many of us still lived like these ignorant peasants, as stagnant and superstitious as the earliest Yangshao savages.

I was still lost in my grand, cultural criticism when I knelt to examine the first patient. She was running a high fever, forty

2. A prewar automobile manufactured in the People's Republic.

degrees centigrade, and she was shivering violently. Barely coherent, she whimpered slightly when I tried to move her limbs. There was a wound in her right forearm, a bite mark. As I examined it more closely, I realized that it wasn't from an animal. The bite radius and teeth marks had to have come from a small, or possibly young, human being. Although I hypothesized this to be the source of the infection, the actual injury was surprisingly clean. I asked the villagers, again, who had been taking care of these people. Again, they told me no one. I knew this could not be true. The human mouth is packed with bacteria, even more so than the most unhygienic dog. If no one had cleaned this woman's wound, why wasn't it throbbing with infection?

I examined the six other patients. All showed similar symptoms, all had similar wounds on various parts of their bodies. I asked one man, the most lucid of the group, who or what had inflicted these injuries. He told me it had happened when they had tried to subdue "him."

"Who?" I asked.

I found "Patient Zero" behind the locked door of an abandoned house across town. He was twelve years old. His wrists and feet were bound with plastic packing twine. Although he'd rubbed off the skin around his bonds, there was no blood. There was also no blood on his other wounds, not on the gouges on his legs or arms, or from the large dry gap where his right big toe had been. He was writhing like an animal; a gag muffled his growls.

At first the villagers tried to hold me back. They warned me not to touch him, that he was "cursed." I shrugged them off and reached for my mask and gloves. The boy's skin was as cold and gray as the cement on which he lay. I could find neither his heart-beat nor his pulse. His eyes were wild, wide and sunken back in their sockets. They remained locked on me like a predatory beast. Throughout the examination he was inexplicably hostile, reaching for me with his bound hands and snapping at me through his gag.

His movements were so violent I had to call for two of the largest villagers to help me hold him down. Initially they wouldn't budge, cowering in the doorway like baby rabbits. I explained that there was no risk of infection if they used gloves and masks. When they shook their heads, I made it an order, even though I had no lawful authority to do so.

That was all it took. The two oxen knelt beside me. One held the boy's feet while the other grasped his hands. I tried to take a blood sample and instead extracted only brown, viscous matter. As I was withdrawing the needle, the boy began another bout of violent struggling.

One of my "orderlies," the one responsible for his arms, gave up trying to hold them and thought it might safer if he just braced them against the floor with his knees. But the boy jerked again and I heard his left arm snap. Jagged ends of both radius and ulna bones stabbed through his gray flesh. Although the boy didn't cry out, didn't even seem to notice, it was enough for both assistants to leap back and run from the room.

I instinctively retreated several paces myself. I am embarrassed to admit this; I have been a doctor for most of my adult life. I was trained and . . . you could even say "raised" by the People's Liberation Army. I've treated more than my share of combat injuries, faced my own death on more than one occasion, and now I was scared, truly scared, of this frail child.

The boy began to twist in my direction, his arm ripped completely free. Flesh and muscle tore from one another until there was nothing except the stump. His now free right arm, still tied to the severed left hand, dragged his body across the floor.

I hurried outside, locking the door behind me. I tried to compose myself, control my fear and shame. My voice still cracked as I asked the villagers how the boy had been infected. No one answered. I began to hear banging on the door, the boy's fist pounding weakly against the thin wood. It was all I could do not to jump at the sound. I prayed they would not notice the color draining from my face. I shouted, as much from fear as frustration, that I *had* to know what happened to this child.

A young woman came forward, maybe his mother. You could tell that she had been crying for days; her eyes were dry and deeply red. She admitted that it had happened when the boy and his father were "moon fishing," a term that describes diving for treasure among the sunken ruins of the Three Gorges Reservoir. With more than eleven hundred abandoned villages, towns, and even cities, there was always the hope of recovering something valuable. It was a very common practice in those days, and also very illegal. She explained that they weren't looting, that it was their own village, Old Dachang, and they were just trying to recover some heirlooms from the remaining houses that hadn't been moved. She repeated the point, and I had to interrupt her with promises not to inform the police. She finally explained that the boy came up crying with a bite mark on his foot. He didn't know what had happened, the water had been too dark and muddy. His father was never seen again.

I reached for my cell phone and dialed the number of Doctor Gu Wen Kuei, an old comrade from my army days who now worked at the Institute of Infectious Diseases at Chongqing University.[3] We exchanged pleasantries, discussing our health, our grandchildren; it was only proper. I then told him about the outbreak and listened as he made some joke about the hygiene habits of hillbillies. I tried to chuckle along but continued that I thought the incident might be significant. Almost reluctantly he asked me what the symptoms were. I told him everything: the bites, the fever, the boy, the arm . . . his face suddenly stiffened. His smile died.

He asked me to show him the infected. I went back into the meeting hall and waved the phone's camera over each of the patients. He asked me to move the camera closer to some of the wounds themselves. I did so and when I brought the screen back to my face, I saw that his video image had been cut.

"Stay where you are," he said, just a distant, removed voice now. "Take the names of all who have had contact with the infected. Restrain those already infected. If any have passed into coma, vacate the room and secure the exit." His voice was flat, robotic, as if he had rehearsed this speech or was reading from something. He asked me, "Are you armed?" "Why would I be?" I asked. He told me he would get back to me, all business again. He said he had to make a few calls and that I should expect "support" within several hours.

They were there in less than one, fifty men in large army Z-8A helicopters; all were wearing hazardous materials suits. They said they were from the Ministry of Health. I don't know who they thought they were kidding. With their bullying swagger, their

3. The Institute of Infectious and Parasitic Diseases of the First Affiliated Hospital, Chongqing Medical University.

intimidating arrogance, even these backwater bumpkins could recognize the Guoanbu.[4]

Their first priority was the meeting hall. The patients were carried out on stretchers, their limbs shackled, their mouths gagged. Next, they went for the boy. He came out in a body bag. His mother was wailing as she and the rest of the village were rounded up for "examinations." Their names were taken, their blood drawn. One by one they were stripped and photographed. The last one to be exposed was a withered old woman. She had a thin, crooked body, a face with a thousand lines and tiny feet that had to have been bound when she was a girl. She was shaking her bony fist at the "doctors." "This is your punishment!" she shouted. "This is revenge for Fengdu!"

She was referring to the City of Ghosts, whose temples and shrines were dedicated to the underworld. Like Old Dachang, it had been an unlucky obstacle to China's next Great Leap Forward. It had been evacuated, then demolished, then almost entirely drowned. I've never been a superstitious person and I've never allowed myself to be hooked on the opiate of the people. I'm a doctor, a scientist. I believe only in what I can see and touch. I've never seen Fengdu as anything but a cheap, kitschy tourist trap. Of course this ancient crone's words had no effect on me, but her tone, her anger . . . she had witnessed enough calamity in her years upon the earth: the warlords, the Japanese, the insane nightmare of the Cultural Revolution . . . she knew that another storm was coming, even if she didn't have the education to understand it.

My colleague Dr. Kuei had understood all too well. He'd even risked his neck to warn me, to give me enough time to call and

4. Guokia Anquan Bu: The prewar Ministry of State Security.

maybe alert a few others before the "Ministry of Health" arrived. It was something he had said . . . a phrase he hadn't used in a very long time, not since those "minor" border clashes with the Soviet Union. That was back in 1969. We had been in an earthen bunker on our side of the Ussuri, less than a kilometer downriver from Chen Bao. The Russians were preparing to retake the island, their massive artillery hammering our forces.

Gu and I had been trying to remove shrapnel from the belly of this soldier not much younger than us. The boy's lower intestines had been torn open, his blood and excrement were all over our gowns. Every seven seconds a round would land close by and we would have to bend over his body to shield the wound from falling earth, and every time we would be close enough to hear him whimper softly for his mother. There were other voices, too, rising from the pitch darkness just beyond the entrance to our bunker, desperate, angry voices that weren't supposed to be on our side of the river. We had two infantrymen stationed at the bunker's entrance. One of them shouted "Spetsnaz!" and started firing into the dark. We could hear other shots now as well, ours or theirs, we couldn't tell.

Another round hit and we bent over the dying boy. Gu's face was only a few centimeters from mine. There was sweat pouring down his forehead. Even in the dim light of one paraffin lantern, I could see that he was shaking and pale. He looked at the patient, then at the doorway, then at me, and suddenly he said, "Don't worry, everything's going to be all right." Now, this is a man who has never said a positive thing in his life. Gu was a worrier, a neurotic curmudgeon. If he had a headache, it was a brain tumor; if it looked like rain, this year's harvest was ruined. This was his way of controlling the situation, his lifelong strategy for always coming out ahead. Now, when reality looked more dire than any of his fatalistic predictions, he had no choice but to turn tail and charge in the opposite direction. "Don't worry, everything's going to be all right." For the first time everything turned out as he predicted. The Russians never crossed the river and we even managed to save our patient.

For years afterward I would tease him about what it took to pry out a little ray of sunshine, and he would always respond that it would take a hell of a lot worse to get him to do it again. Now we were old men, and something worse was about to happen. It was right after he asked me if I was armed. "No," I said, "why should I be?" There was a brief silence, I'm sure other ears were listening. "Don't worry," he said, "everything's going to be all right." That was when I realized that this was not an isolated outbreak. I ended the call and quickly placed another to my daughter in Guangzhou.

Her husband worked for China Telecom and spent at least one week of every month abroad. I told her it would be a good idea to accompany him the next time he left and that she should take my granddaughter and stay for as long as they could. I didn't have time to explain; my signal was jammed just as the first helicopter appeared. The last thing I managed to say to her was "Don't worry, everything's going to be all right."

[Kwang Jingshu was arrested by the MSS and incarcerated without formal charges. By the time he escaped, the outbreak had spread beyond China's borders.]

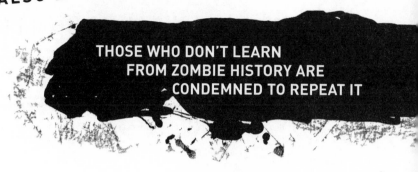

TOOLS THAT CAN SAVE YOUR LIFE!

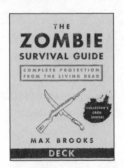